IMAGES
of America

VIETNAMESE IN ORANGE COUNTY

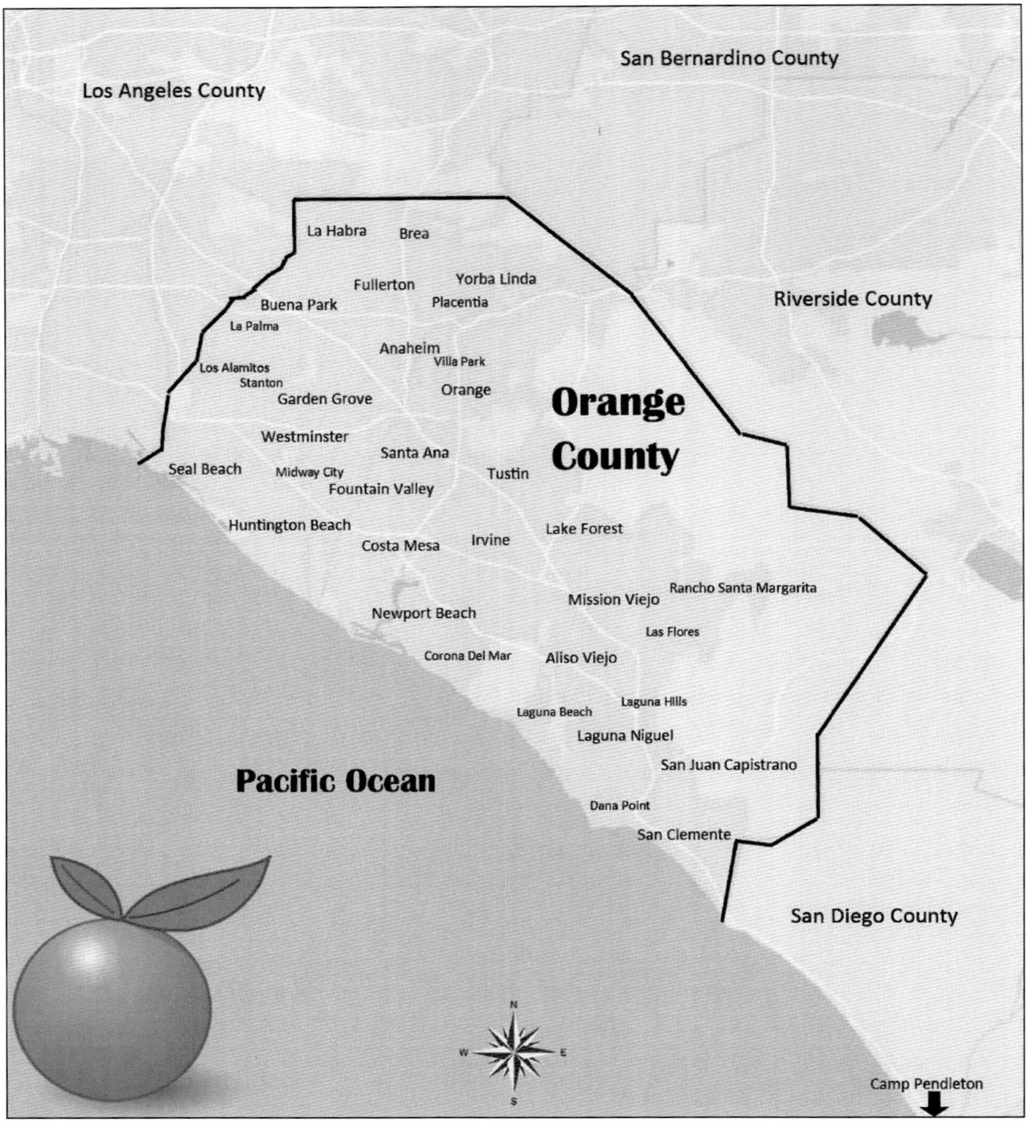

This map of Orange County, California, includes the cities of Westminster, Garden Grove, and Santa Ana, collectively known as "Little Saigon."

On the Cover: Community leaders and elected officials celebrate Tet (Vietnamese lunar new year) in the late 1980s outside Hoa Binh Supermarket, which is located at the crossroads of Westminster and Garden Grove. (Courtesy of Ho Dang.)

IMAGES
of America

VIETNAMESE IN ORANGE COUNTY

Thuy Vo Dang, Linda Trinh Vo,
and Tram Le

ARCADIA
PUBLISHING

ISBN 978-1-4671-3321-0

Published by Arcadia Publishing
Charleston, South Carolina

Printed in the United States of America

Library of Congress Control Number: 2014952136

For all general information, please contact Arcadia Publishing:
Telephone 843-853-2070
Fax 843-853-0044
E-mail sales@arcadiapublishing.com
For customer service and orders:
Toll-Free 1-888-313-2665

Visit us on the Internet at www.arcadiapublishing.com

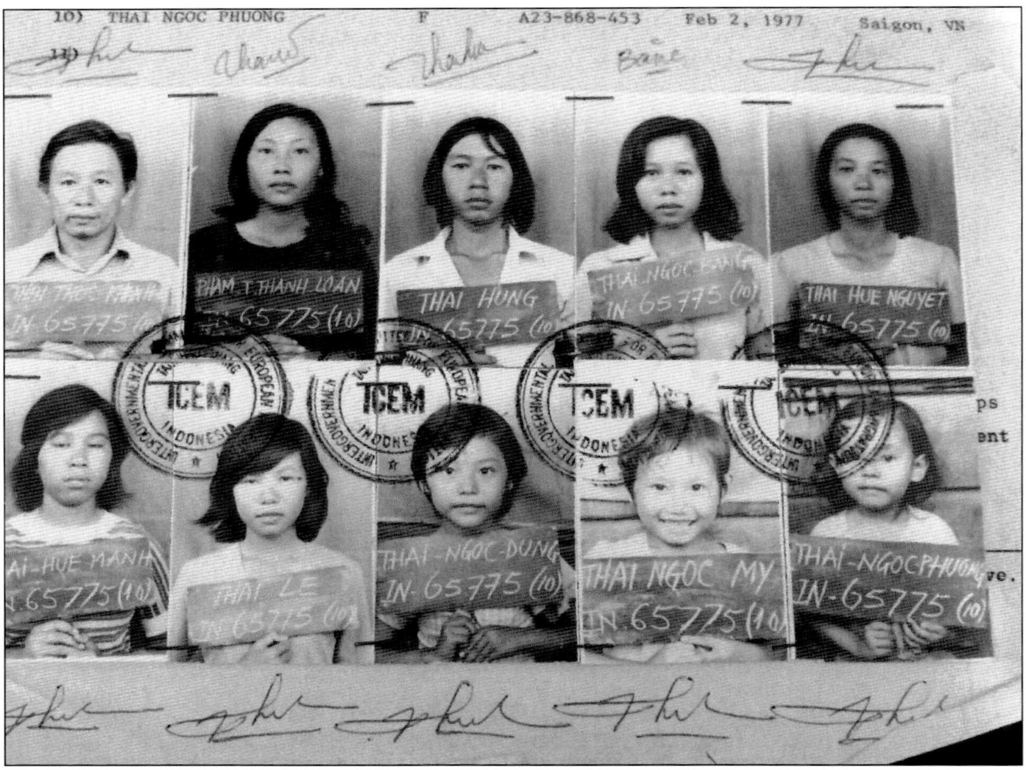

These are identification card photographs issued to refugees by authorities such as the United Nations High Commissioner for Refugees, International Rescue Committee, or the Intergovernmental Committee for Migration (later changed to the Intergovernmental Organization for Migration). The people shown are members of the Loan Pham Thai family on December 28, 1979, in Indonesia. (Courtesy of the UCI Vietnamese American Oral History Project, VAOHP0041.)

Contents

Acknowledgments

This book is the culmination of our community work in Southern California and generated by our affiliations with the UC Irvine Libraries' Southeast Asian Archive and the Vietnamese American Oral History Project (VAOHP) at UC Irvine. The royalties from this book project will be donated to VAOHP to support the preservation of our histories. Although we are unable to capture all stories or perspectives, we hope this collection contributes to a more inclusive portrayal of a diverse and vibrant community.

We thank Dr. Georges van den Abbeele and the VAOHP Advisory Board: Dr. Vicki L. Ruiz, Dr. James K. Lee, Christina J. Woo, Michelle Light, Caroline McGuire, Kasey Ning, and Daniel Do-Khanh. We are indebted to our University of California, Irvine, Libraries colleagues Lorelei Tanji, John Renaud, Audra Eagle Yun, Matthew McKinley, Anne Frank, Prany Sananikone, the Special Collections and Archives department, and the Vietnamese American Community Ambassadors—a UCI alumni chapter.

We are grateful to those who donated their stories and archival materials and assisted us in finding images or completing captions. We received invaluable assistance from Dr. Jonathan H. X. Lee, Dr. Nhu-Ngoc Ong, Pham Phu Thien Giao, and the Vietnamese American Arts & Letters Association.

We thank our research assistants Pauline Dong and Claire Cella, as well as the students in our Vietnamese American Experience and Research Methodologies/Field Research courses.

We acknowledge VAOHP donors, especially the Jao Foundation, Wells Fargo Foundation (Jack Toan), and Edison International (Edward Robinson, Qiana Charles, Tammy Tran, Tami Bui).

Thuy would like to thank her parents and siblings for having the courage to leave Vietnam and the strength to persevere in America. She would also like to thank Duc, Allyse Minh Kieu, and Austen for their love. Linda appreciates her family in Vietnam and the United States who made sacrifices to raise her and inspired her to collect stories, especially her parents, Thuy and Bob Hanlon. Tram is grateful to her parents and brother for giving her the loving, funny, sometimes incomprehensible, but never dull memories of growing up Vietnamese American and to her rock, Wolfgang Shane.

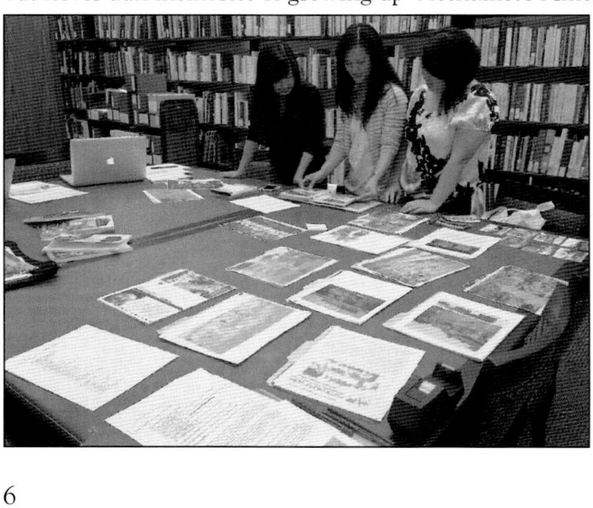

The co-authors are working on an early concept for this book in the Southeast Asian Archive reading room, located in Langson Library on the UC Irvine campus. (Courtesy of Howard Diep.)

One

History

Vietnam is an S-shaped country bordered by China to the north, Laos and Cambodia to the west, and the South China Sea on the south and the east. In the mid-19th century, France colonized the country and greatly influenced its culture and politics. After World War II, the Viet Minh, a nationalist group, defeated the French in 1954, and the country was divided at the 17th parallel into North and South Vietnam. This partition resulted in a mass displacement of approximately one million Vietnamese from north to south. Connected to Cold War–era politics, the Soviet and Chinese-backed North and US-backed South fought a war for two decades. While 58,000 American military personnel lost their lives, millions of Vietnamese soldiers and civilians were killed during the war. The conflict also spread to neighboring Laos and Cambodia, causing millions of additional casualties. The war also led to countless numbers of injuries and major displacement of populations in the country. The South Vietnamese government surrendered on April 30, 1975, with the Fall of Saigon, which led to the mass exodus of Vietnamese from their homeland. In the closing days of the war, thousands of Vietnamese fled the country for fear of the brutality of the communist regime. In the ensuing decades, many more risked their lives to escape Vietnam. Presently, there are close to two million Vietnamese in the United States.

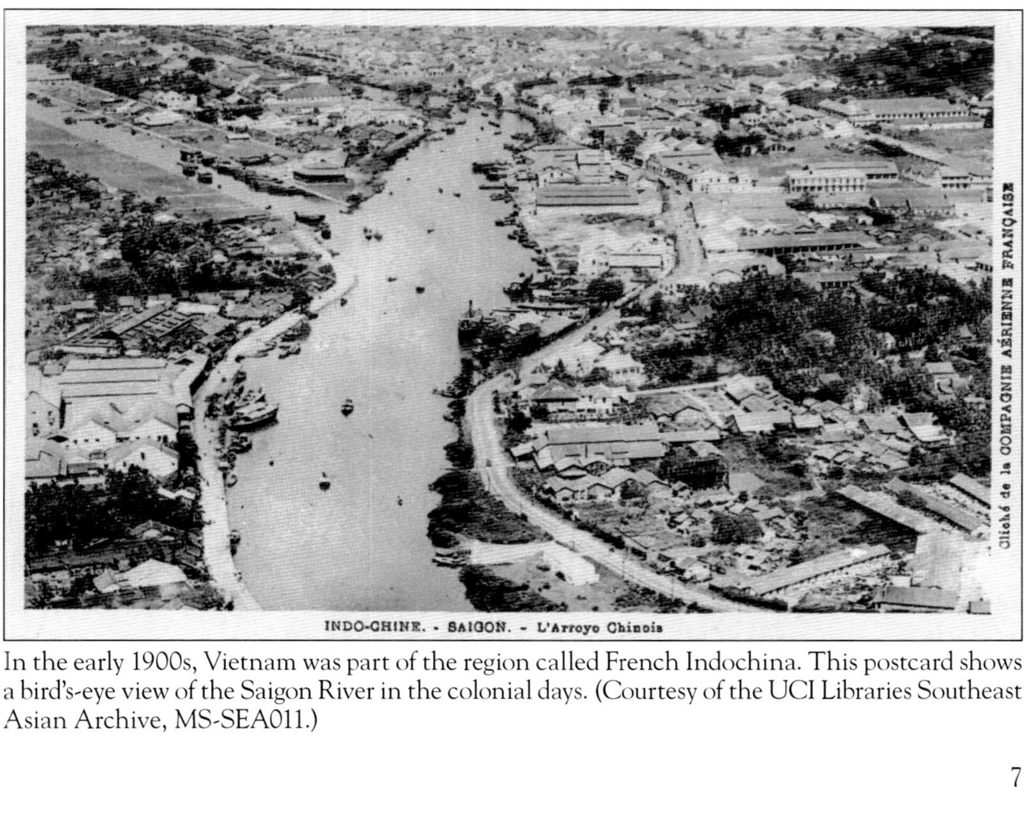

In the early 1900s, Vietnam was part of the region called French Indochina. This postcard shows a bird's-eye view of the Saigon River in the colonial days. (Courtesy of the UCI Libraries Southeast Asian Archive, MS-SEA011.)

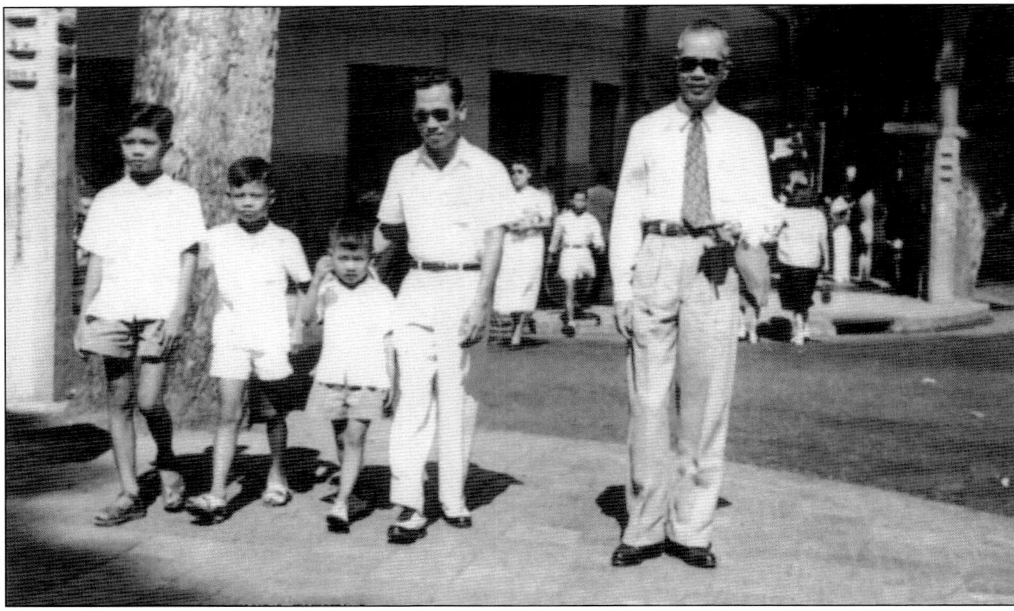

In 1954, Le Huu Khoan, a Garden Grove resident, walks with his father and brothers outside a courthouse in South Vietnam. Khoan's father, Le Huu Tham, served as a judge in Rach Gia, Vietnam. (Courtesy of the UCI Vietnamese American Oral History Project, VAOHP0055.)

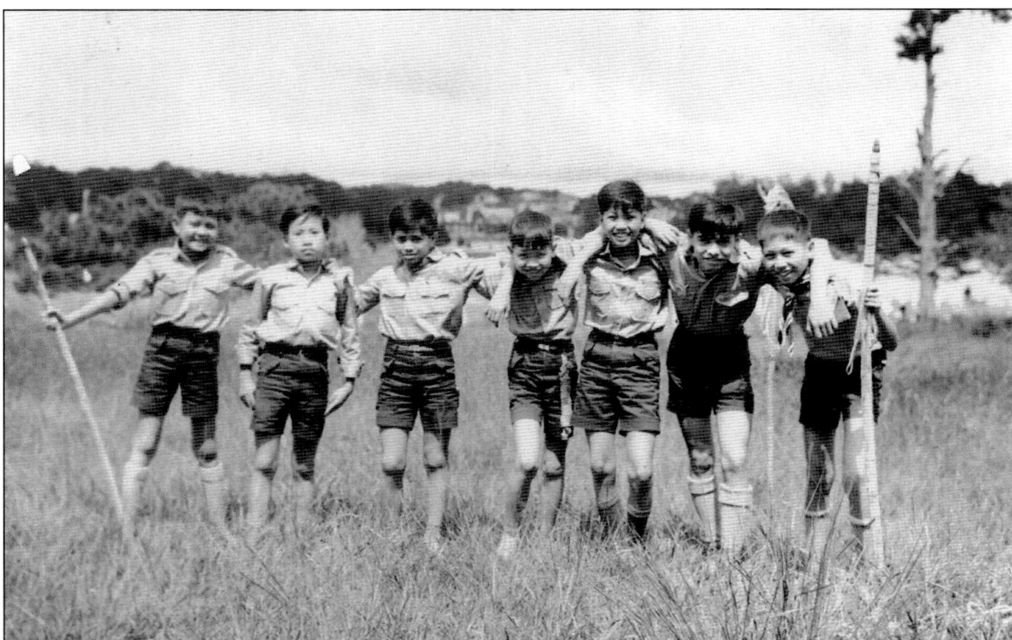

Steve Pho (center) is with his friends on their first school camping trip in Da Lat, Vietnam, in 1964. He later joined the military, moved to Saigon to fight for South Vietnam, and became a boatperson refugee in the 1980s. (Courtesy of the UCI Vietnamese American Oral History Project, VAOHP0164.)

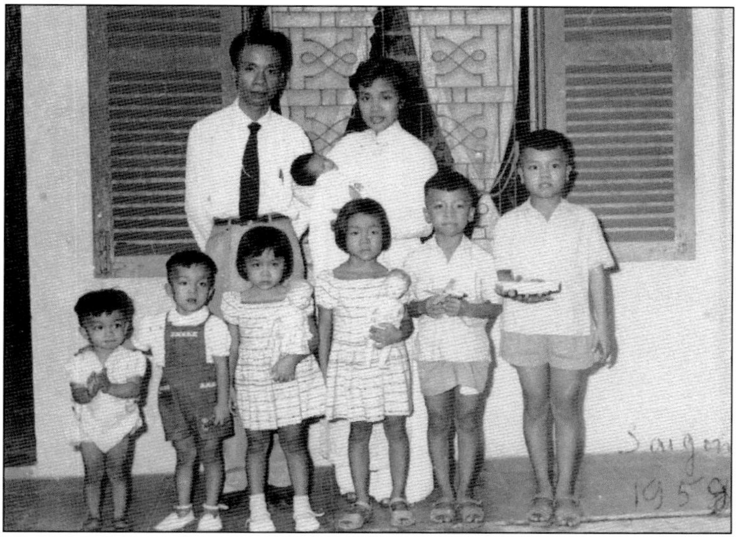

In 1959, this photograph was taken the day of Phan Anh Huy's baptism in front of the family home in Saigon on Truong Minh Giang Street. Catholicism took root in Vietnam due to the influence of the French. All the children in the front row are her older siblings; some would later leave Vietnam as refugees. (Courtesy of the UCI Vietnamese American Oral History Project, VAOHP0038.)

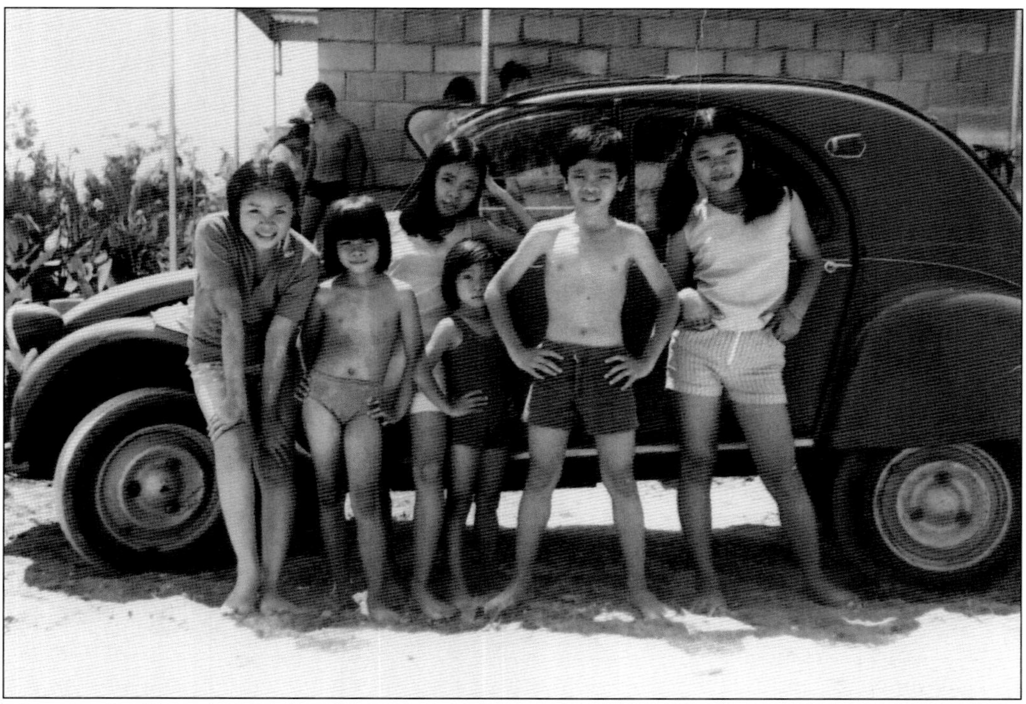

This was the Phan family's yearly vacation, taken in the early 1970s at Cape Saint Jacques Beach, which is now Vung Tau, a popular tourist destination in Vietnam. Phan Anh Huy (far right) poses with some of her siblings. She and her family have since immigrated to the United States, and several family members live in Orange County. (Courtesy of Trinh Mai.)

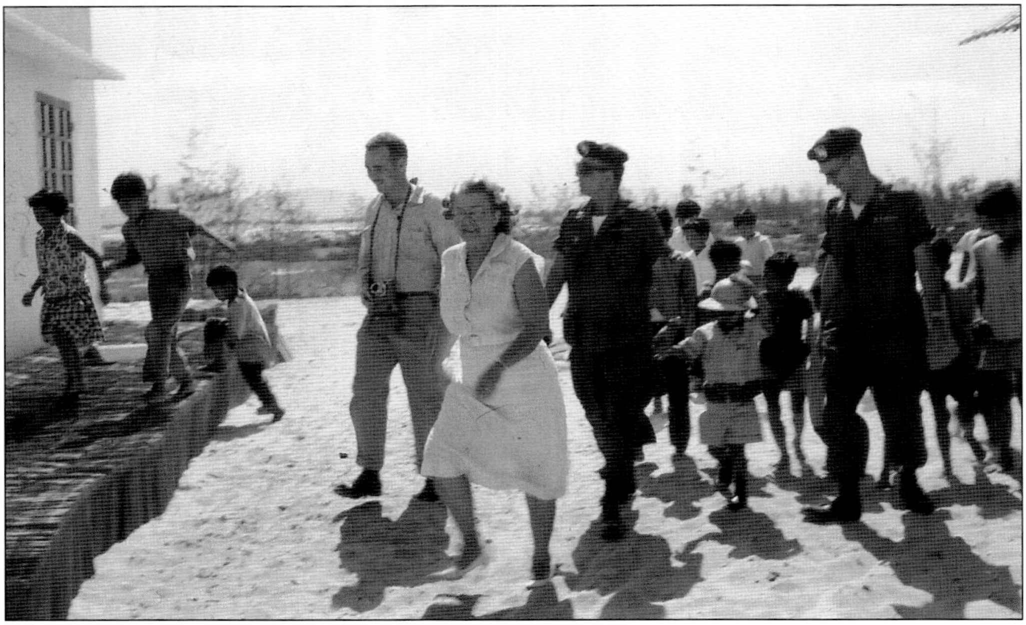

Laura Smith, an American missionary (center), is pictured here outside of a Da Nang orphanage in 1967. She ran a small orphanage that took in Vietnamese and nearby tribal children. The Vietnam War created a large number of orphans, many who lived on the streets and had to fend for themselves. (Courtesy of Joe Carrier.)

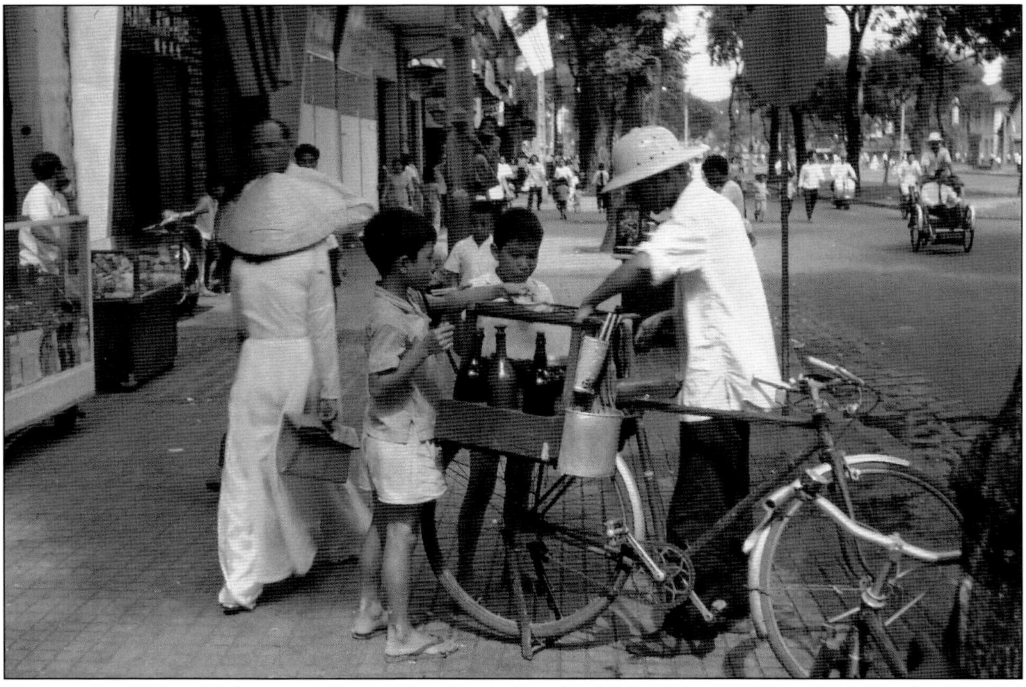

As war was raging in the country, this scene of everyday life on Nguyen Hue Boulevard in Saigon in 1966 depicts boys gathering around a street peddler to buy some refreshments. (Courtesy of Joe Carrier.)

Pictured here with a fellow soldier in Nha Trang, Thomas Toan Phan was an Army of the Republic of Vietnam officer who was drafted in 1972 at age 20. He trained in the United States and then returned as an officer in the central region. After the South fell, he was sent to a re-education camp. He escaped Vietnam by boat in 1986 and arrived in a refugee camp in Phanat Nikhom, Thailand. After his resettlement in America, he sponsored his wife and children. (Courtesy of the UCI Vietnamese American Oral History Project, VAOHP0100.)

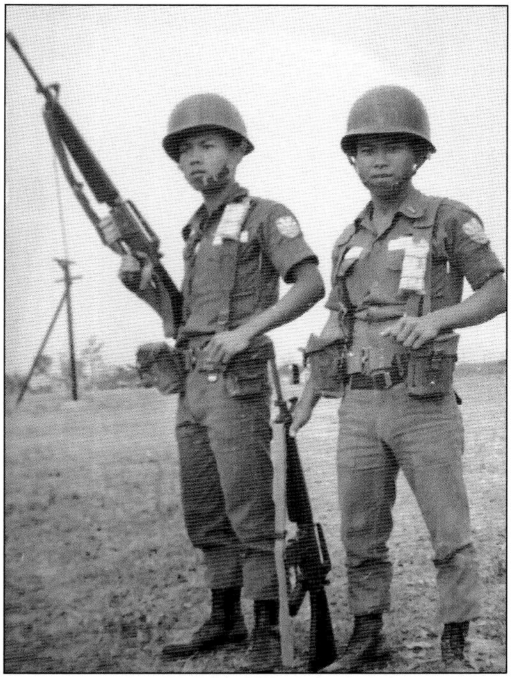

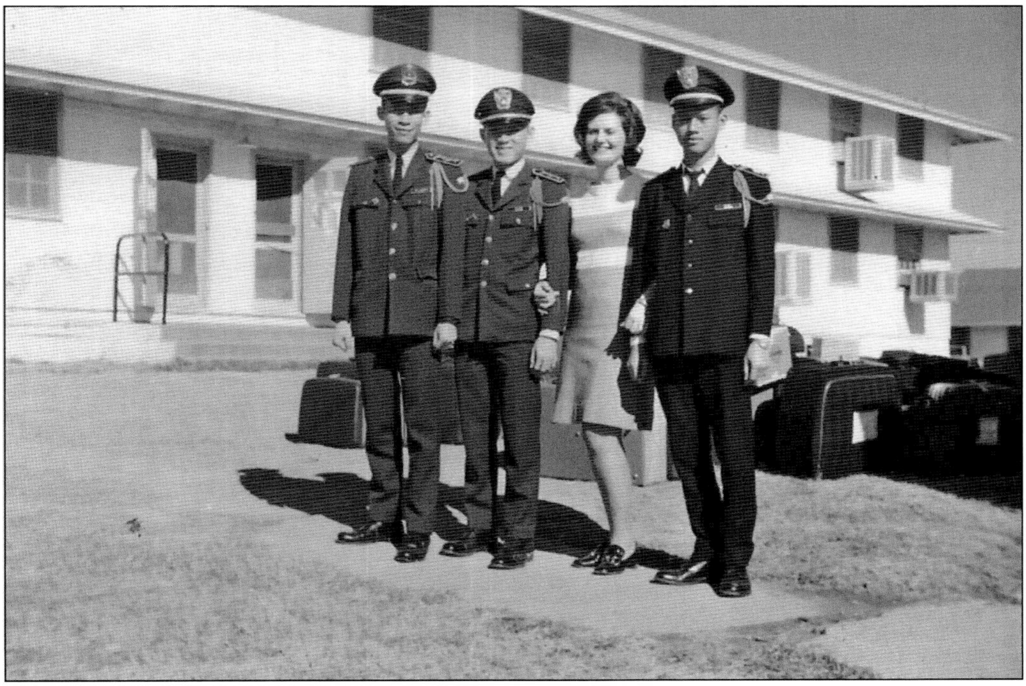

In 1969, Tu Anh Vu, a South Vietnamese helicopter pilot, received formal fighter pilot training by the US military in Texas. He is featured here (far right) with other officers-in-training. He escaped Vietnam on April 30, 1975, with his wife and daughter, and they resettled in Georgia. He found a career as an airline avionics technician for United Airlines and settled in Huntington Beach with his family. (Courtesy of the UCI Vietnamese American Oral History Project, VAOHP0024.)

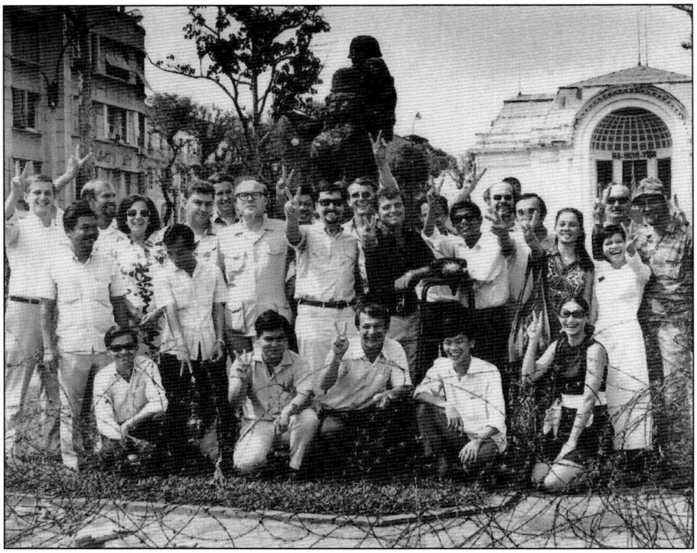

The Vietnam War was the first televised war in US history. Pulitzer Prize–winning photographer Nick Ut (front row, second from left) captured iconic images from the war, including "The Terror of War" photographs, which showed children after a napalm bombing. In this 1966 photograph, he is with the Associated Press staff in front of the Vietnam National Assembly building. (Courtesy of the UCI Vietnamese American Oral History Project, VAOHP0204.)

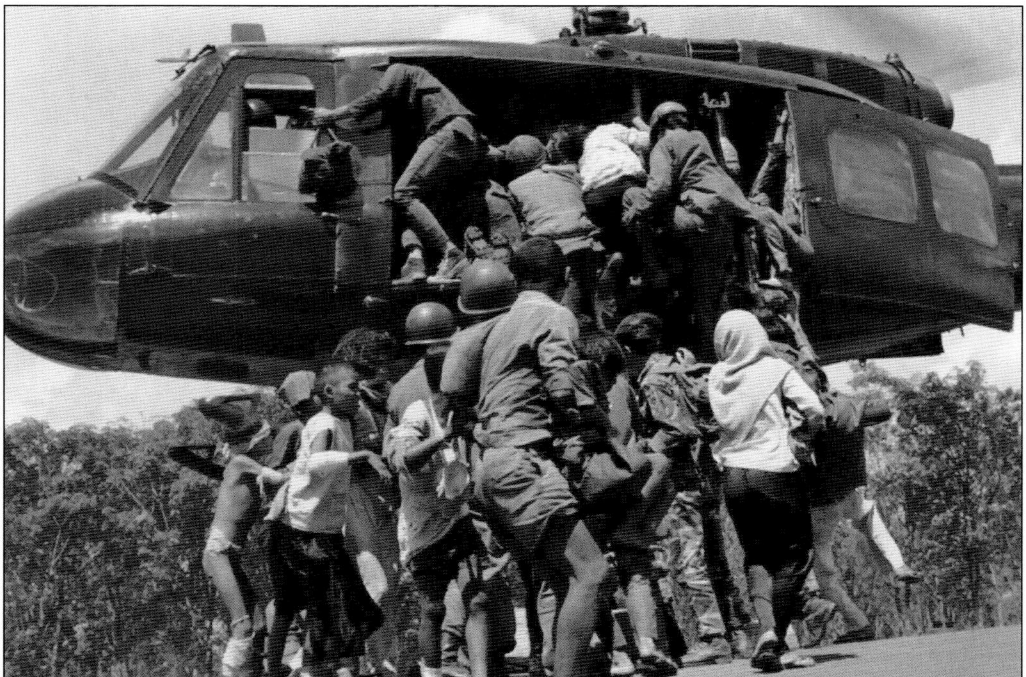

On June 25, 1972, Nick Ut captured this image of wounded civilians and troops pushing their way aboard a South Vietnamese evacuation helicopter hovering over a stretch of Highway 13 near An Loc. (Courtesy of the UCI Vietnamese American Oral History Project, VAOHP0204.)

Anti-war demonstrations were part of American life in the late 1960s and early 1970s. The Vietnam War Moratorium was held across the United States on October 15, 1969. On the newly built UC Irvine campus, demonstrations occurred, including alternative education classes in Aldrich Park, a march to nearby institutions involved in war production and research, and a memorial service for those who died in the war. (Courtesy of UCI Libraries Special Collections and Archives, AS-061.)

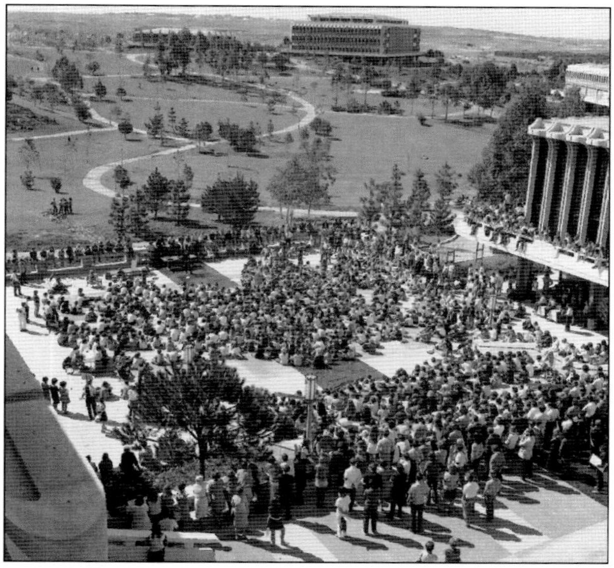

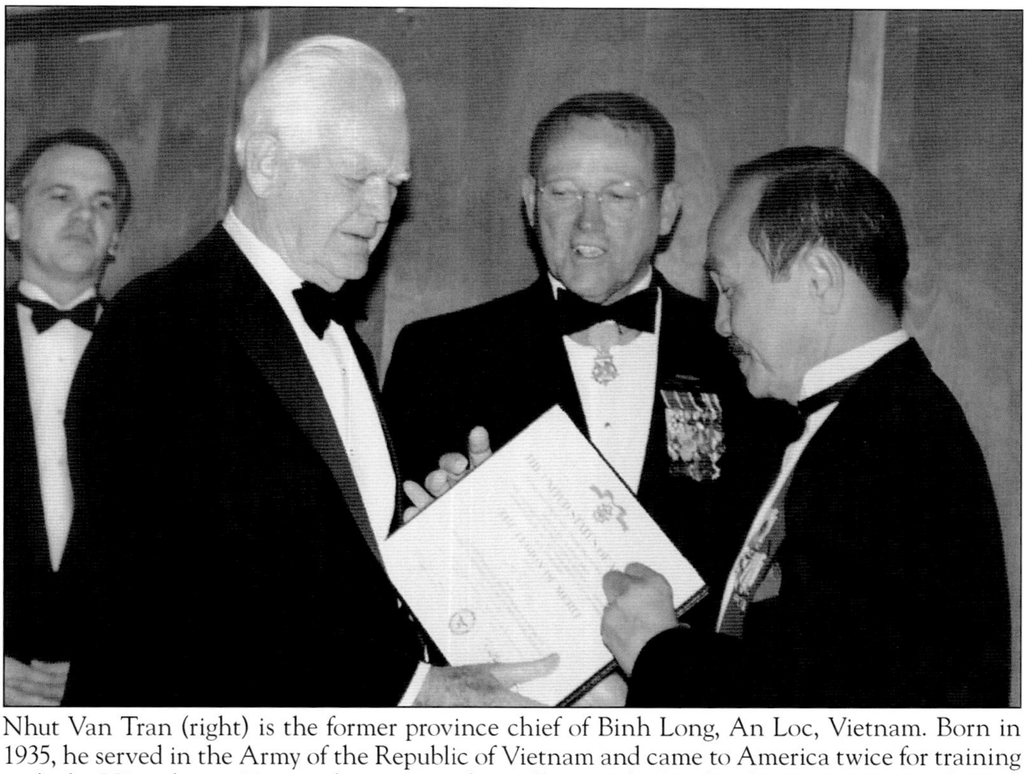

Nhut Van Tran (right) is the former province chief of Binh Long, An Loc, Vietnam. Born in 1935, he served in the Army of the Republic of Vietnam and came to America twice for training with the US military. He was the commanding officer at the Battle of An Loc. In 1975, he and his family were evacuated to Camp Pendleton, and they were sponsored to Texas before eventually moving to Orange County. He held a variety of jobs, including being a gardener as well as working at an oil refinery and a Navy shipyard. In this 1998 photograph, he is being awarded the Legion of Merit by William Westmoreland, a controversial four-star general during the Vietnam War. (Courtesy of the UCI Vietnamese American Oral History Project, VAOHP0134.)

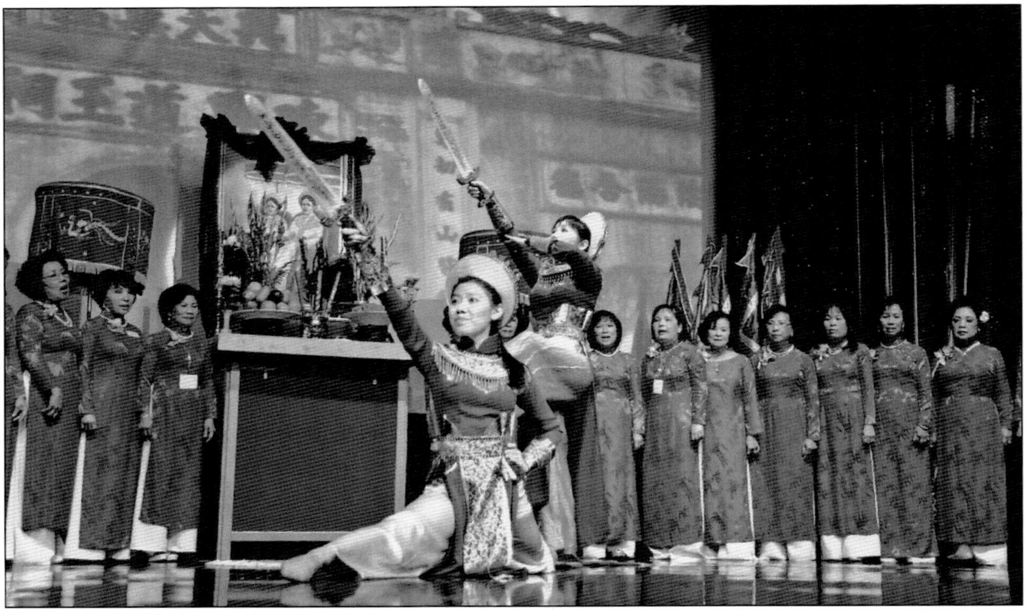

Alumni of Trung Vuong High School hosted a commemoration of the Trung Sisters at the Saigon Performing Arts Center in Fountain Valley on March 10, 2013. Performance group Viet Cam and martial arts group Vo Vi Nam performed at this event for over 300 attendees. (Courtesy of Nguyen Van Liem/*Viet Tide*.)

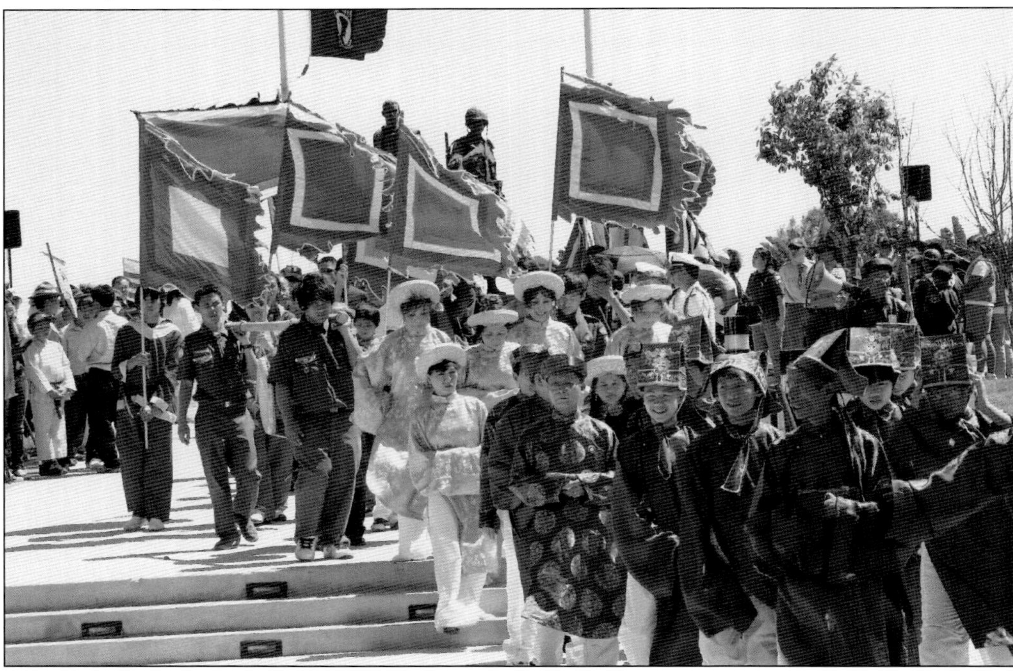

In Little Saigon, Vietnamese Americans honor their history through an annual celebration of the founding father, King Hung Vuong. According to Vietnamese legend, the people are descendants of the original 100 children born from a dragon king and fairy queen. (Courtesy of Kimberly Pham.)

Two

RESETTLEMENT

Vietnamese refugees and immigrants in Orange County come from varying backgrounds. Before 1975, a small number of Vietnamese in the United States were international students, war brides, international brides, diplomats, or military personnel receiving training. During the Fall of Saigon at the end of April 1975, approximately 130,000 refugees were evacuated by sea and air by the US military during Operation Frequent Wind. They were temporarily housed in four military bases, including Camp Pendleton in San Diego County, until they found individuals, religious groups, and charitable organizations willing to sponsor them. Among this group were employees of the South Vietnamese military or the American government who feared persecution of their families when the new regime took over. During this time, Vietnamese orphans were also airlifted to America and adopted through Operation Babylift.

Beginning in the late 1970s, the majority of Vietnamese refugees escaped by fishing boats or ships to Hong Kong, Indonesia, Malaysia, the Philippines, Singapore, and Thailand; however, some travelled by land to Cambodia or Thailand. A fair number of the boat people refugees were ethnic Chinese who were forced to flee for fear of persecution. Those who fled by sea often faced piracy, rape, starvation, and death and disappearance, and those captured were imprisoned. Some escapees languished for years in crowded refugee camps waiting for sponsorship in resettlement countries, including the United States. The United Nations High Commissioner for Refugees (UNHCR) created the Orderly Departure Program (ODP) to safely process the departure of Vietnamese immigrants. Former South Vietnamese veterans who survived imprisonment in the reeducation camps were allowed passage to the United States through the Humanitarian Operation (HO). Additionally, Amerasians, mixed-race children of American servicemen and Vietnamese women, were permitted to immigrate to the United States along with their relatives. A number of immigrants arriving today are sponsored by family members or are international students.

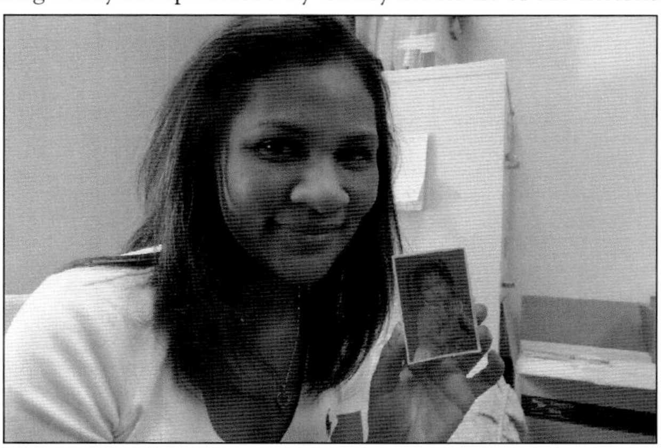

Tamara Hill, with a photograph of herself, was an orphan who was evacuated from Vietnam in April of 1975 as part of Operation Babylift; many were children of Vietnamese mothers and American fathers. She was adopted by a family in Northridge and currently lives in Irvine. (Courtesy of the UCI Vietnamese American Oral History Project, VAOHP0176.)

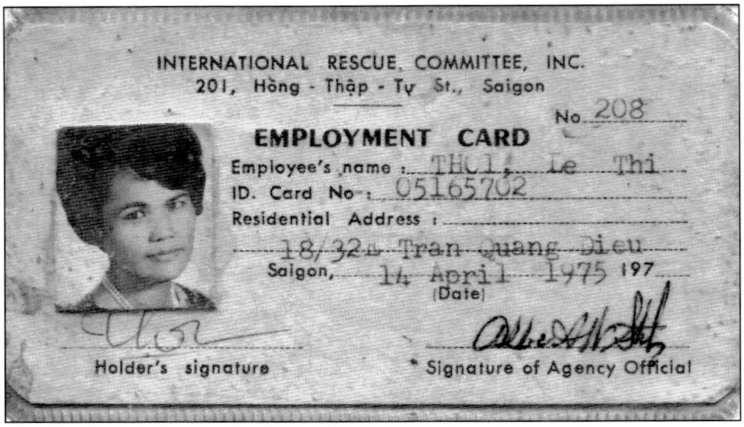

INTERNATIONAL RESCUE COMMITTEE, INC.
201, Hòng - Thập - Tự St., Saigon

No. 208

EMPLOYMENT CARD

Employee's name : THOI, Le Thi
ID. Card No : 05165702
Residential Address :
18/32 Tran Quang Dieu
Saigon, 14 April 1975 197
(Date)

Holder's signature
* Signature of Agency Official

A Vietnamese employee of the International Rescue Committee, Le Thi Thoi, was issued an employment card on April 14, 1975, just a few weeks before the Fall of Saigon. (Courtesy of Le Thi Thoi.)

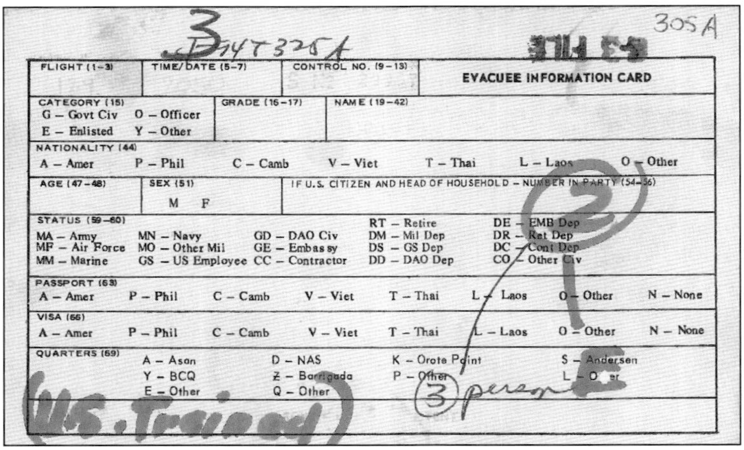

305A

EVACUEE INFORMATION CARD

FLIGHT (1–3) | TIME/DATE (5–7) | CONTROL NO. (9–13)

CATEGORY (15): G – Govt Civ, O – Officer, E – Enlisted, Y – Other | GRADE (16–17) | NAME (19–42)

NATIONALITY (44): A – Amer, P – Phil, C – Camb, V – Viet, T – Thai, L – Laos, O – Other

AGE (47–48) | SEX (51) M F | IF U.S. CITIZEN AND HEAD OF HOUSEHOLD – NUMBER IN PARTY (54–56)

STATUS (59–60): MA – Army, MF – Air Force, MM – Marine, MN – Navy, MO – Other Mil, GS – US Employee, GD – DAO Civ, GE – Embassy, CC – Contractor, RT – Retire, DM – Mil Dep, DS – GS Dep, DD – DAO Dep, DE – EMB Dep, DR – Ret Dep, DC – Cont Dep, CO – Other Civ

PASSPORT (63): A – Amer, P – Phil, C – Camb, V – Viet, T – Thai, L – Laos, O – Other, N – None

VISA (66): A – Amer, P – Phil, C – Camb, V – Viet, T – Thai, L – Laos, O – Other, N – None

QUARTERS (69): A – Ason, Y – BCQ, E – Other, D – NAS, Z – Barrigada, Q – Other, K – Orote Point, P – Other, S – Andersen, L – Other

(U.S. Trained)

3 person

Information cards like this were used to prioritize departures from Vietnam during the chaotic days before Saigon fell. Those with affiliations to the American government were given higher priority for airlifts and sponsorships. (Courtesy of Nguyen Thi Kim Anh.)

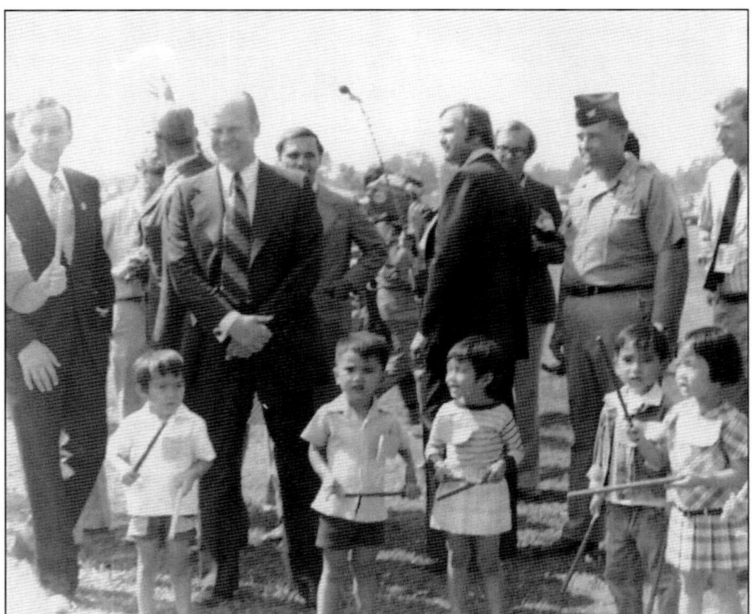

President Gerald Ford poses with refugee children at Fort Chaffee, Arkansas, in 1975. The Ford administration passed the Indochina Migration and Refugee Act of 1975, allocating funding to the resettlement. (Courtesy of UCI Libraries Southeast Asian Archive, MS-SEA025, B1:9.)

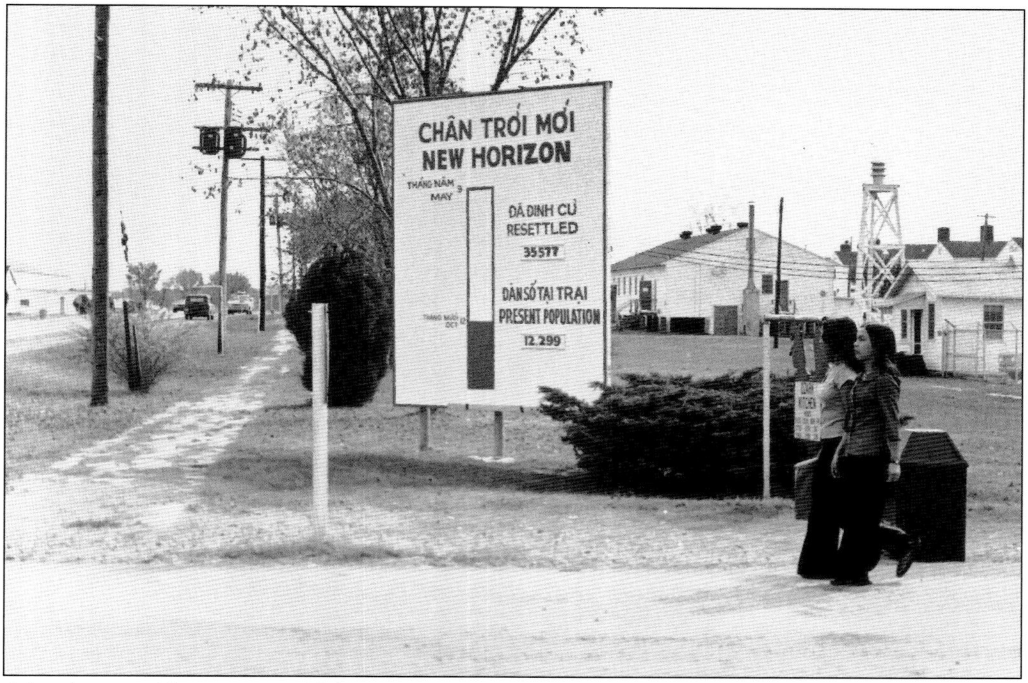

After leaving Vietnam in 1975, evacuees were processed in Guam and the Philippines before being flown to one of four temporary resettlement centers: Camp Pendleton (California), Fort Chaffee (Arkansas), Eglin Air Force Base (Florida), and Fort Indiantown Gap (Pennsylvania). This sign outside Fort Chaffee displays the numbers of those at the center and those already resettled. (Courtesy of UCI Libraries Southeast Asian Archive, MS-SEA025, Box1:8.)

A Vietnamese family arrives in America through Fort Chaffee in 1975. Refugees could not leave the military base until they found sponsors who would be responsible for their resettlement. Refugees were dispersed across the country, but through secondary migration many later moved to areas with higher Vietnamese concentrations, including Orange County. (Courtesy of UCI Libraries Southeast Asian Archive, MS-SEA025, Box1:11.)

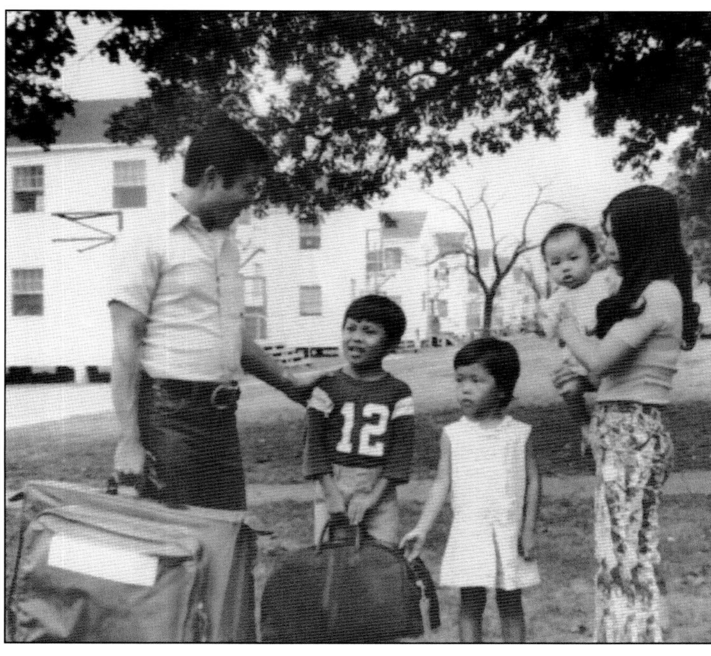

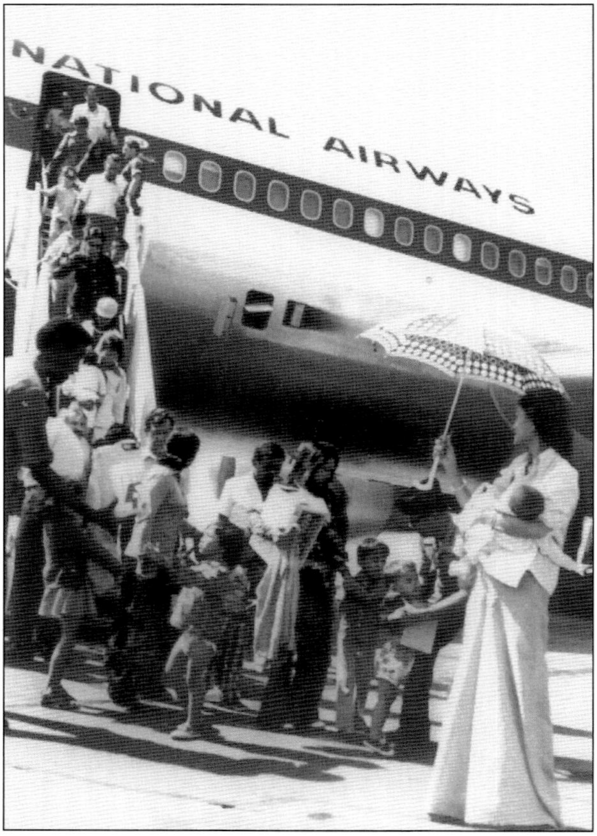

In 1975, refugees arrive at El Toro Airbase before being transported to Camp Pendleton for processing. (Official Marine Corps photograph.)

Upon their arrival to Camp Pendleton, refugees were checked in by Marine Corps personnel, distributed rations of clothing, and assigned housing. (Official Marine Corps photograph.)

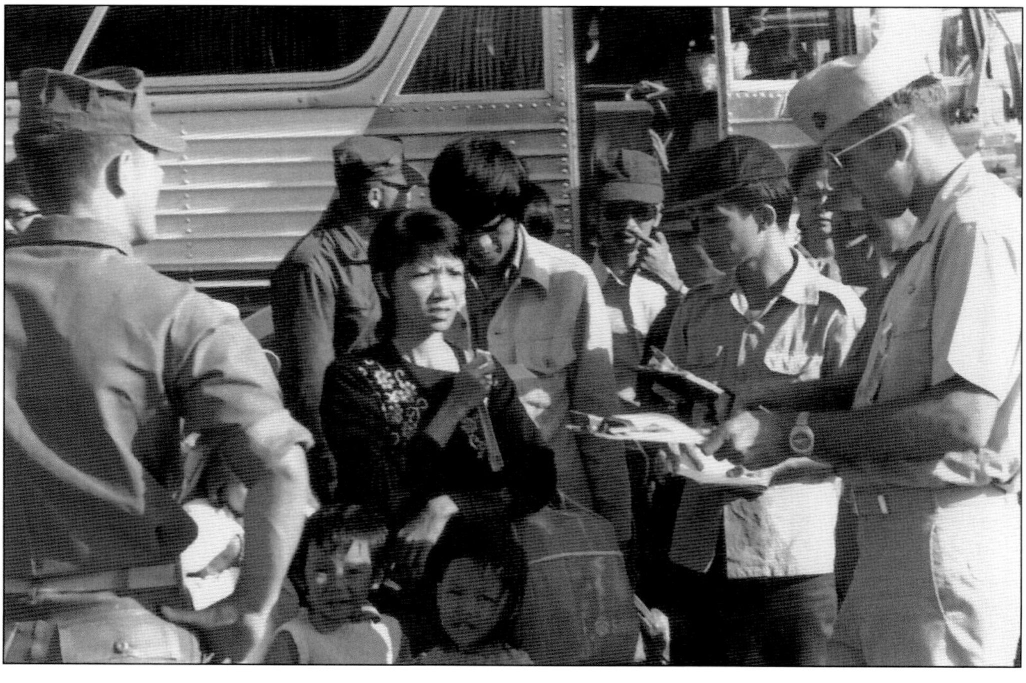

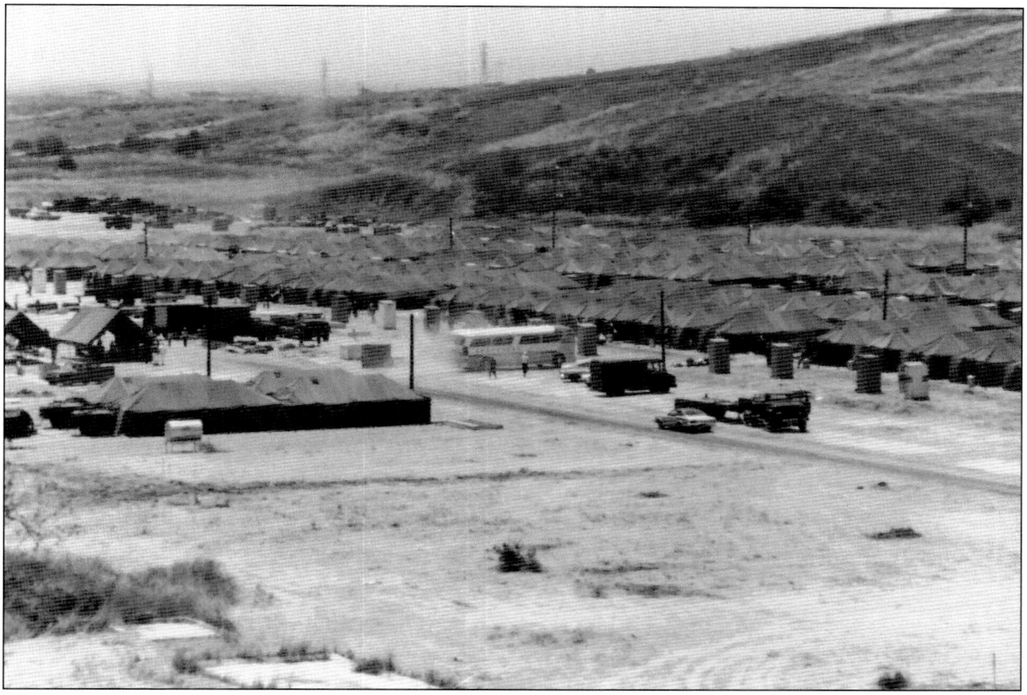

This photograph shows the tent cities that appeared almost overnight at Camp Pendleton to accommodate over 50,000 refugees entering the United States. They arrived from April to October 1975, with a peak of 18,000 refugees at one time. (Courtesy of UCI Libraries Southeast Asian Archive, MS-SEA034, Box1:1.)

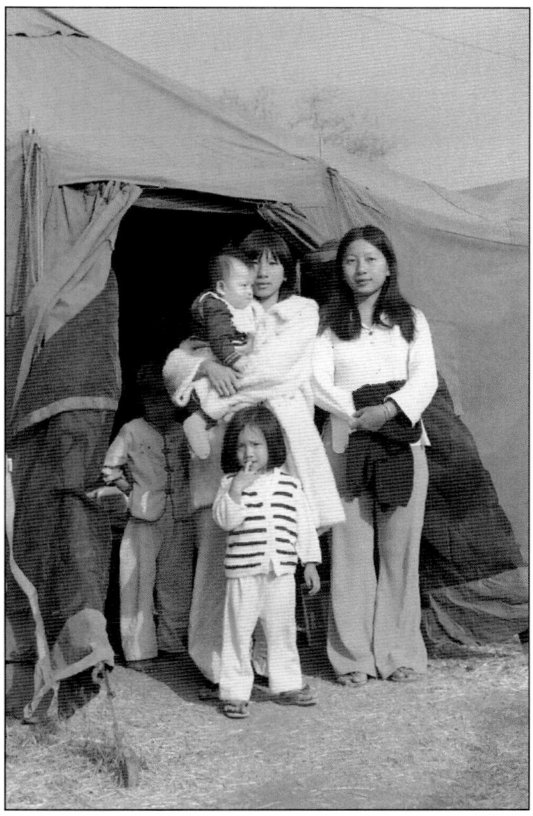

Members of Nhan Thi Nguyen's family stand in front of their tent at Camp Pendleton in 1975. She brought her nine children from Vietnam to America and raised them as a single mother until her husband, Duong Dinh Thu, was released from a re-education camp. He was able to reunite with them after 12 years. (Courtesy of the UCI Vietnamese American Oral History Project, VAOHP0143.)

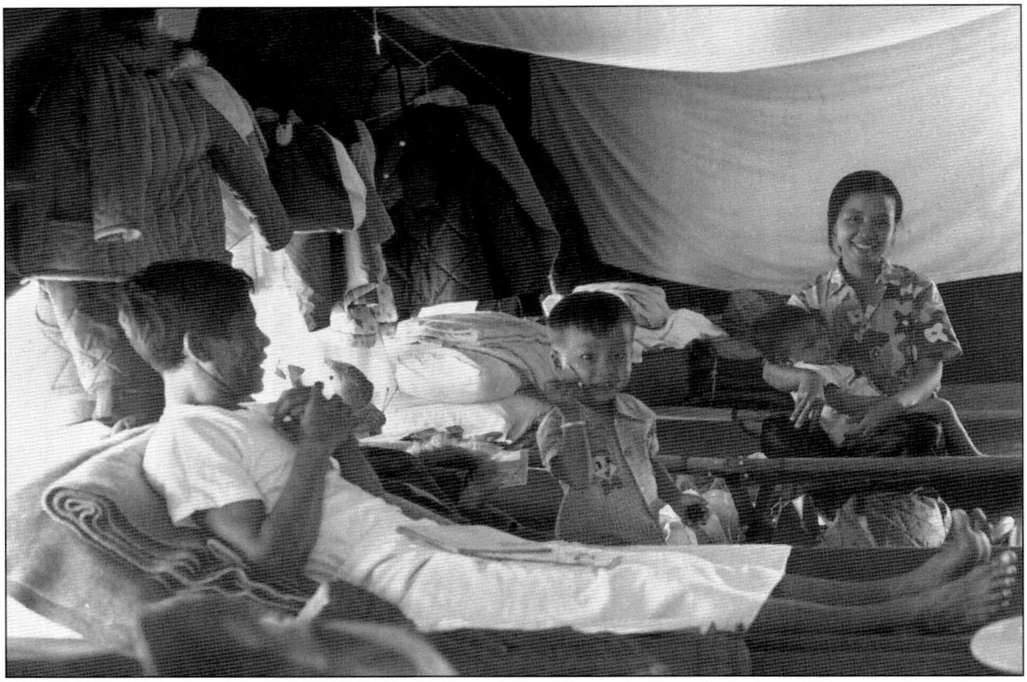
Inside one of the tents at Camp Pendleton, a Vietnamese family adjusts to their temporary living quarters. Many refugees were used to Vietnam's tropical and humid climate and had a hard time adapting to the cold nights. (Official Marine Corps photograph.)

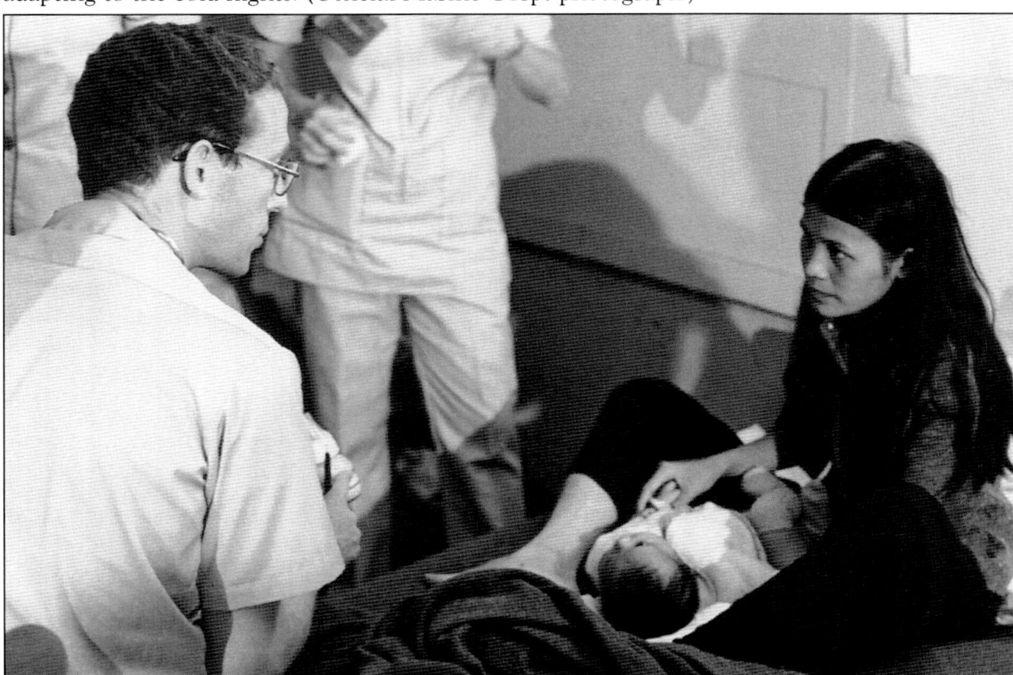
Medical examinations were part of the required screening process for Vietnamese refugees. (Official Marine Corps photograph.)

Truong Quang To (far right) built his own boat to escape Vietnam with his wife and children in 1987. After seven days at sea, they ended up in Thailand and eventually resettled in Huntington Beach. (Courtesy of Truong Quang To.)

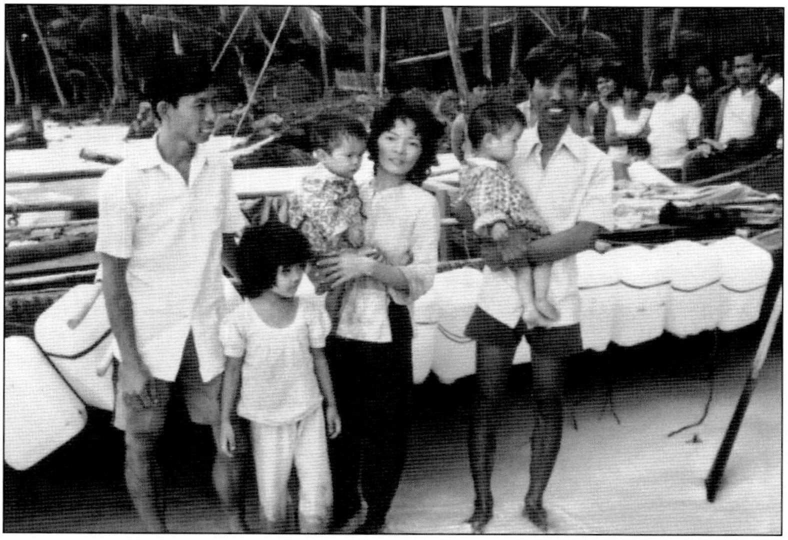

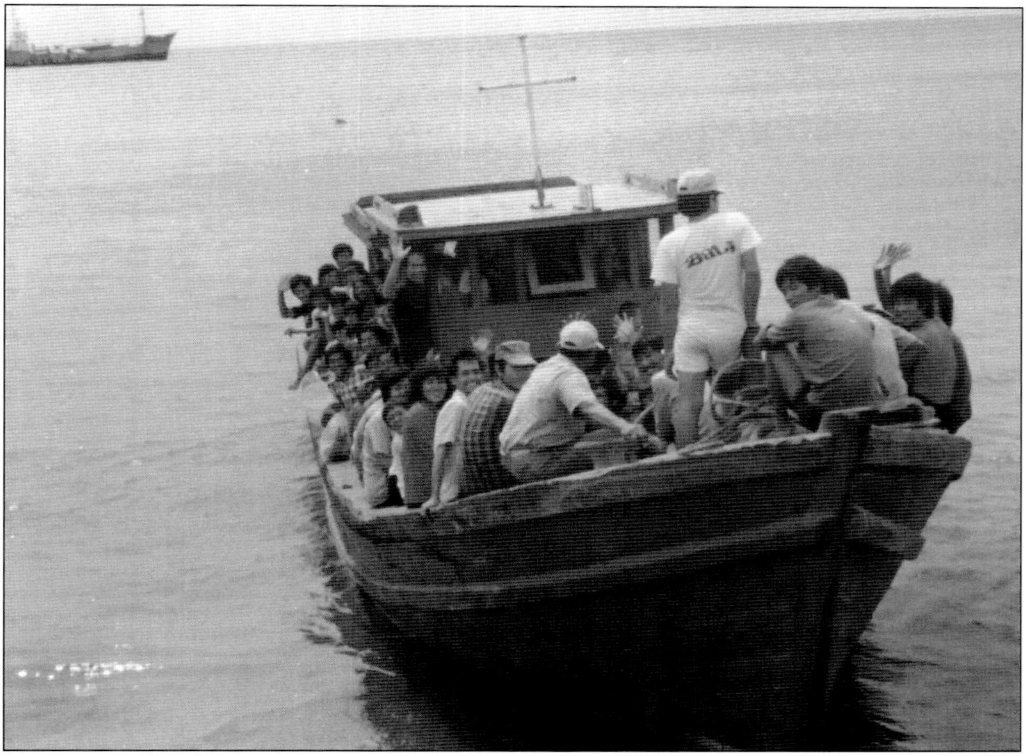

A German oil tanker in the South China Sea came to the assistance of this refugee boat. The refugees, relieved that their difficult journey was nearly over, were taken to Kuku Island and admitted to Galang I refugee camp in Indonesia. Overcrowded boats capsized during bad weather, and other groups that were adrift at sea ran out of food and water. The most ominous threats were Thai pirates who robbed, beat, raped, and kidnapped the refugees and then sank the boats to destroy evidence of their crimes. (Courtesy of UCI Vietnamese American Oral History Project, VAOHP0016.)

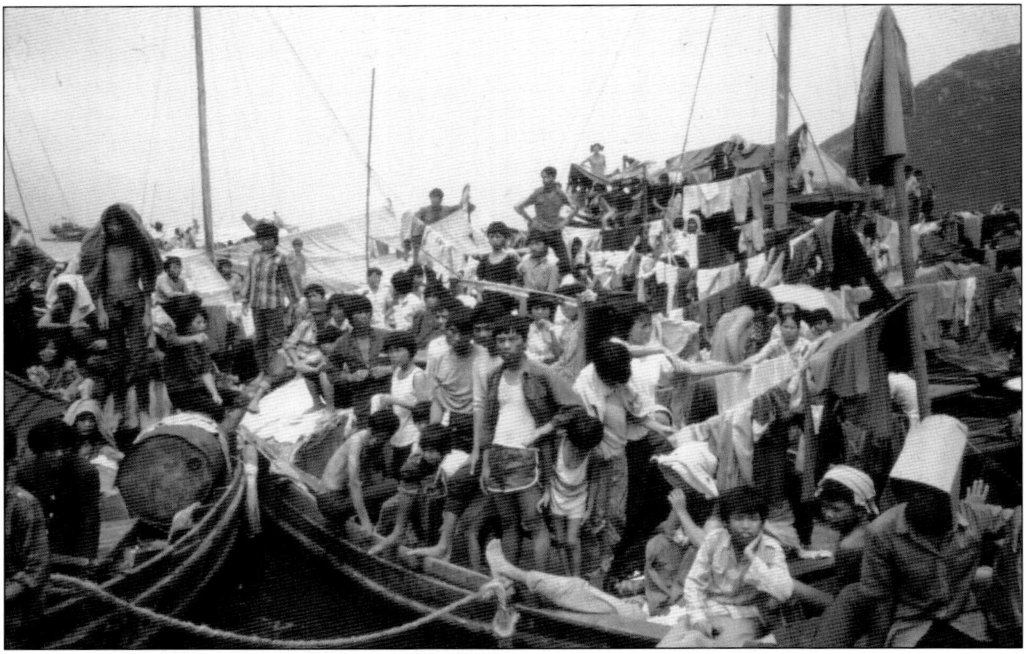

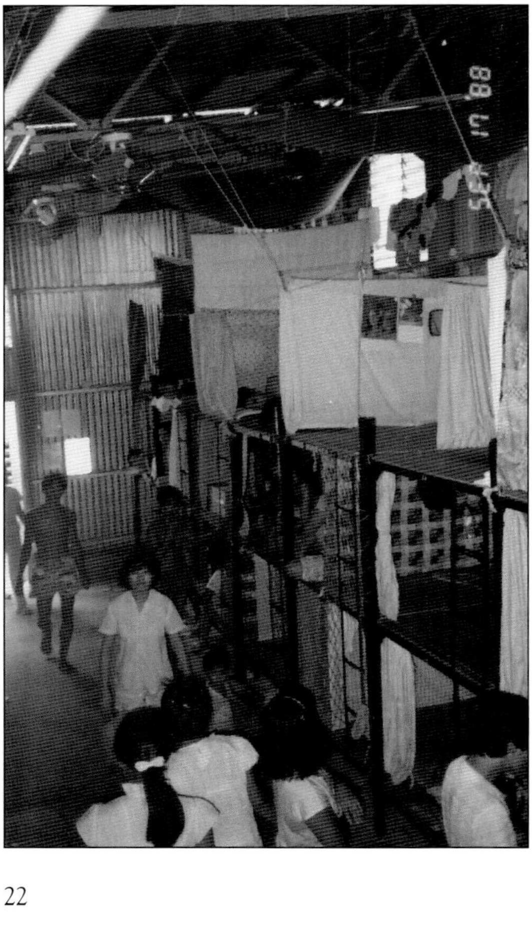

The boat people exodus began in the late 1970s with the mass departure of Vietnamese seeking political refugee status. In the decade that followed, the dangerous journeys of land and boat refugees became an international crisis. Due to overcrowding, these refugees are living aboard their boats waiting for a space in the camps. (Courtesy of the UCI Libraries Southeast Asian Archive, MS-SEA016, Box6:4.)

Whitehead and Chimawan Detention Centres were refugee camps in Hong Kong infamous for their hazardous and cramped conditions. In 1982, the Hong Kong government introduced a closed camp policy where refugees arriving after that date were no longer allowed to leave the refugee camps to work in the surrounding community. This policy was aimed at deterring and discouraging more Vietnamese from coming to Hong Kong. (Courtesy of UCI Libraries Southeast Asian Archive, MS-SEA016, Box10:16.)

Children are playing in front of a day-care center at the Cape Collinson camp in Hong Kong around 1988 or 1989. This camp was managed by the Hong Kong Correctional Services Department. At the time of this photograph, the numbers of refugees seeking admittance dramatically increased to an estimated 300 per day. (Courtesy of UCI Libraries Southeast Asian Archive, MS-SEA016, Box9:7.)

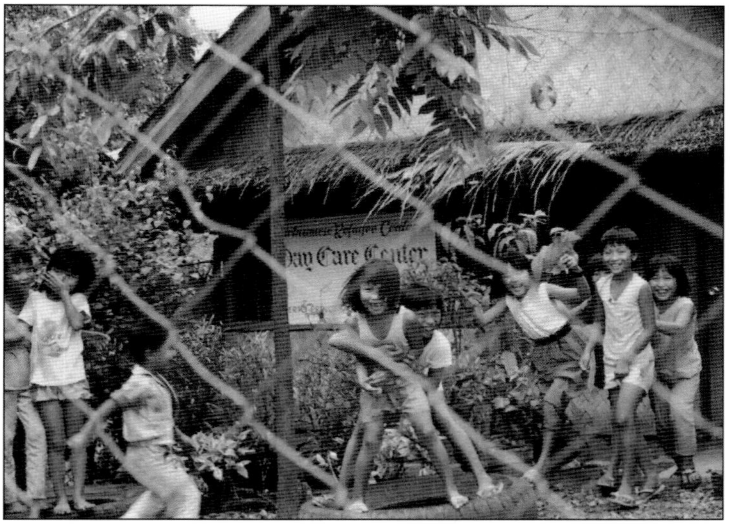

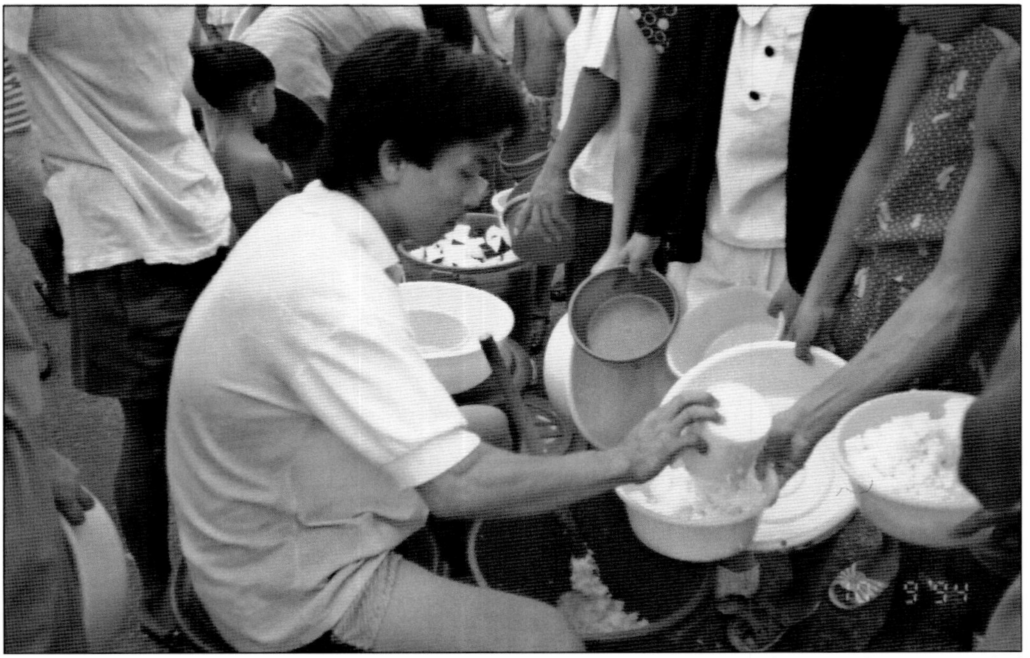

A camp worker distributes food rations to a crowd of refugees. This 1994 photograph was provided by a UC Irvine student-led humanitarian organization called Project Ngoc. Student volunteers documented the deteriorating conditions and lobbied in Washington, DC, and the United Nations for refugee rights. (Courtesy of UCI Libraries Southeast Asian Archive, MS-SEA016.)

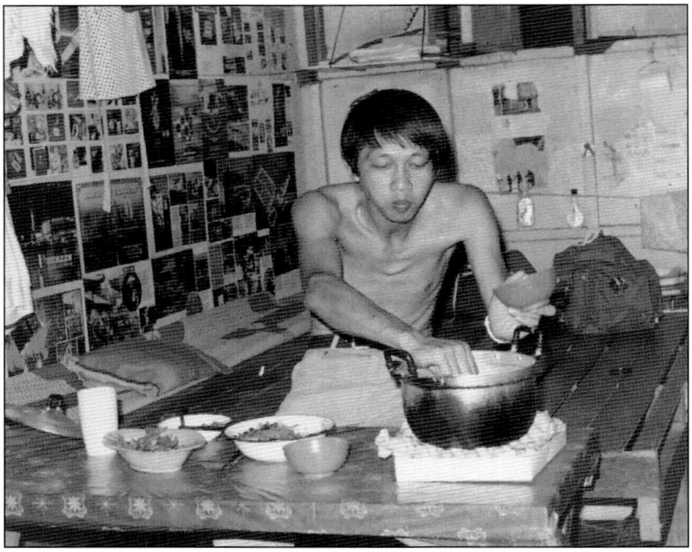

Steve Pho cooks in his private room in the Bataan Refugee Camp. A small stove allowed him to prepare his own food during his six months in the camp. Besides teaching English to other refugees, he made money taking photographs of people and events around camp. He eventually settled in Garden Grove, where he became a community activist and assisted in opening a performing-arts center. (Courtesy of the UCI Vietnamese American Oral History Project, VAOHP0164.)

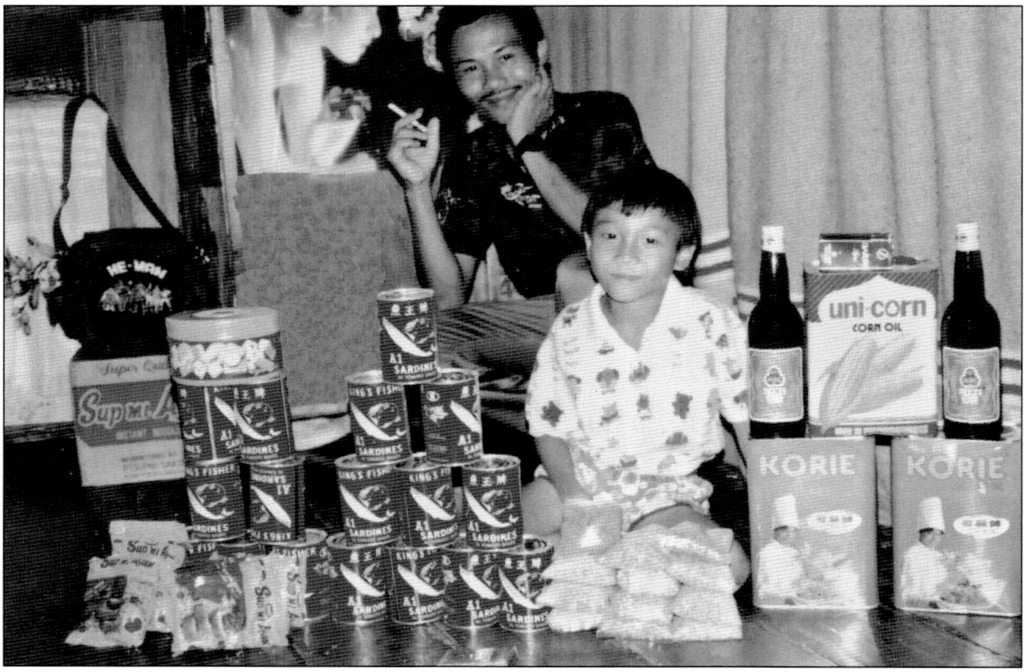

The Office of the United Nations High Commissioner for Refugees provided food staples such as corn oil, canned foods, instant noodles, and rice, depending on the size of refugee families. Tho Nguyen and his son Lam pose with their rations in Galang II, Indonesia, in 1990. (Courtesy of Tho Nguyen.)

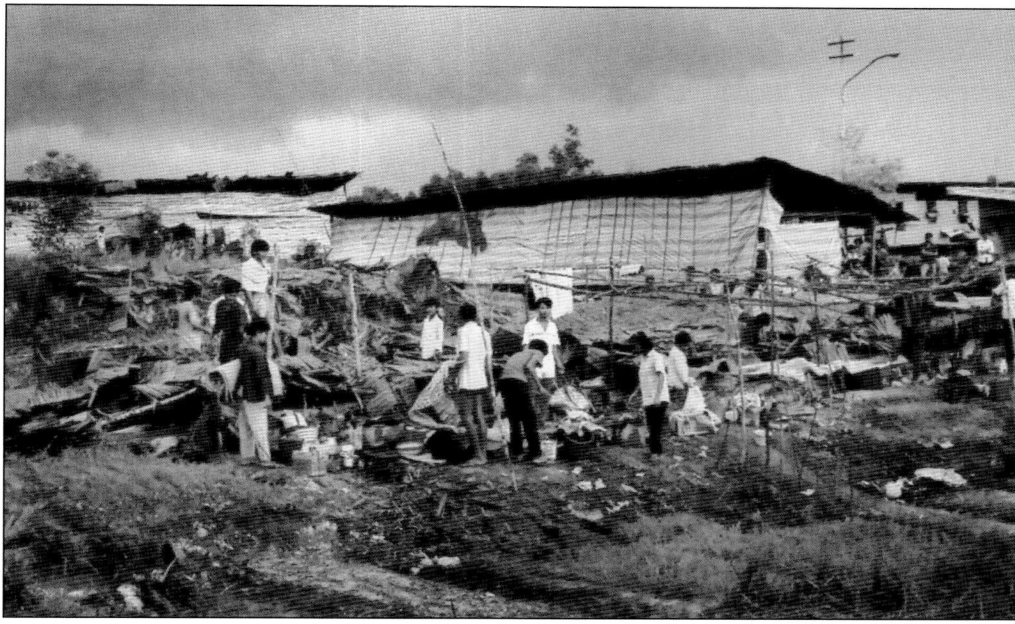

Makeshift housing structures in refugee camps were poorly constructed and unable to withstand strong rainfall or high winds. In Galang, Indonesia, one structure collapsed overnight, and the tenants are salvaging their possessions from the wreckage. (Courtesy of Tho Nguyen.)

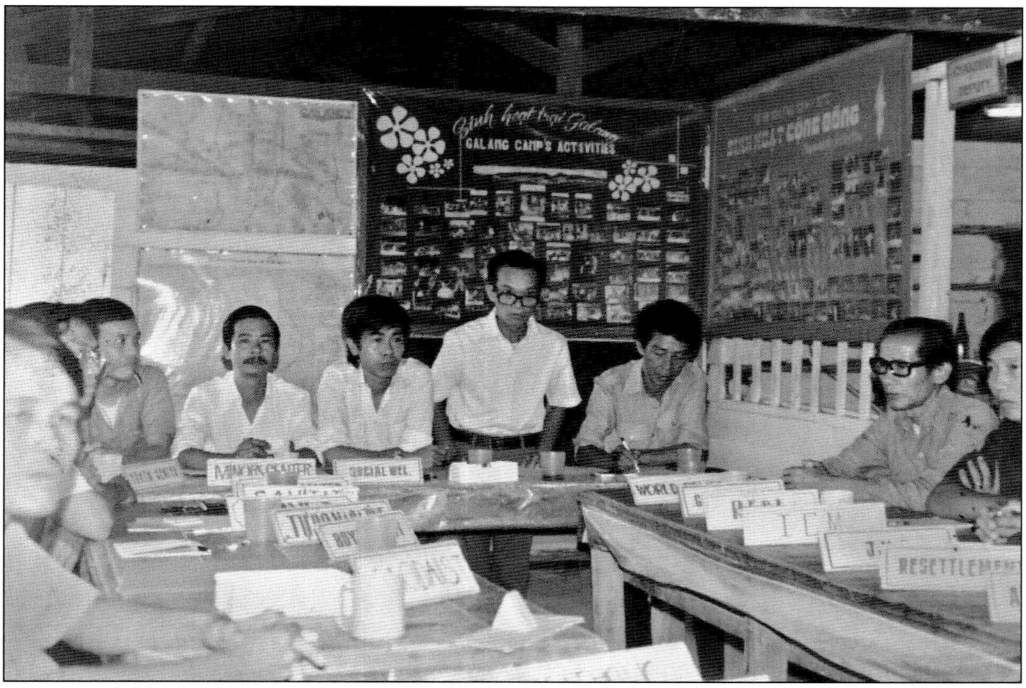

International humanitarian aid workers and volunteers from within the refugee camps in Southeast Asia organized to improve conditions in the camps. This photograph was taken during a 1984 meeting of representatives in a refugee camp in Galang, Indonesia. (Courtesy of the UCI Vietnamese American Oral History Project, VAOHP0142.)

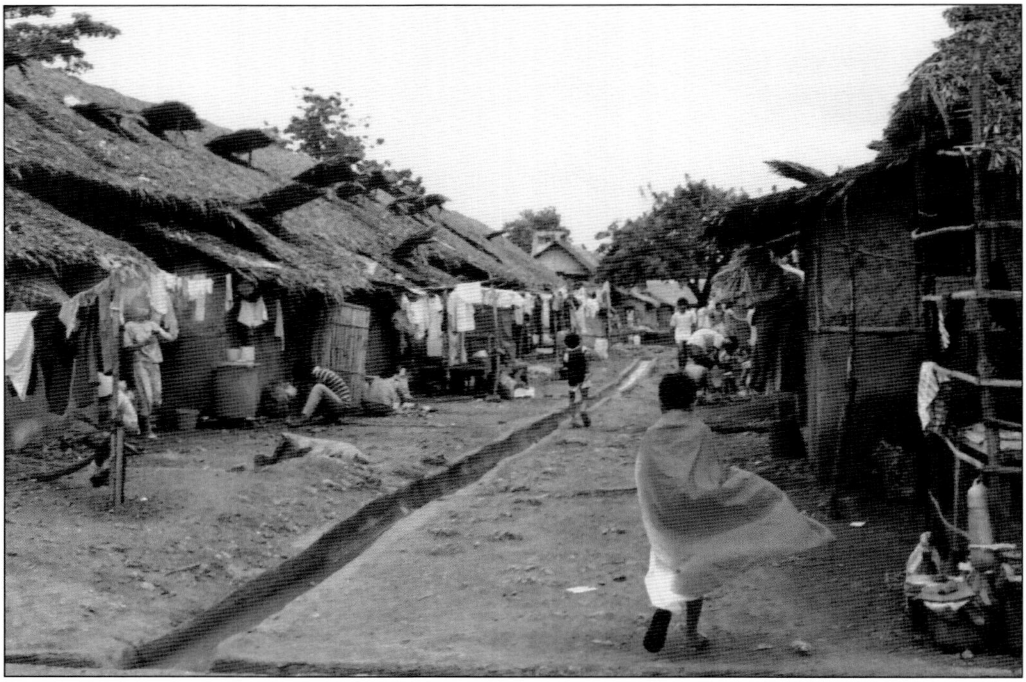

A child runs through a refugee camp in Palawan, Philippines. This image depicts a typical refugee camp zone, where there are 75 huts with about 12 people in each hut. (Courtesy of UCI Libraries Southeast Asian Archive, MS-SEA016, Box9:7.)

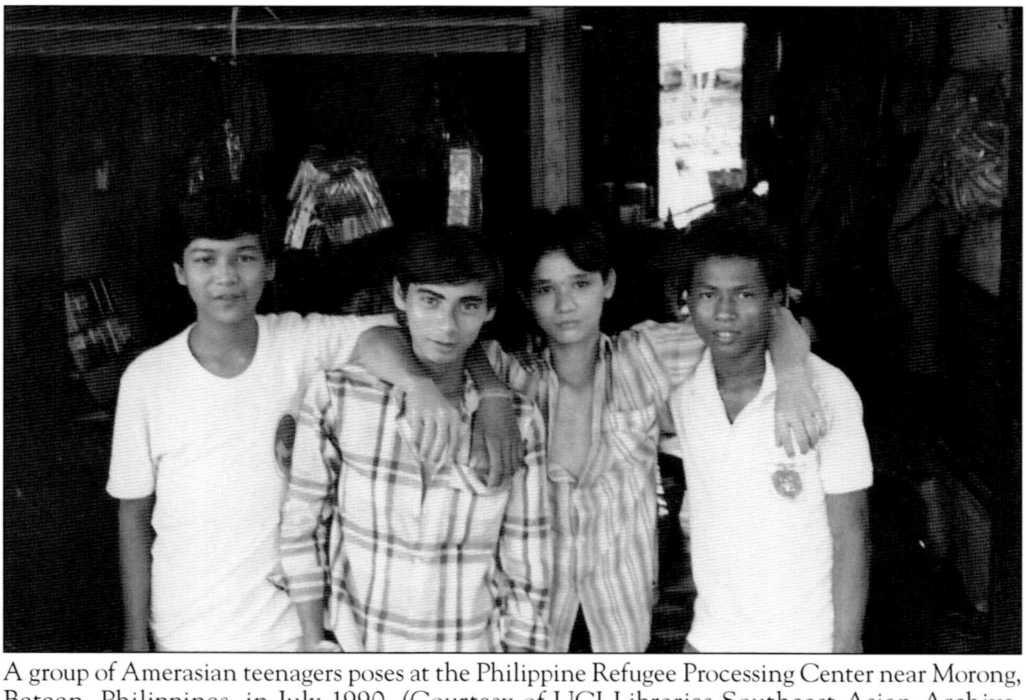

A group of Amerasian teenagers poses at the Philippine Refugee Processing Center near Morong, Bataan, Philippines, in July 1990. (Courtesy of UCI Libraries Southeast Asian Archive, MS-SEA016, Box9:13.)

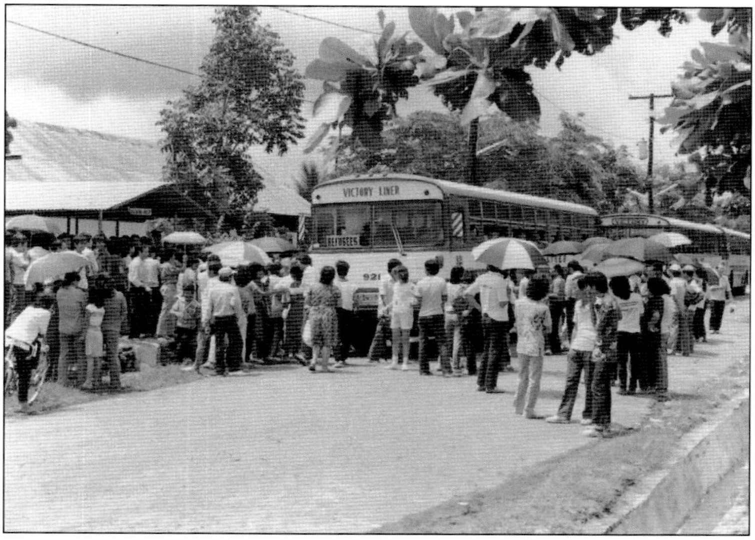

Refugees leave the Bataan Refugee Camp on July 1986 on a bus that will take them to the airport to fly to the United States. (Courtesy of the UCI Vietnamese American Oral History Project, VAOHP0164.)

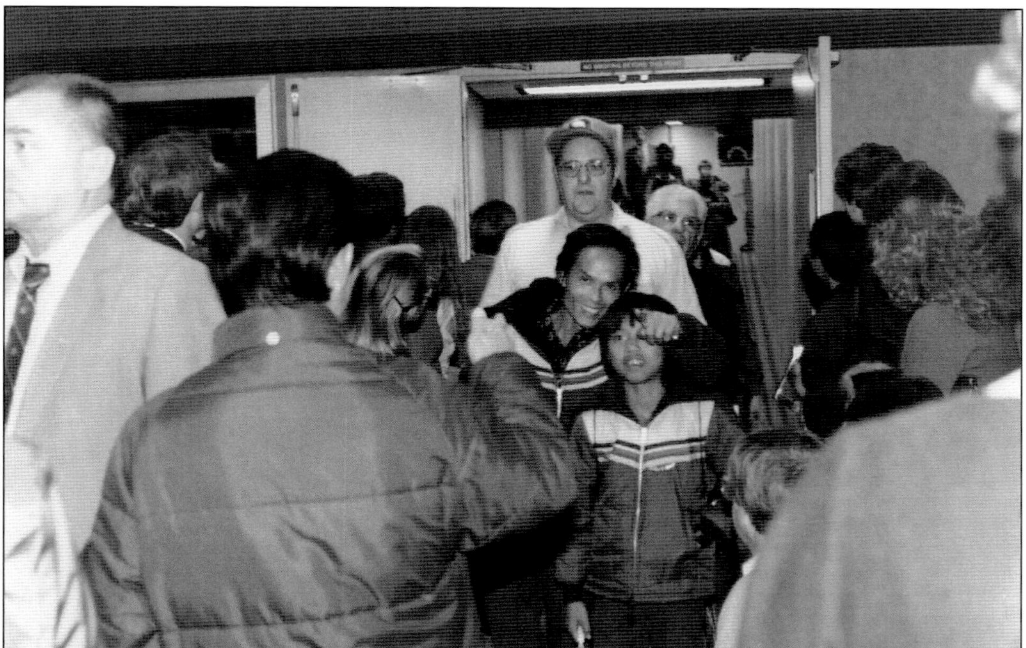

In 1984, Huy Tran arrived in Austin, Texas, with this father, Hien Tran, from a Galang, Indonesia, refugee camp and was greeted by Huy's uncle. The jackets worn by father and son were issued by the International Committee on Migration (ICM) and were standard issue for refugees at the time. Huy grew up in Orange County, graduated from UC Irvine, and became a junior high school math teacher in the Anaheim Union High School District. (Courtesy of UCI Vietnamese American Oral History Project, VAOHP0016.)

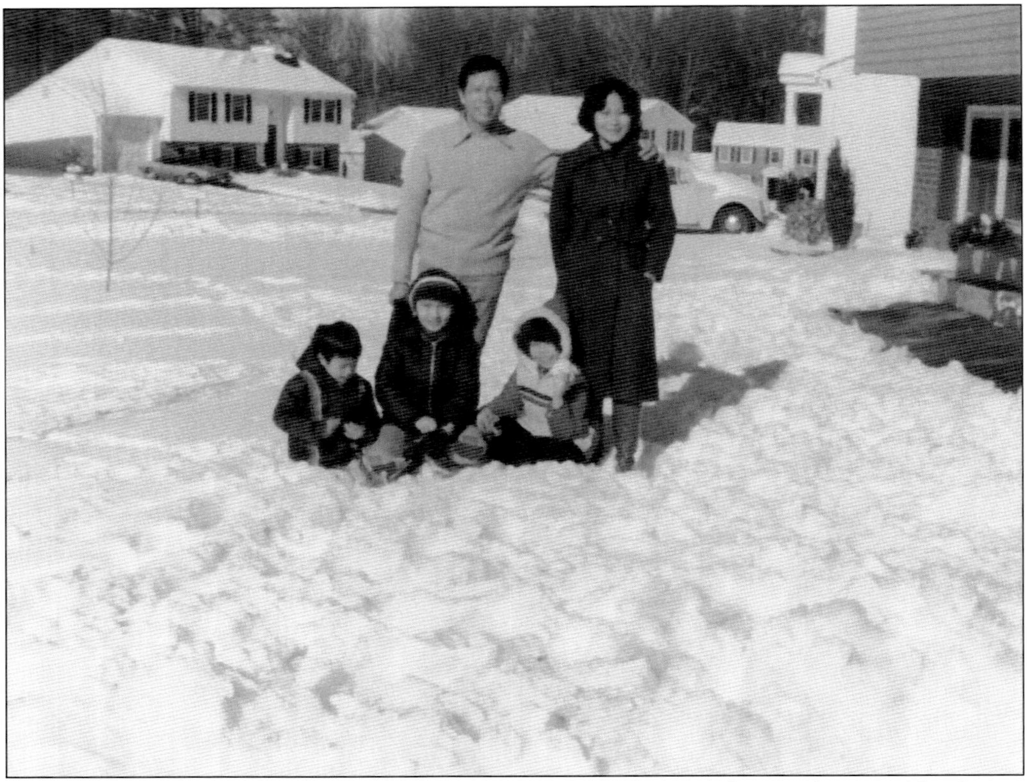

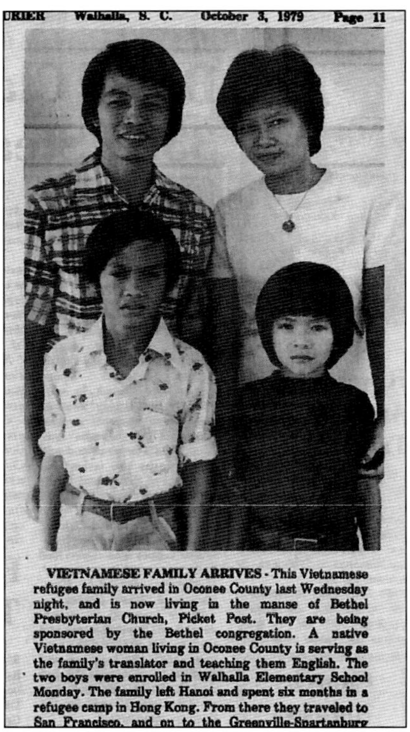

URIER Walhalla, S. C. October 3, 1979 Page 11

VIETNAMESE FAMILY ARRIVES - This Vietnamese refugee family arrived in Oconee County last Wednesday night, and is now living in the manse of Bethel Presbyterian Church, Picket Post. They are being sponsored by the Bethel congregation. A native Vietnamese woman living in Oconee County is serving as the family's translator and teaching them English. The two boys were enrolled in Walhalla Elementary School Monday. The family left Hanoi and spent six months in a refugee camp in Hong Kong. From there they traveled to San Francisco, and on to the Greenville-Spartanburg

The Refugee Dispersion Policy implemented by the US government in 1975 scattered individuals and families all over the country. This was done to ease the economic impact on any given region, force refugees to assimilate quickly, facilitate sponsorships, and prevent ethnic concentrations from forming. In December 1979, the Nguyen family settled in Virginia before moving to Orange County. Reunification with families, employment opportunities, and warmer climates were the main reasons for secondary migration. (Courtesy of Tu-Uyen Nguyen.)

Jack Khu Dang Toan (front left) is featured with his family after they were sponsored by Bethel Presbyterian Church and resettled in South Carolina in 1979. They eventually relocated to Orange County. (Courtesy of the *Keowee Courier.*)

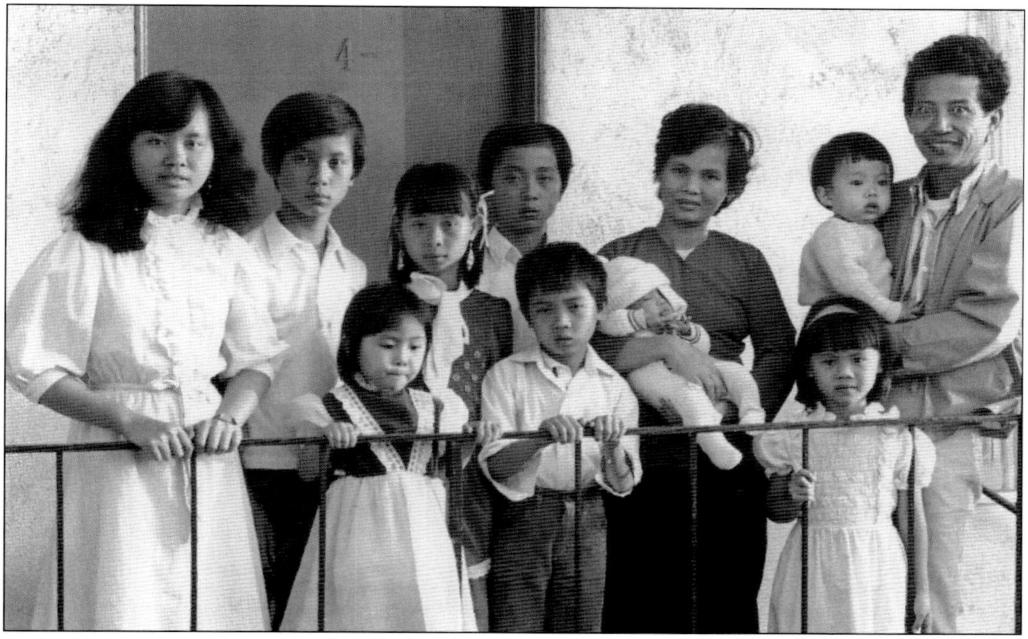

The Vo family escaped Vietnam by boat and was sponsored by a Lutheran church in Jamestown, New York, but shortly thereafter moved to Orange County. In this 1984 photograph, they are in front of their two-bedroom apartment in Garden Grove, where the family of 11 lived on Hazard Avenue alongside other refugee families. Neighbors coined the pejorative phrase "Gooks of Hazard" to describe the refugee families. (Courtesy of UCI Vietnamese American Oral History Project, VAHF0014.)

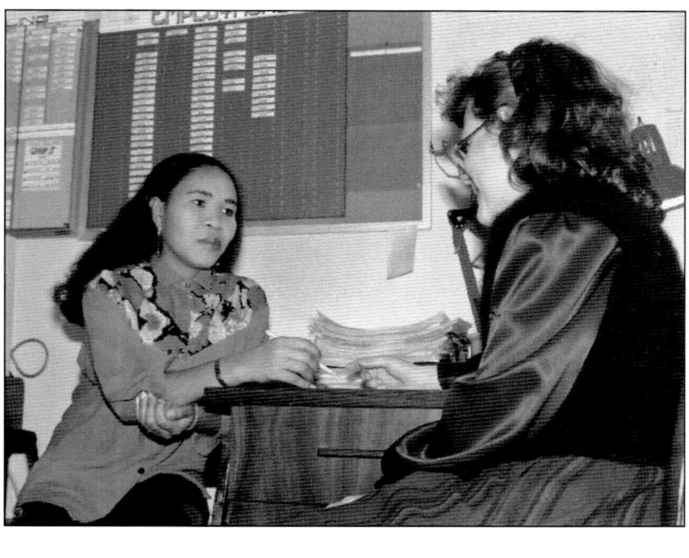

In Orange County, Saint Anselm's Cross-Cultural Community Center opened its doors in 1976 and worked with individual sponsors in addition to other religious groups, organizations, and voluntary agencies (VOLAGs) to assist refugees, including the Vietnamese. In 2012, the organization changed its name to Horizon Cross Cultural Center and tailored its services to assist newer immigrants. (Courtesy of Horizon Cross Cultural Center.)

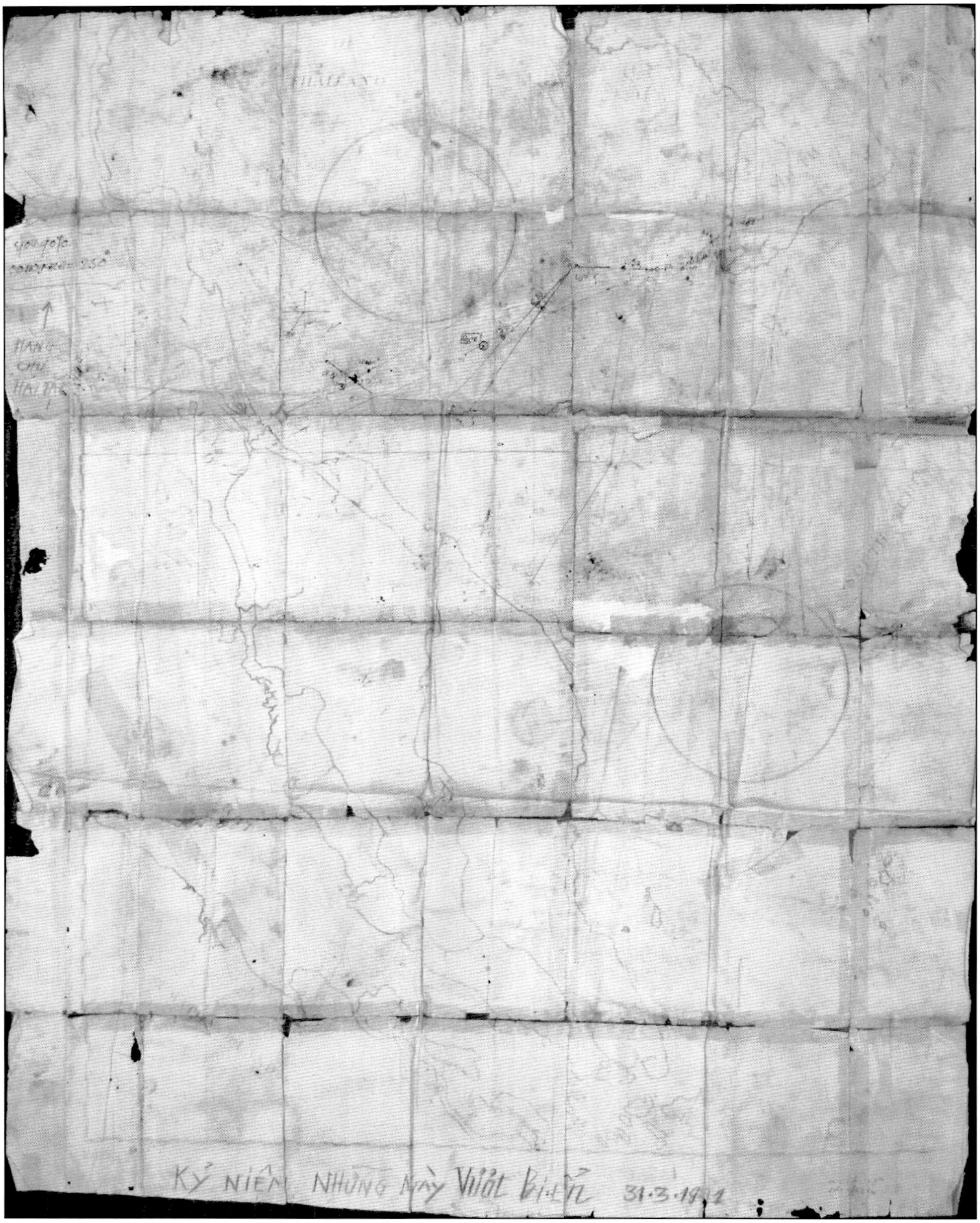

Dung Tran saved this tattered hand-drawn map, which he used to escape Vietnam in the early 1980s with his brother. They encountered Thai fishermen at sea who drew arrow marks directing them toward land. They arrived in Songkhla, Thailand, and resettled in Fountain Valley. (Courtesy of Dung Tran.)

Three

LITTLE SAIGON

Starting with a few residents and businesses in the late 1970s, Little Saigon in Orange County developed into the largest community of Vietnamese outside of Vietnam, commonly known as the capital of this exiled population. Thousands of Vietnamese businesses as well as cultural, social, political, and religious organizations emerged to serve the needs and interests of refugees and immigrants, most providing services in Vietnamese. Saigon was the former capital of South Vietnam, and exiles named it Little Saigon as a way to remember their homeland. As a result of community advocacy, "Welcome to Little Saigon" signs were erected in the cities of Westminster, Garden Grove, and Santa Ana, although the boundaries continue to expand into surrounding cities. In the late 1970s, the area was blighted, so real estate was relatively affordable compared to the rest of the county, allowing the newcomers to transform it into a thriving residential community and commercial center. The area serves not only locals, but also attracts visitors and tourists, some who have moved here to be close to their relatives and to the ethnic community. Its proximity to Camp Pendleton in San Diego County where the refugees were temporarily settled, accessibility to public education, availability of social services, and temperate climate and miles of beautiful beaches contribute to the continued growth of the community.

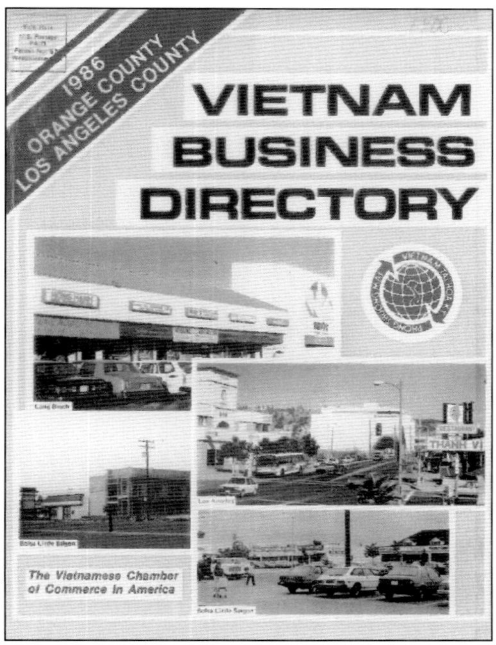

Starting in the 1980s, different organizations began compiling phone books listing thousands of businesses in Little Saigon. This one, produced by the Vietnamese American Chamber of Commerce, reflects the growing commercial and professional development of the community. (Courtesy of the UCI Libraries Southeast Asian Archive, MS-SEA020.)

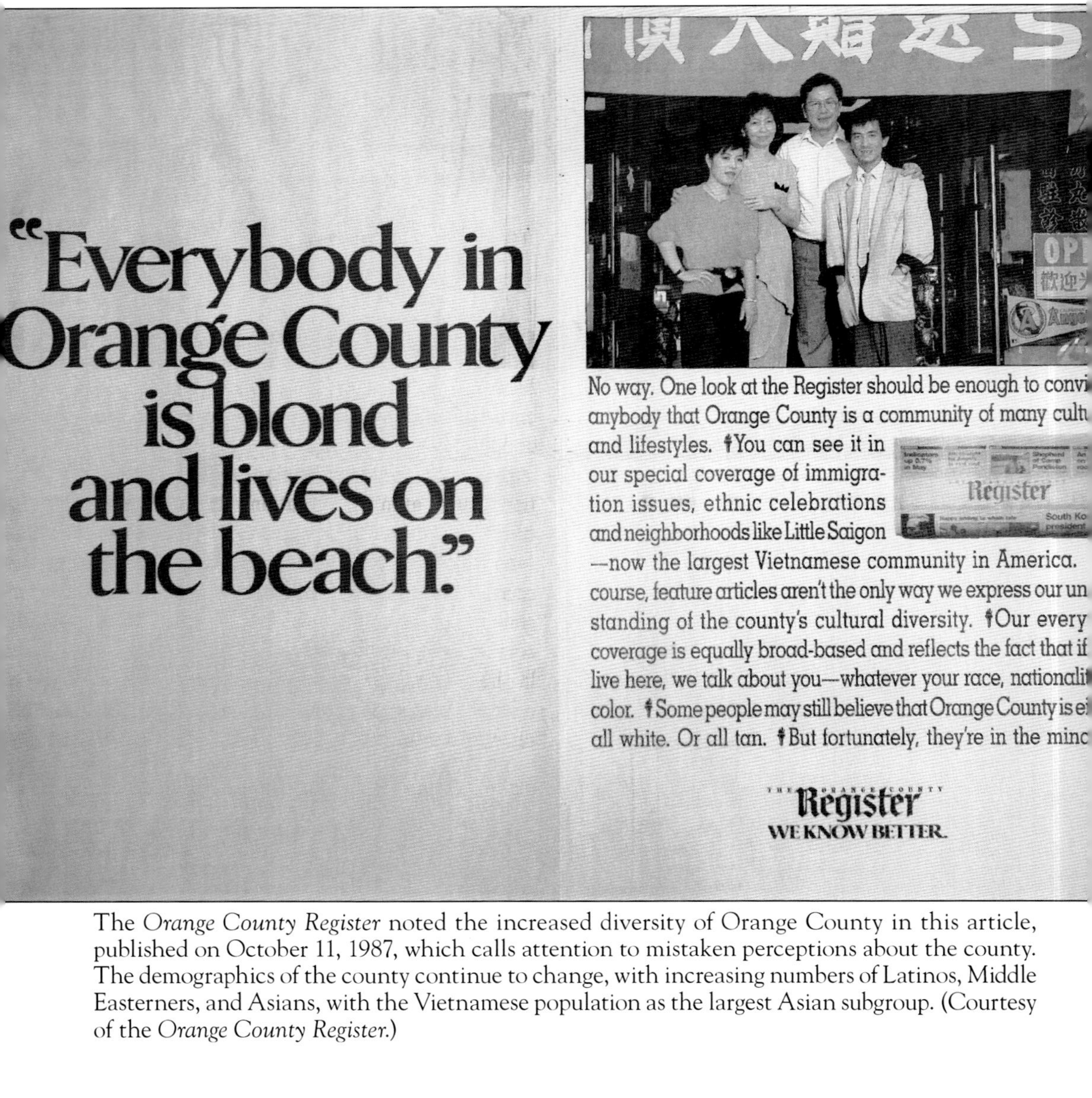

The *Orange County Register* noted the increased diversity of Orange County in this article, published on October 11, 1987, which calls attention to mistaken perceptions about the county. The demographics of the county continue to change, with increasing numbers of Latinos, Middle Easterners, and Asians, with the Vietnamese population as the largest Asian subgroup. (Courtesy of the *Orange County Register*.)

Land along Bolsa Avenue in Westminster was purchased by Bridgecreek Realty Investment Corporation in the 1980s, ushering in an era of rapid development for a region of Orange County that was in economic decline. This construction site would later become the Asian Garden Mall (Phuoc Loc Tho). (Courtesy of the Jao Foundation.)

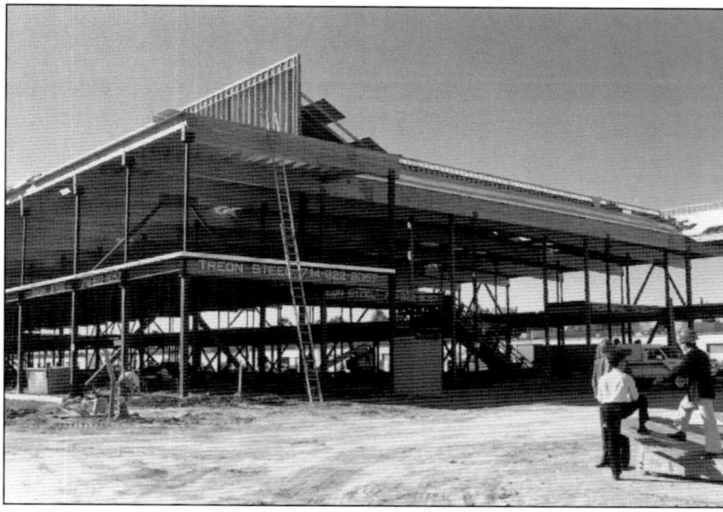

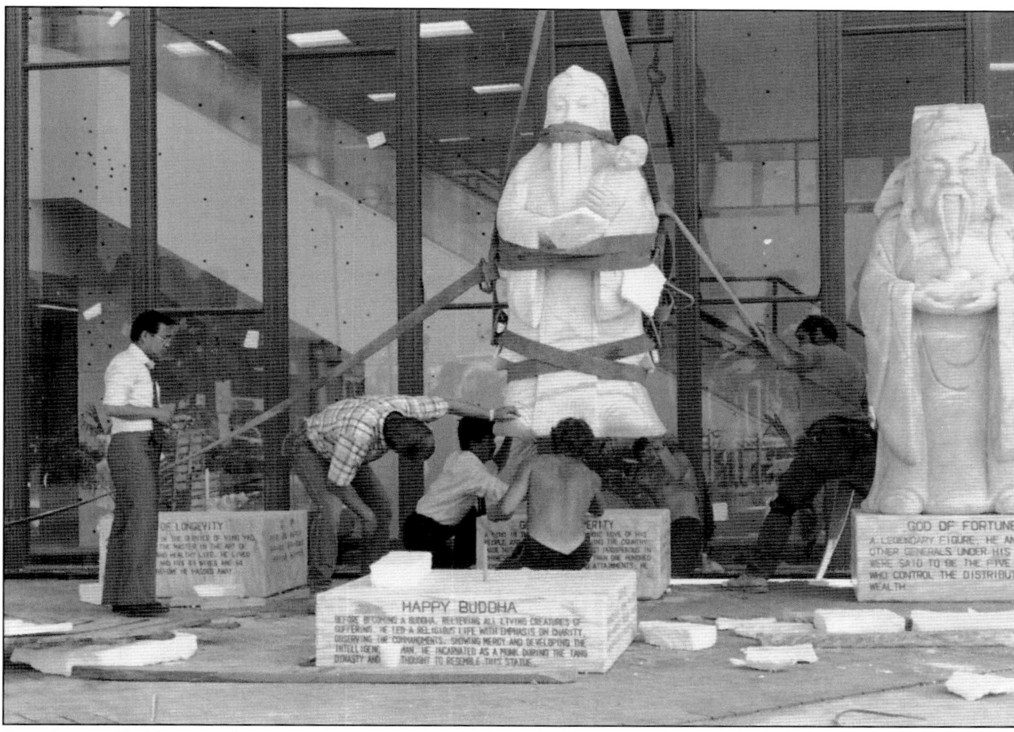

Frank Jao (left), president and CEO of Bridgecreek Development, is overseeing the placement of statues in front of his Asian Garden Mall. He and his partner Danh Quach developed numerous shopping plazas in Little Saigon. The mall, completed in 1987, is a prime attraction for visitors to the Little Saigon business district and includes a large food court as well as jewelry, clothing, and other retail shops. In 1975, Frank arrived in the United States as a refugee through Camp Pendleton, worked as a vacuum cleaner salesman, and took real estate classes at Coastline Community College before becoming an entrepreneur. (Courtesy of the Jao Foundation.)

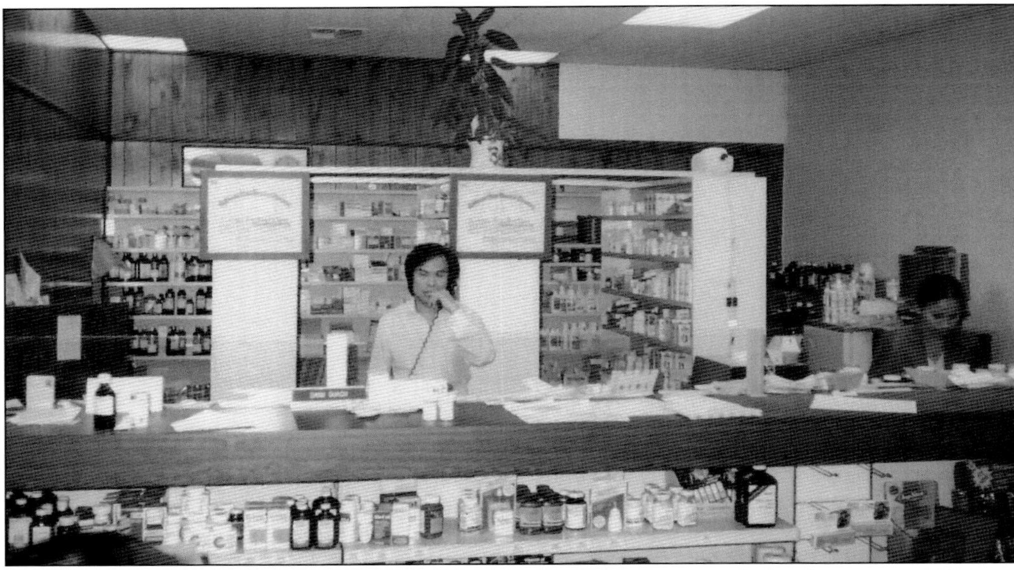

Pharmacist Danh Quach opened the first Vietnamese pharmacy on Bolsa Avenue in 1978, and his wife opened up Linh's Pharmacy, which not only sold medicine but also a variety of household goods. Their businesses were among the first to open in what would become known as Little Saigon. (Courtesy of the UCI Vietnamese American Oral History Project, VAOHP0047.)

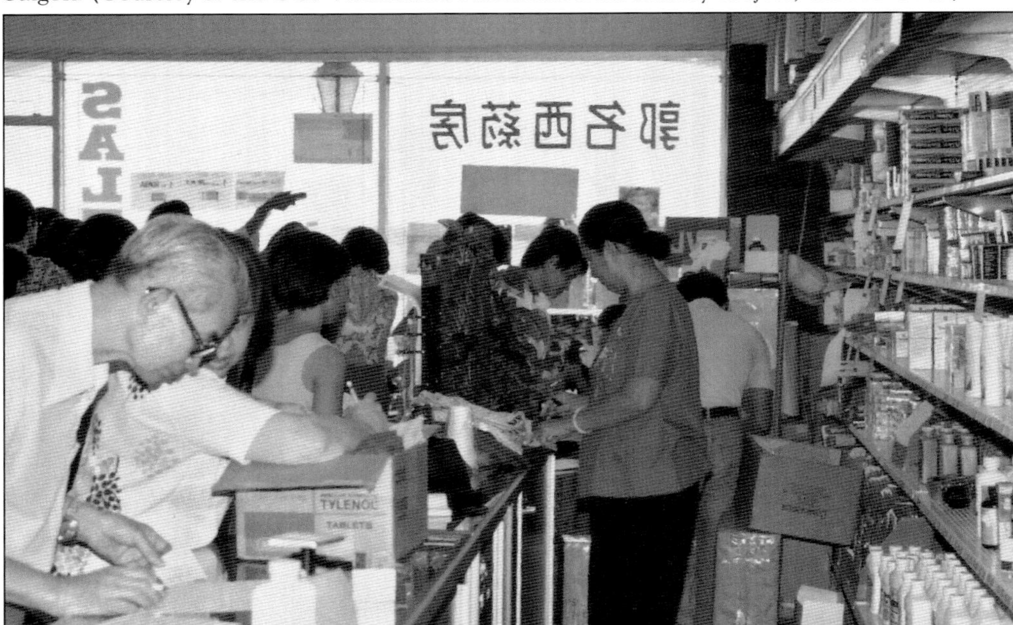

After the war in Vietnam, basic products such as toiletries, cloth, baby formula, and over-the-counter medicine were in short supply. Vietnamese-owned stores in America sold these products, packaged them, and shipped them for refugees, who could send these goods to their relatives in Vietnam to use or sell on the black market. Presently, money transfer shops such as Hoa Phat are more commonly used to send cash to relatives, as consumer goods and medicine are no longer scarce in Vietnam. (Courtesy of the UCI Vietnamese American Oral History Project, VAOHP0047.)

Le Dinh Dieu is pictured in front of the *Nguoi Viet Daily News* main office, where he worked after arriving in the United States, helping to turn the paper from a weekly to a daily newspaper. He began serving as editor-in-chief of *Nguoi Viet* in 1983 and is known as a community leader and patron of the arts. (Courtesy of the UCI Vietnamese American Oral History Project, VAOHP0202.)

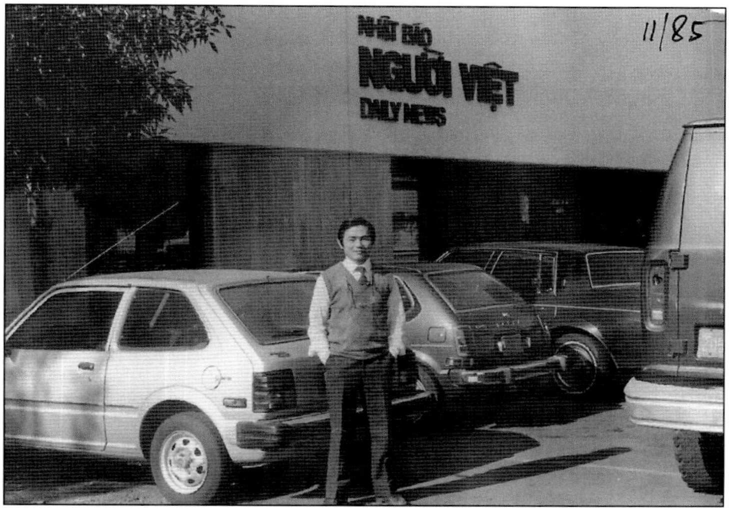

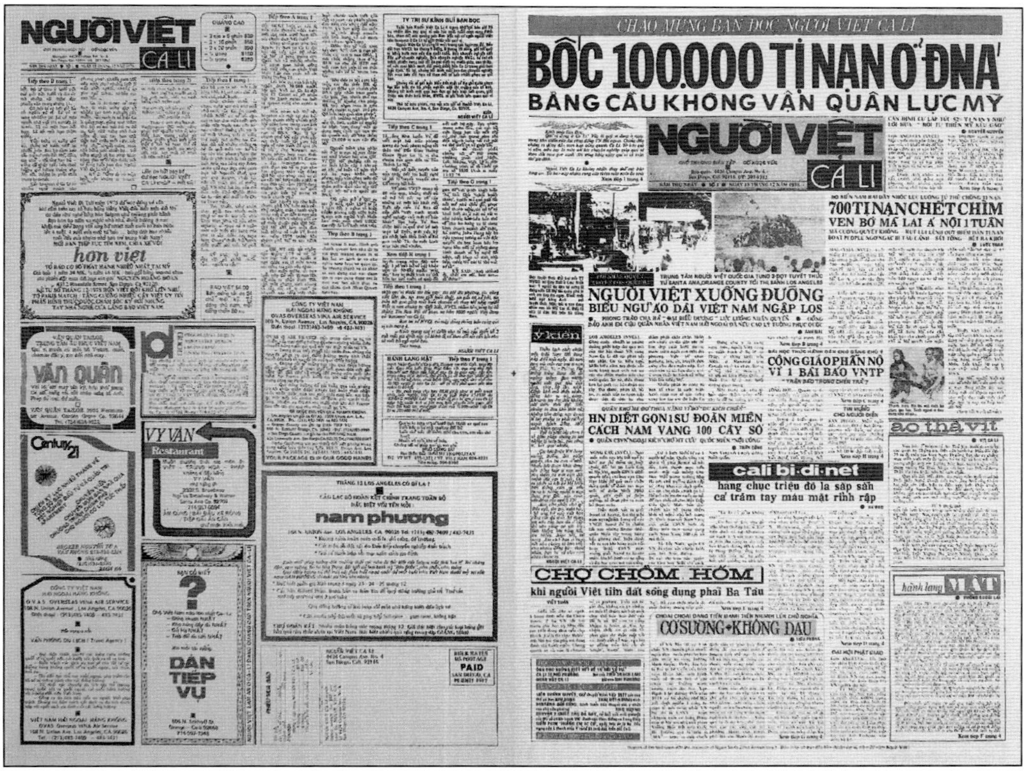

NGƯỜI VIỆT CA LI

CHÀO MỪNG BẠN ĐỌC NGƯỜI VIỆT CA LI

BỐC 100.000 TỊ NẠN Ở ĐNÁ

BẰNG CẦU KHÔNG VẬN QUÂN LỰC MỸ

700 TỊ NẠN CHẾT CHÌM

VEN BỜ MÃ LAI Á NỘI 1 TUẦN

NGƯỜI VIỆT XUỐNG ĐƯỜNG

BIỂU NGỮ ÁO DÀI VIỆT NAM NGẬP LOS

CÔNG GIÁO PHẪN NỘ VÌ 1 BÀI BÁO VNTP

HN DIỆT GỌN 1 SƯ ĐOÀN MIỀN

CÁCH NAM VANG 100 CÂY SỐ

cali bi-di-net

hàng chục triệu đô la sắp sửa cả trăm tay máu mặt rình rập

CHỢ CHỒM HỔM

khi người Việt tìm đất sống dụng phải Ba Tàu

CÓ SƯƠNG • KHÔNG ĐAU

hơn việt

văn quân

VY VÂN Restaurant

Century 21

nam phương

DÂN TIẾP VỤ

Nguoi Viet, started by Do Ngoc Yen from his Garden Grove home, is the first and largest Vietnamese-language newspaper printed in the United States. Pictured here is the first issue, a four-page newspaper published on December 15, 1978. Later renamed *Nguoi Viet Daily News*, it is currently headquartered in the heart of Little Saigon on Moran Street in Westminster, California, which has become a famous media hub for the community. (Courtesy of ThienGiao Pham.)

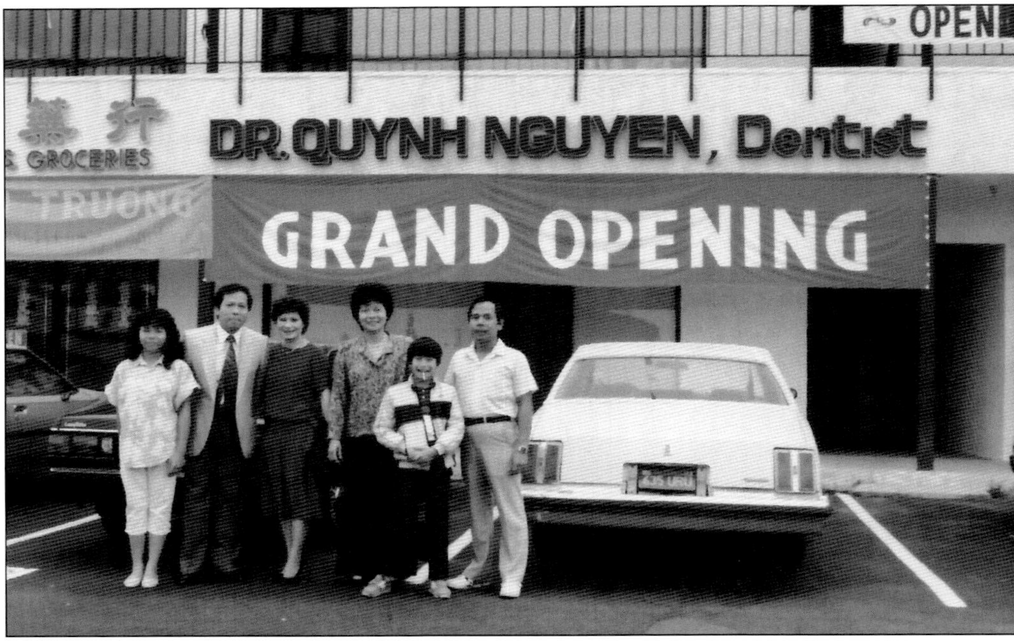

Dr. Quynh Nguyen's family celebrates the grand opening of his dental office in Westminster, located near the corner of Bolsa and Bushard Streets, in 1985. (Courtesy of Tu-Uyen Nguyen.)

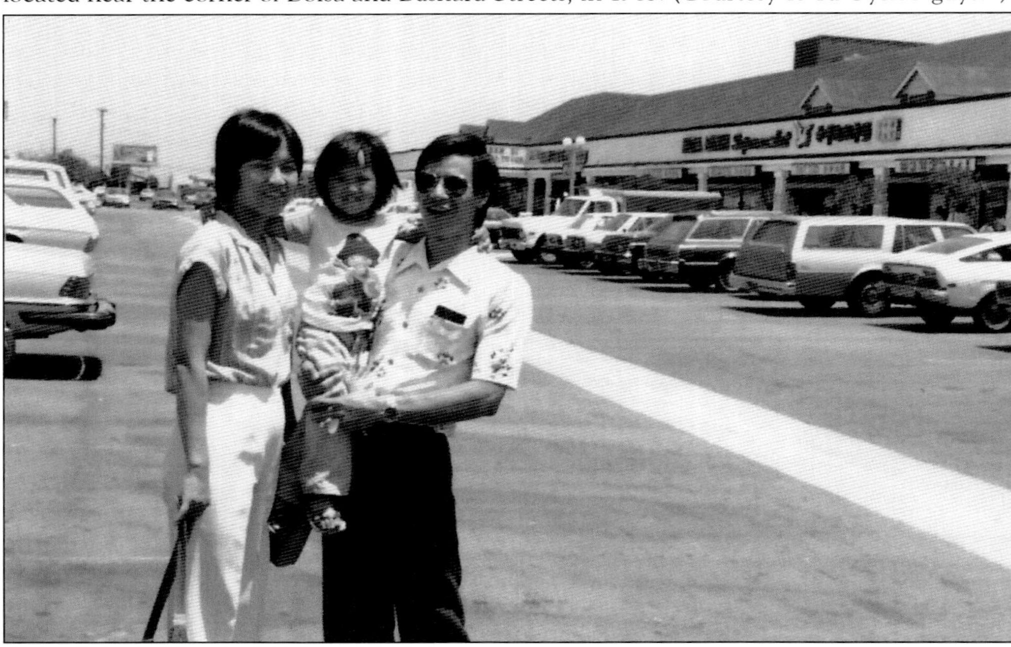

Vietnamese families throughout Southern California take excursions to Little Saigon for shopping, dining, and entertainment. By the late 1980s, mini-malls and shopping centers were ubiquitous throughout Little Saigon. Vietnamese Americans bought many of the dilapidated structures, remodeled them, opened businesses, and revitalized the area. Seen here from left to right are Nguyen Thi Bich Thuy, Lilly Nguyen, and Nguyen Kim Giang in the 1980s. (Courtesy of the UCI Vietnamese American Oral History Project, VAOHP0181.)

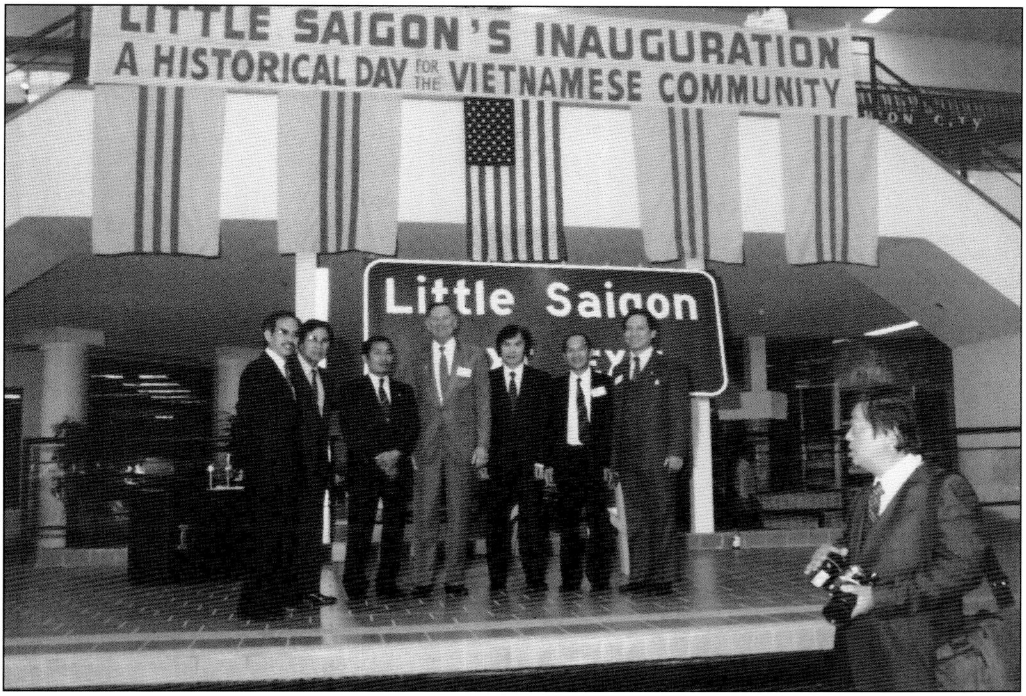

On June 17, 1988, Gov. George Deukmejian (center) stands on a stage in Asian Garden Mall, announcing "Little Saigon" as the official name of the business district, with signs on the 405 and 22 Freeways. (Courtesy of the Jao Foundation.)

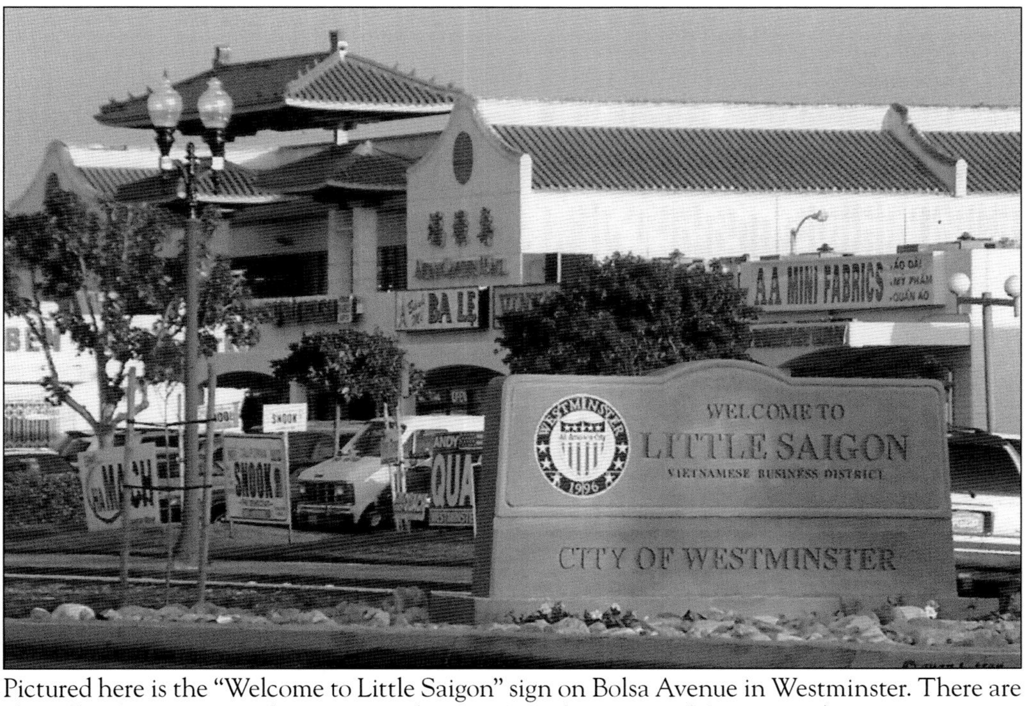

Pictured here is the "Welcome to Little Saigon" sign on Bolsa Avenue in Westminster. There are also official signs in Garden Grove and Santa Ana. (Courtesy of Quan Tran.)

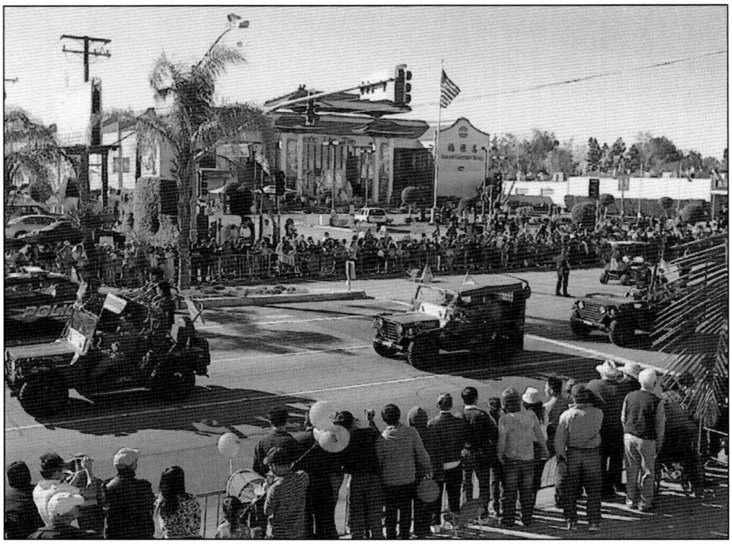

Part of an annual tradition to celebrate the lunar New Year, the Vietnamese American community organizes a Tet Parade that includes civic and business leaders and organizations. (Courtesy of Thuy Vo Dang.)

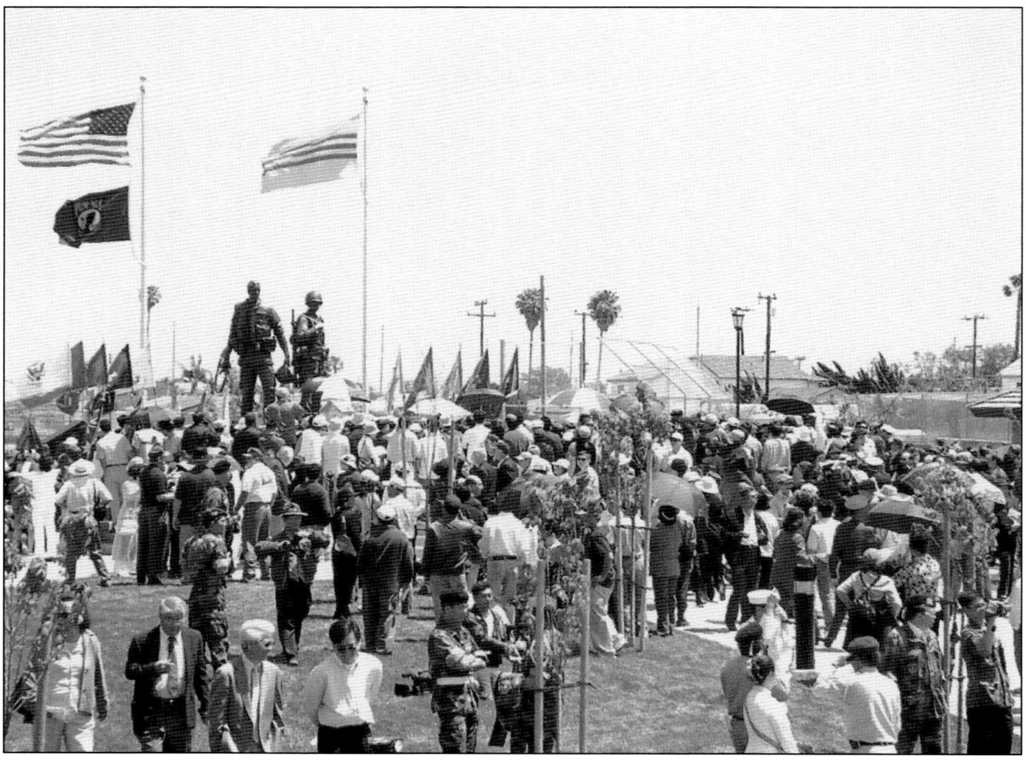

The Vietnam War Memorial located in the Sid Goldstein Freedom Park in Westminster was unveiled on April 27, 2003. While most of these memorials feature only American soldiers, this is one of the few that highlights an American and South Vietnamese soldier standing side by side as allies. The sculptor, Tuan Nguyen, was born in Vietnam in 1963 and escaped as a refugee to the United States in 1988. (Courtesy of Linda Trinh Vo.)

Yen Dang, the Tu Quynh Bookstore owner, poses inside her shop around 1985. The bookstore, opened in 1979, is a meaningful place where displaced newcomers can find Vietnamese-language literature and music. Tu Quynh supported the refugee advocacy movement by sending books to the camps. (Courtesy of Yen Dang.)

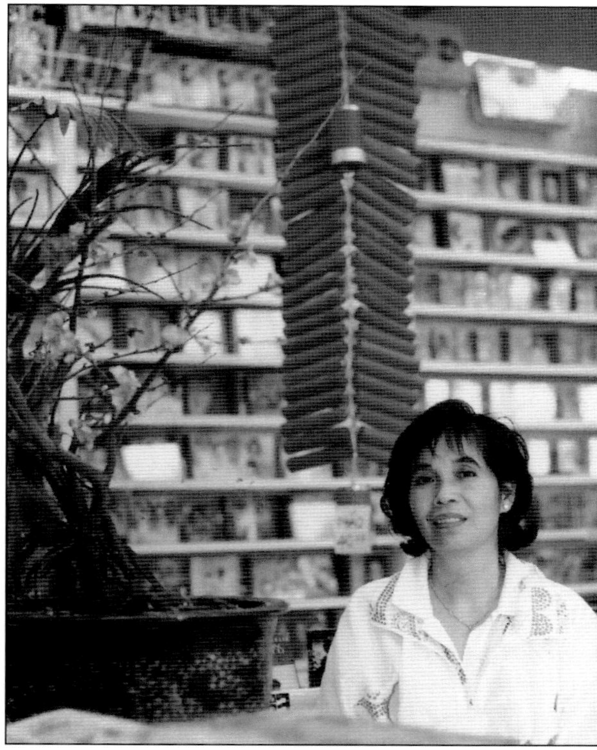

Jewelry stores are abundant in the Little Saigon area, and 24-karat gold is popular in these shops. A partial explanation for their popularity is the Vietnamese community's distrust of banks and their desire to invest in and buy gold. (Courtesy of Hang Phung and Lala Truong.)

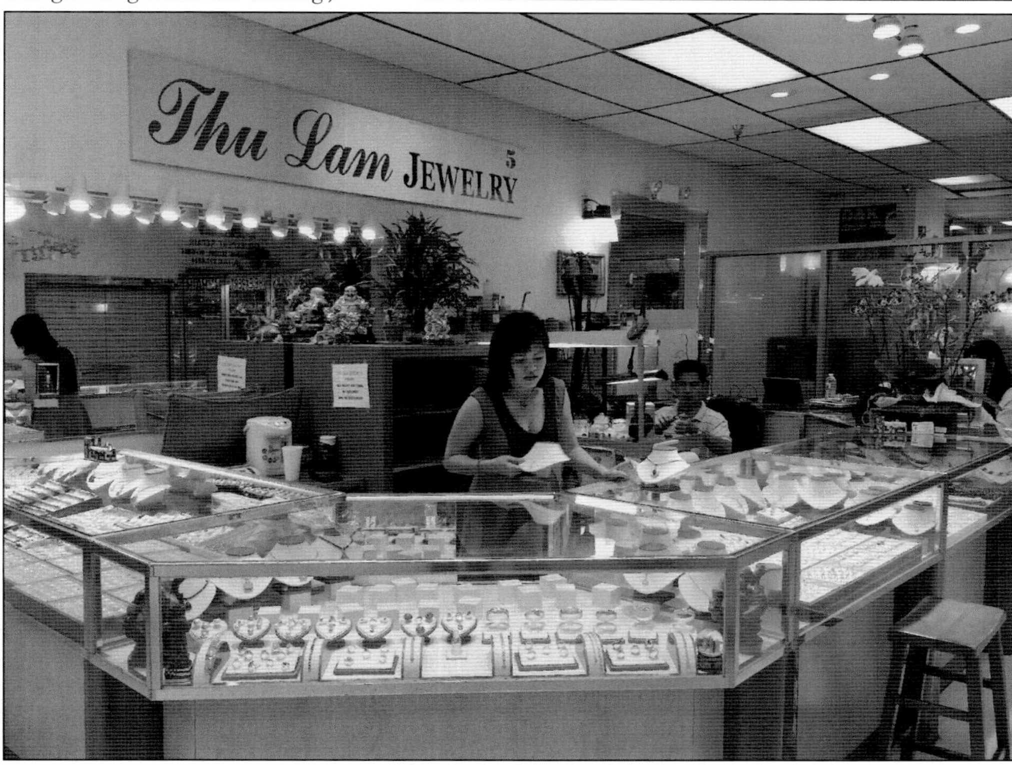

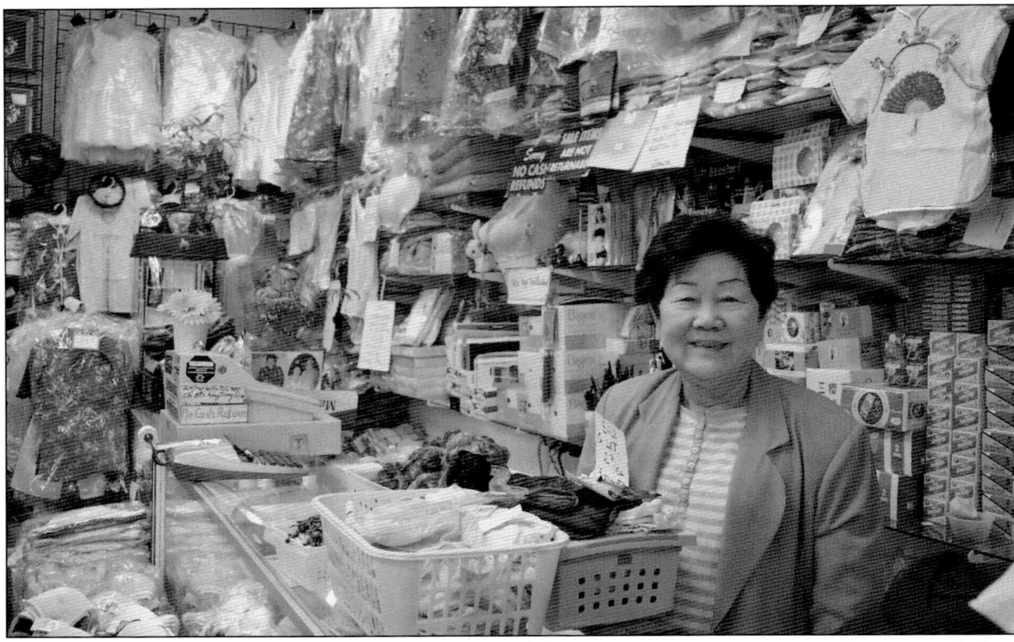

Overcrowded gift shops, such as the one pictured here, carry an assortment of items, including undergarments, children's clothing, phone cards, pain relief balm, and other personal-care items. Mom-and-pop small businesses are the foundation on which Little Saigon is built. (Courtesy of Kim Chu and Uyen Huynh.)

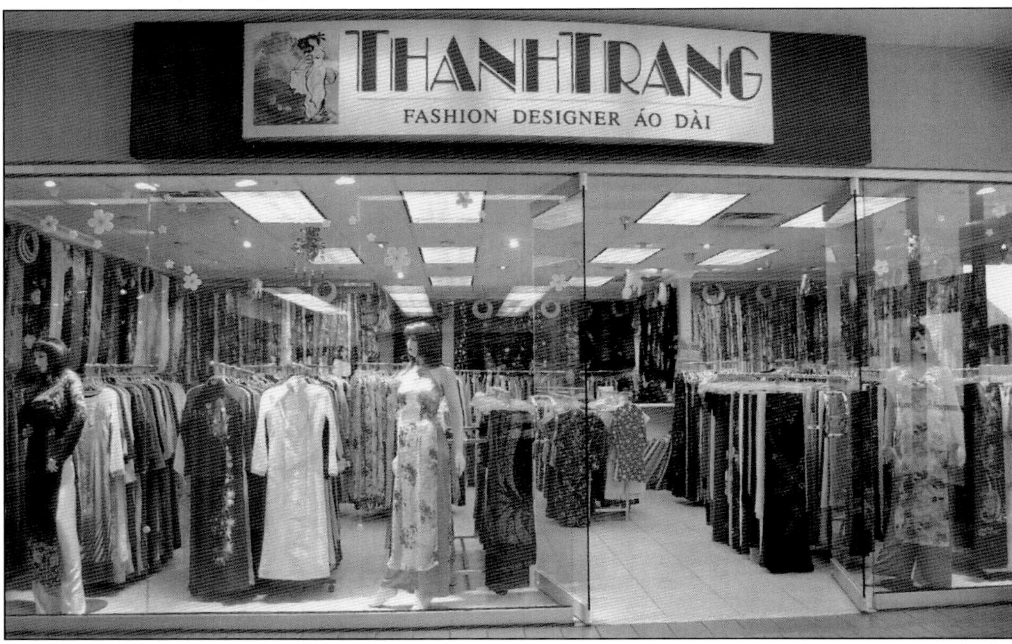

Little Saigon is the destination for Vietnamese Americans to get custom-made, traditional clothes like *ao dai* for special occasions such as weddings and festival celebrations. The Thanh Trang clothing store pictured here, located in the Asian Garden Mall, is one example of many. (Courtesy of Joyce Ang and Sandy Vu.)

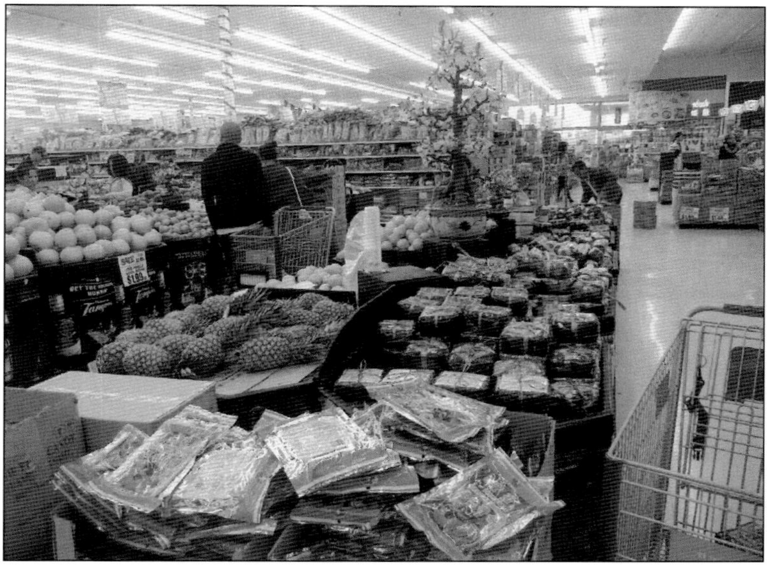

Supermarkets, such as My Thuan Supermarket in Westminster, attract Vietnamese as well as non-Vietnamese shoppers for their variety of fresh and affordable seafood, meats, produce, and specialty items not found in mainstream grocery stores. (Courtesy of Nairi Davidian and Allen Chen.)

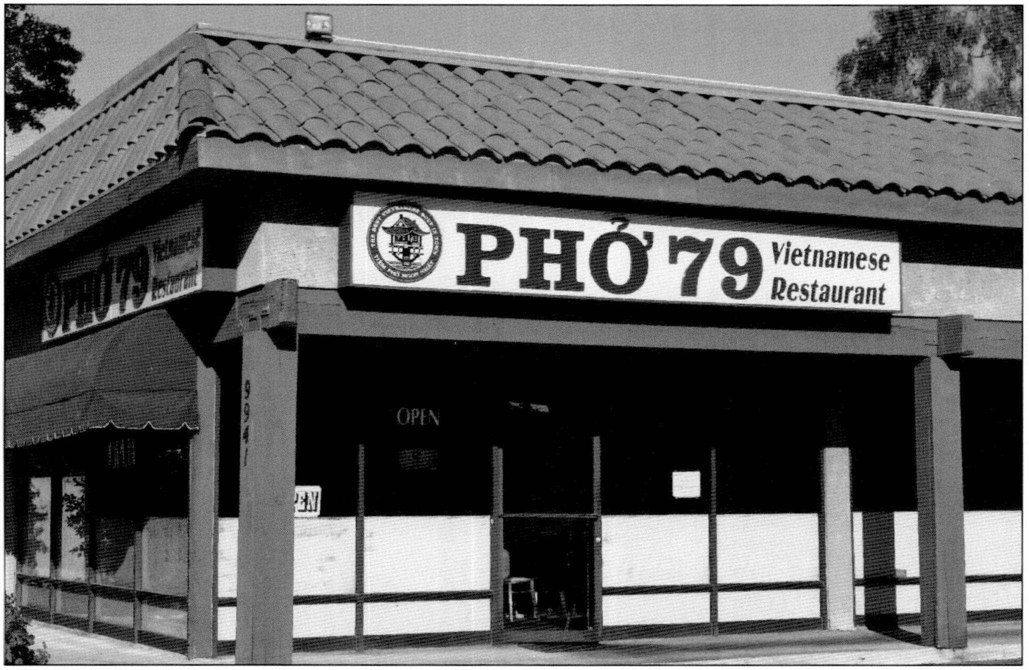

Located in Garden Grove, the popular Pho 79 restaurant serves *pho*, a traditional Vietnamese soup of rice noodles, meats, and vegetables. The restaurant, whose name references its former location at 79 Vo Tanh Street in Saigon, opened in 1982. (Courtesy of Thuy Vo Dang.)

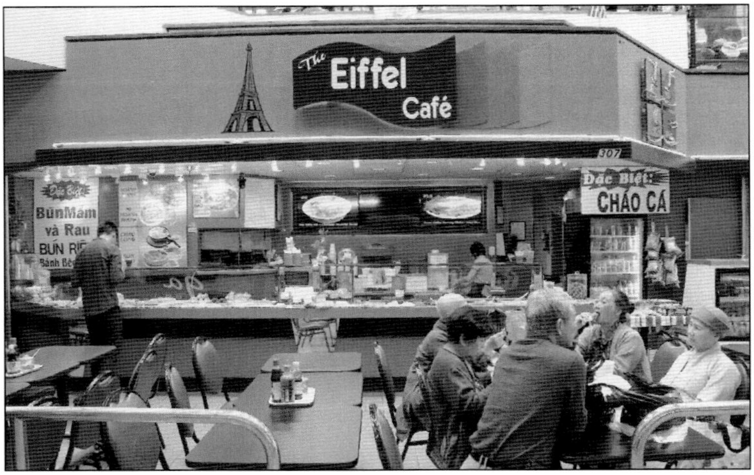

Numerous food-to-go stalls inside supermarkets or stand-alone shops cater to Vietnamese living in nearby neighborhoods looking for fast, affordable, and convenient dining options. (Courtesy of Taylor Weik and Eric Chau.)

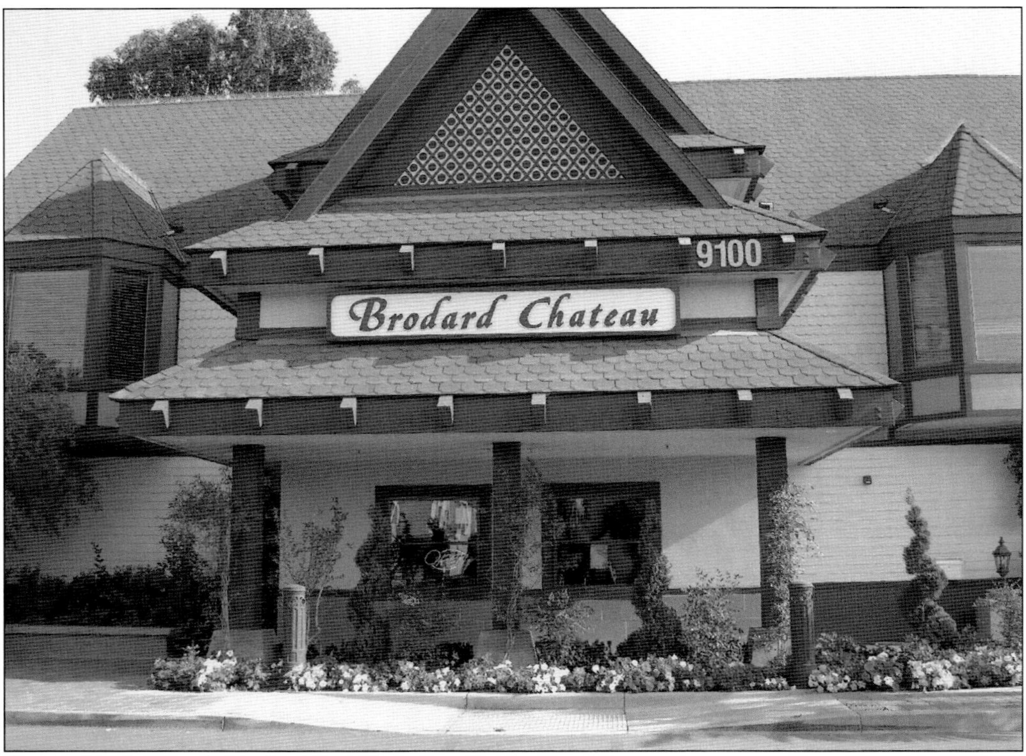

The Dang family, who owned the famed Hoa Binh boulangeries in Vietnam, came to America in the late 1980s and opened restaurants in Garden Grove, Westminster, and Corona del Mar. Although mom-and-pop pho and *banh mi* sandwich shops are abundant, more upscale Vietnamese restaurants have opened in the county. Their restaurants are known for their *nem nuong*, char-grilled pork rolled with vegetables and herbs in rice paper. Brodard Chateau occupies the Victorian house that used to be Pinnacle Peak Steakhouse, once a popular American dining spot. (Courtesy of Linda Trinh Vo.)

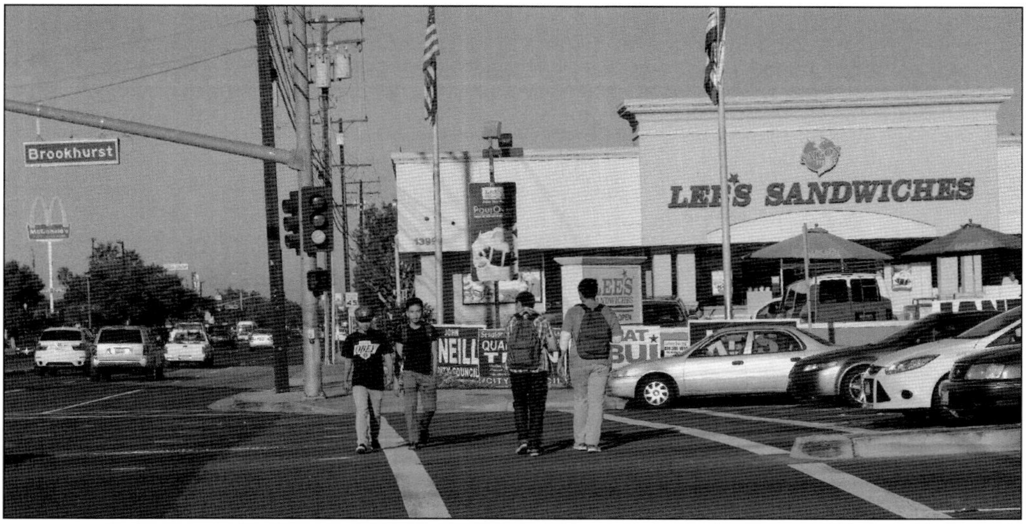

Lee's Sandwiches was founded by Chieu Le, an entrepreneur who resettled in San Jose in 1980 and started a food truck business in 1981 selling banh mi, a Vietnamese sandwich influenced by French cuisine. The first Lee's was opened in 2001 in Orange County, and now there are over 40 locations in California and other states. (Courtesy of Thuy Vo Dang.)

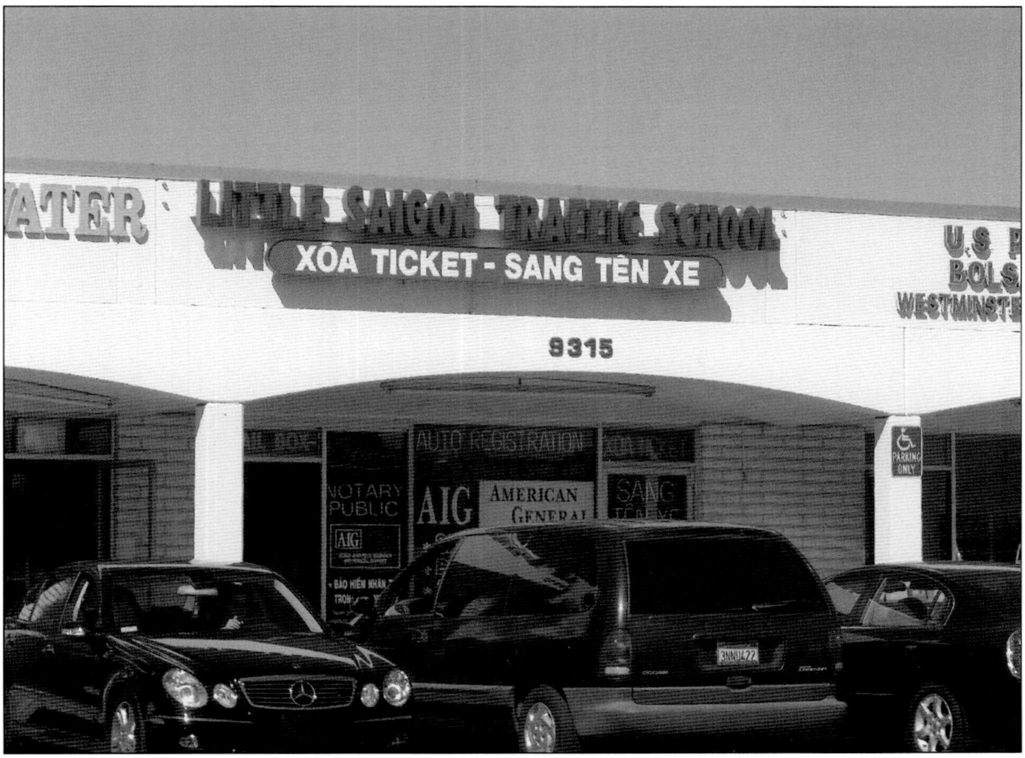

Michael Vo opened Little Saigon Traffic School in 1989 after reading a newspaper article about a Vietnamese person who was kicked out of a drivers' education course due to language barriers. Michael became the first Vietnamese mayor of Fountain Valley in 2013. (Courtesy of Linda Trinh Vo.)

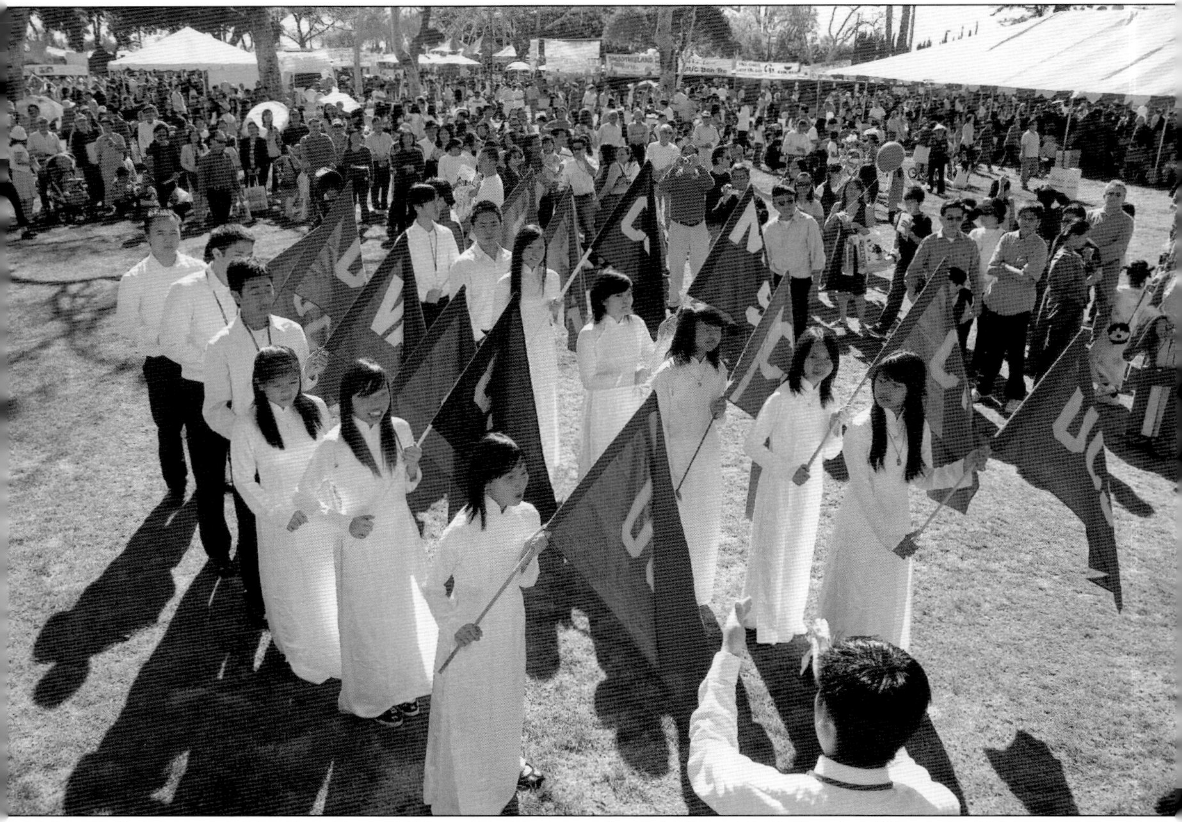

The annual Tet Parade in Westminster was founded in 1982 by the Union of Vietnamese Students Association (UVSA), which hosts social and leadership activities for Vietnamese students and the community. This organization represents college and high school Vietnamese Student Associations in the Little Saigon area. The UVSA Tet Festival, the largest in the country, has generated high revenues, which they redistribute to nonprofit organizations. (Courtesy of Brian Dang.)

Four

Family

War and forced migration have resulted in the disruptions and displacements of Vietnamese families. During the war and in its aftermath, many were imprisoned in re-education camps and separated from their families. Refugee status may also present an opportunity to forge new identities in order to pass screening requirements or to escape previous relationships. In the process of rebuilding their lives in America, Vietnamese women and men have reconstructed family in hybrid ways. Some women have become key contributors to the family income and, consequently, the primary decision-makers, displacing traditional male power and authority. Rather than the multi-generational household as the norm, more and more senior citizens are living by themselves. Children who learn English in school must often act as translators for their parents, thus subverting the tradition of reverence towards elders. In resettlement, flexible formations of family or kinship were often necessary, so friends were treated like kin and assisted each other in finding housing and employment. Social networks were useful in forming *hui*, or rotating credit associations, in which trusted friends and family would pool their financial resources so that members could take turns receiving a lump sum of money to open a business or pay for a funeral. Families often extend across the ocean, evidenced by the high volume of care packages and money (called remittances) sent by Vietnamese Americans to support relatives remaining in the homeland. Refugee and immigrant parents and their children face generational, linguistic, and cultural barriers. As new generations of Vietnamese Americans emerge, the struggle to maintain Vietnamese language and customs remain important issues in the community.

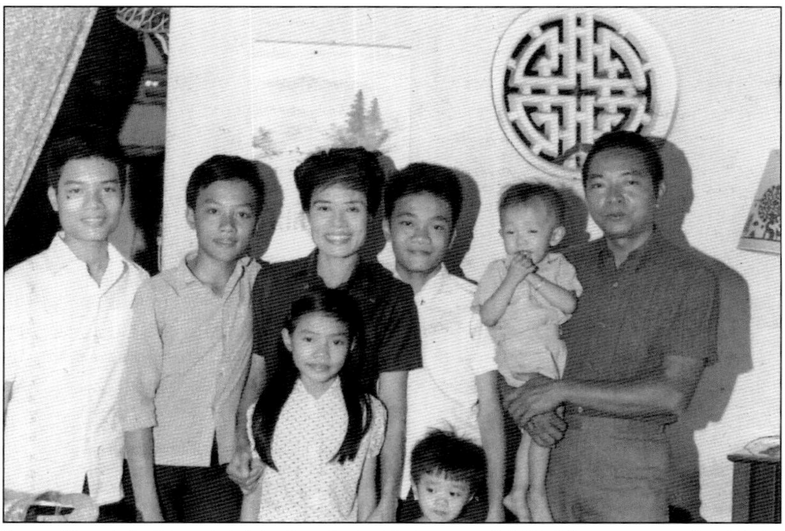

Pham Boi Hoan (far right) is with his family in Saigon in 1968. He came to the United States by himself in 1975 and worked as a librarian for the Library of Congress in Washington, DC. In 2007, he was able to sponsor 12 members of his family, who resettled in Orange County. (Courtesy of Danthu Pham.)

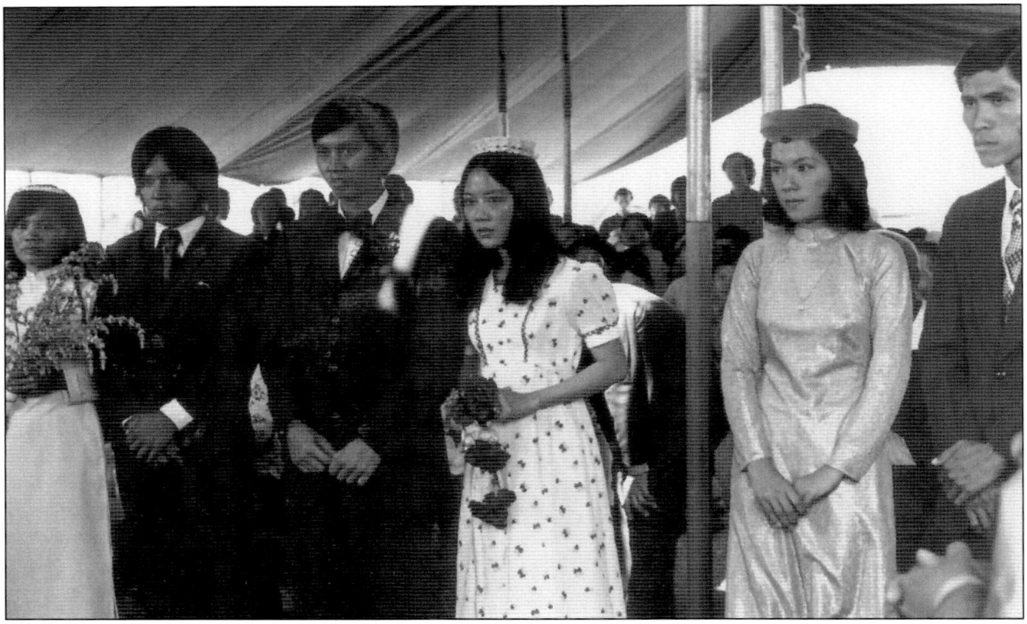

This photograph shows a group wedding at one of the "tent cities" at Camp Pendleton in 1975. (Official Marine Corps photograph.)

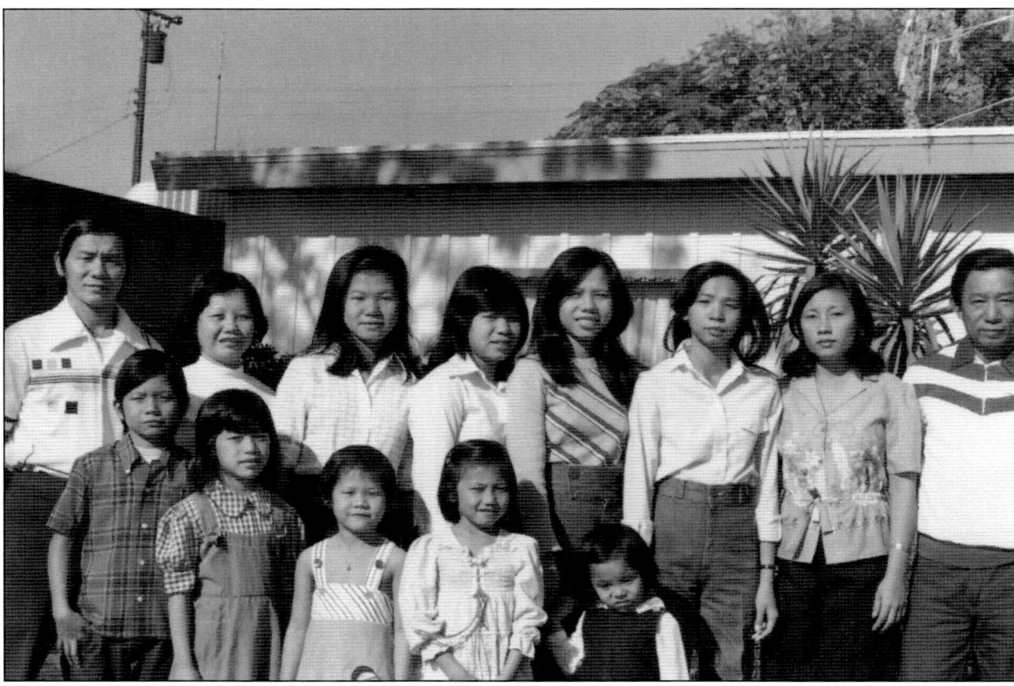

Taken in 1980, this image shows the Loan Pham Thai family, who escaped Vietnam and were sponsored by a church in Bakersfield, California. Work opportunities drew them to Massachusetts, but after six cold winters, the family settled in Huntington Beach. Their identification card photographs are on page four. (Courtesy of the UCI Vietnamese American Oral History Project, VAOHP0041.)

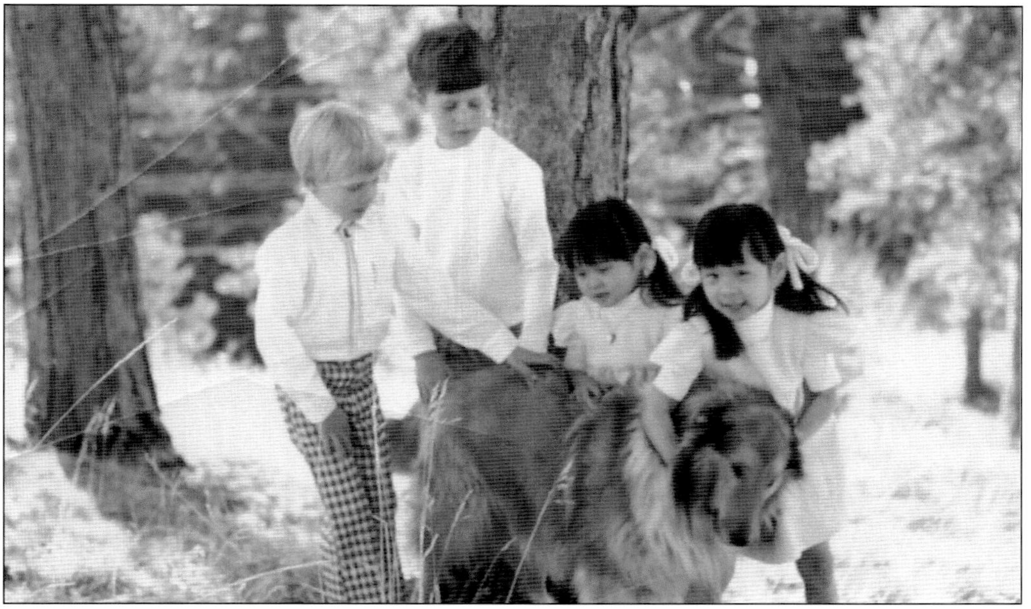

Truong Le Chi's husband, Hoang Dai Ba, passed away in 1969, leaving her to care for their six children. As the war ended, Chi gave up her five youngest children for international adoption so they could have a better life. Her oldest son, Hoang Dai Hai, stayed behind and helped her sell medicine on the black market until he escaped by land to Cambodia in 1986. Two of Chi's daughters, Hoang Thi Minh Khue and Hoang Thi Thanh Truc, were adopted by an American family. Here, the sisters are pictured with their American brothers. (Courtesy of the UCI Vietnamese American Oral History Project, VAOHP0108.)

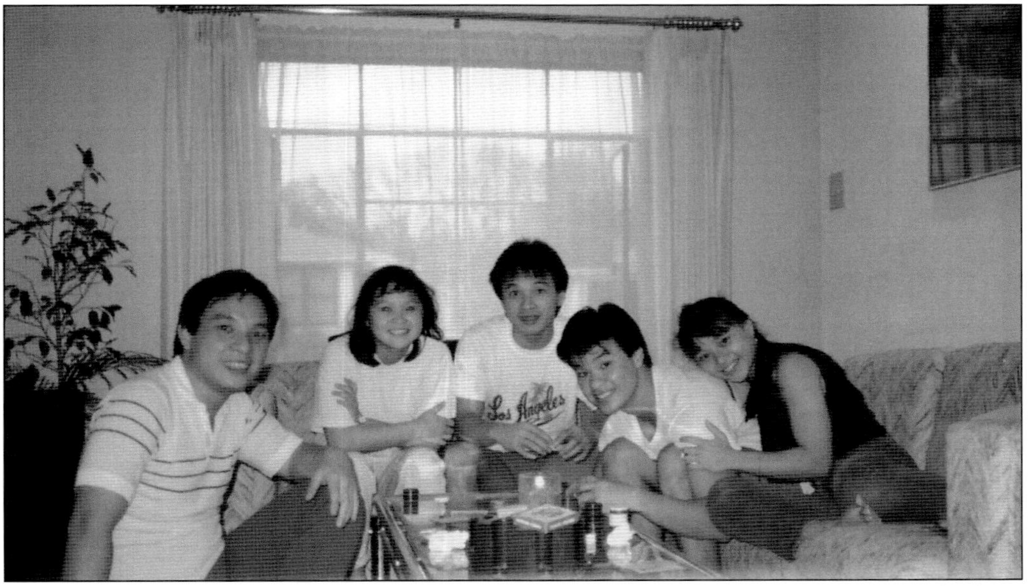

Five of Truong Le Chi's six children reunited in Texas in the 1990s. Even within one family, there were diverse refugee experiences. The eldest, Hoang Dai Hai (far left), escaped Vietnam in the 1980s while the others were all adopted by American families in 1975. (Courtesy of the UCI Vietnamese American Oral History Project, VAOHP0108.)

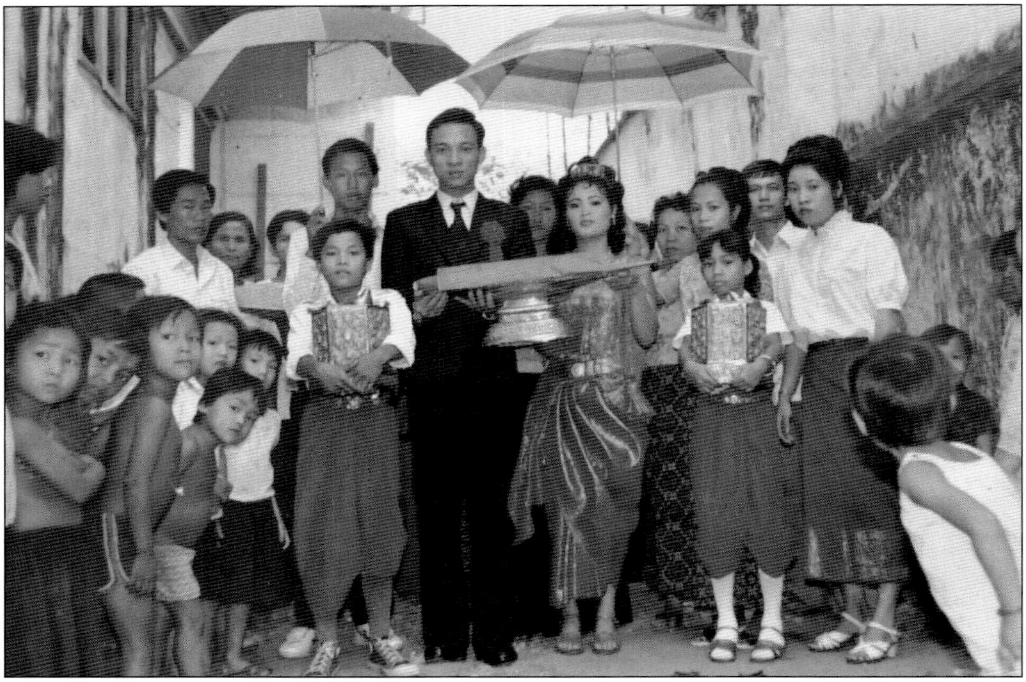

In 1987, Hoang Dai Hai married a Khmer woman named Kim in Phnom Penh, Cambodia. He attempted to escape Vietnam by boat at least 10 times without success until he finally left by land to Cambodia in 1986. He made a living by selling medicine, performing acupuncture, and working as a healer. There he met Kim, and the two of them escaped Cambodia by boat. They arrived at a Thai refugee camp and then were sent to a refugee camp in Bataan, Philippines, before resettling in America. He went to dental school and practiced dentistry in Washington before moving to Fountain Valley. (Courtesy of the UCI Vietnamese American Oral History Project, VAOHP0125.)

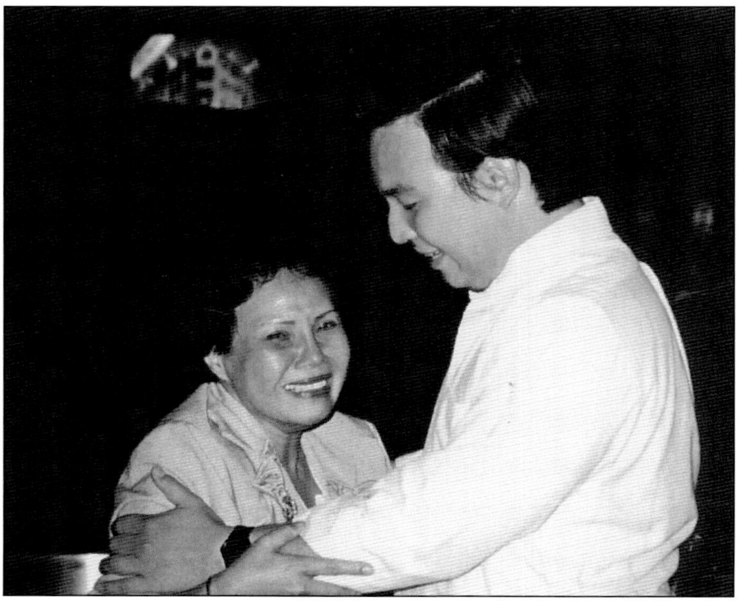

Truong Le Chi, a Garden Grove resident, left Vietnam in 1990 via the Orderly Departure Program through her second marriage to a South Vietnamese veteran who had returned from re-education camp prison. She is finally reunited with her eldest son, Hoang Dai Hai, and has reconnected with her other children in America. (Courtesy of the UCI Vietnamese American Oral History Project, VAOHP0108.)

In 1962, Dung Pham was a nursing student at Texas Women's University and completed her clinical practice at Parkland Memorial Hospital in Dallas, where she resided in the staff quarters. She is knitting in front of a framed picture of her fiancé, who was in Vietnam. (Courtesy of the UCI Vietnamese American Oral History Project, VAOHP0202.)

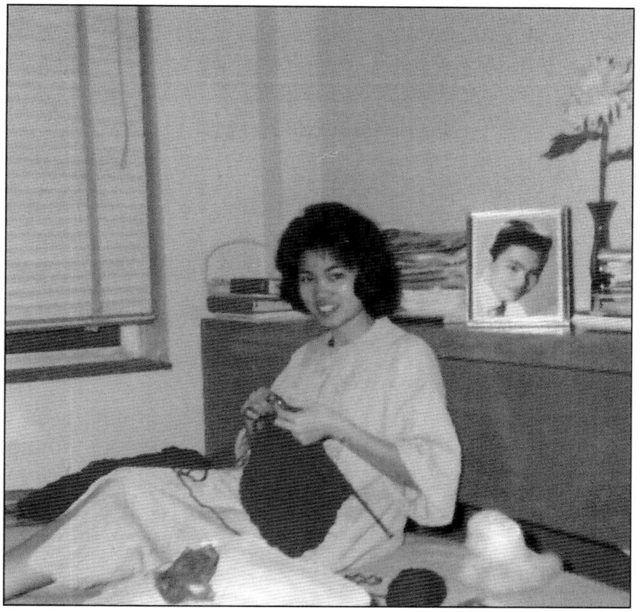

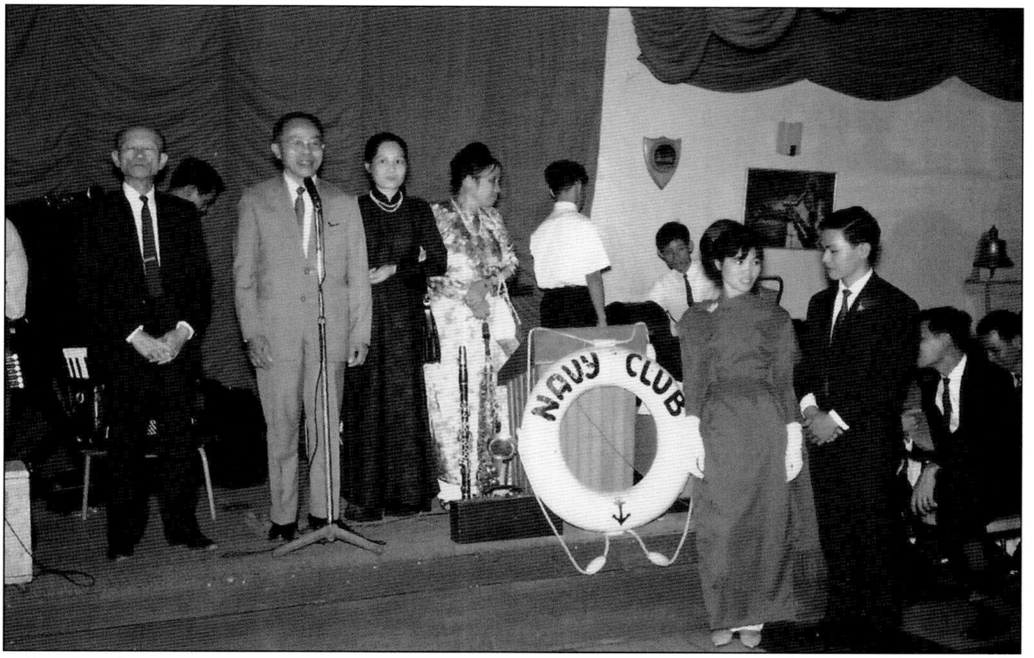

After finishing her nursing program in Texas, Dung Pham returned to Vietnam to marry her fiancé. At the Navy Club in Saigon, both sets of parents are giving their welcome remarks at the wedding reception on September 18, 1966. (Courtesy of the UCI Vietnamese American Oral History Project, VAOHP0202.)

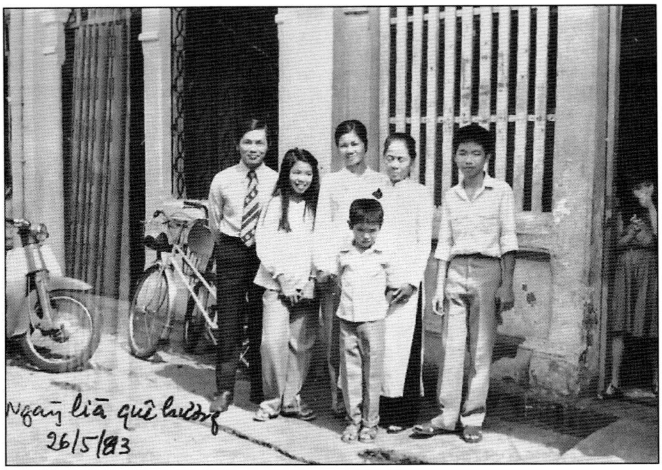

Pictured here is Dung Pham's family in front of their house just before leaving Vietnam on May 26, 1983. As part of the Vietnamese communist government policy, they had to forfeit their house to the government. She did not care at the time, remarking, "Happy, happy day! Released from the huge prison—Vietnam under communism." (Courtesy of the UCI Vietnamese American Oral History Project, VAOHP0202.)

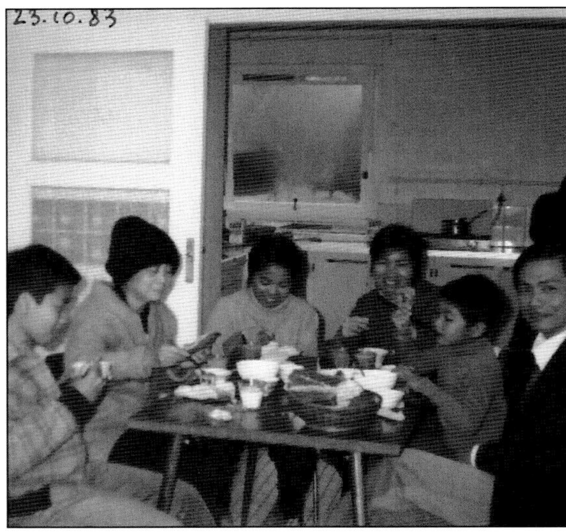

Dung Pham and her family share a meal at the Centre de Réfugiés (Refugee Center) in Miribel, France, on October 23, 1983. She explains, "As with millions of Vietnamese people, I tried to escape by boat nine times with my three young children while my husband was in prison. In four of those trips we got caught and put in prison. Failed in all tries! Finally, the French government sponsored the whole family to France, thanks to my father-in-law who had served in the French military before 1954. So our family could get out of Vietnam safely by airplane in May 1983." (Courtesy of the UCI Vietnamese American Oral History Project, VAOHP0202.)

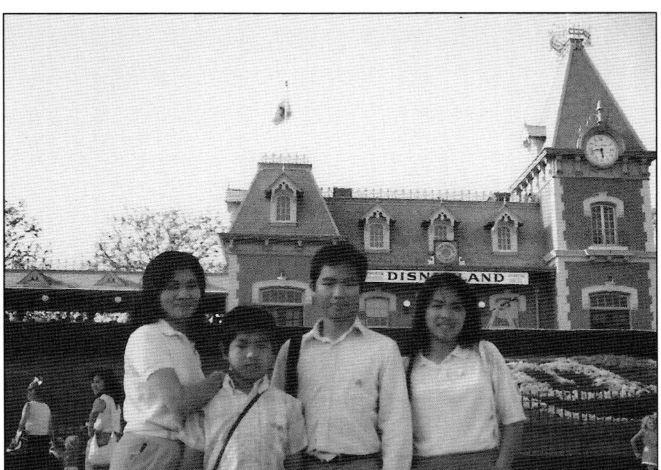

Dung Pham and her three children, Nhat Linh, Nhat Lan, and Ysa visit Disneyland, located next to Little Saigon, in the late 1980s after they finally settled in Orange County. (Courtesy of the UCI Vietnamese American Oral History Project, VAOHP0202.)

Tu-Uyen Nguyen (center) opens Christmas presents in 1981 at her home in Huntington Beach with her brother Quang (right) and cousin Tam Bui (left). When they first lived in the United States, they did not have enough money to buy a Christmas tree, so the children made their own out of construction paper with Christmas cards for decoration. (Courtesy of Tu-Uyen Nguyen.)

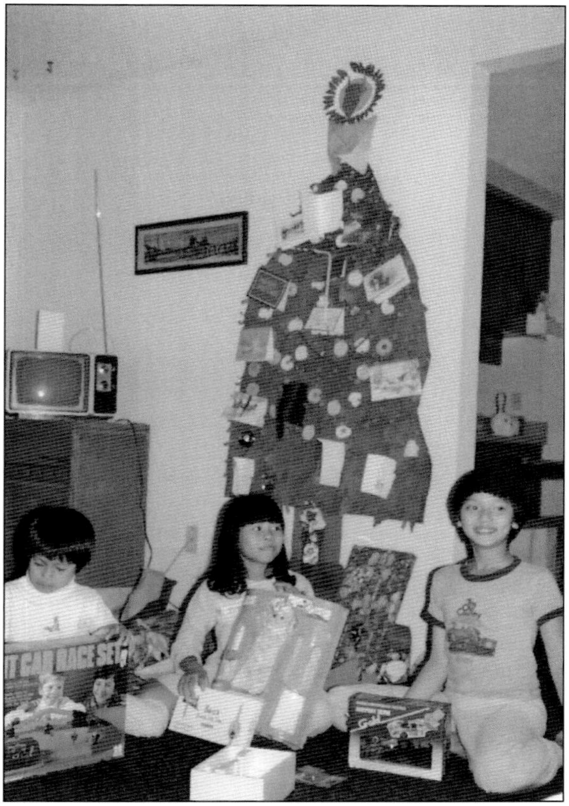

Liem Le (center), her daughter Tu-Uyen (left), and son Quang (right) pose in front of the first car they purchased in the United States, a used 1971 Dodge Dart they bought in 1981 for $1,500. It was a luxury for refugees in their early years to have a car. (Courtesy of Tu-Uyen Nguyen.)

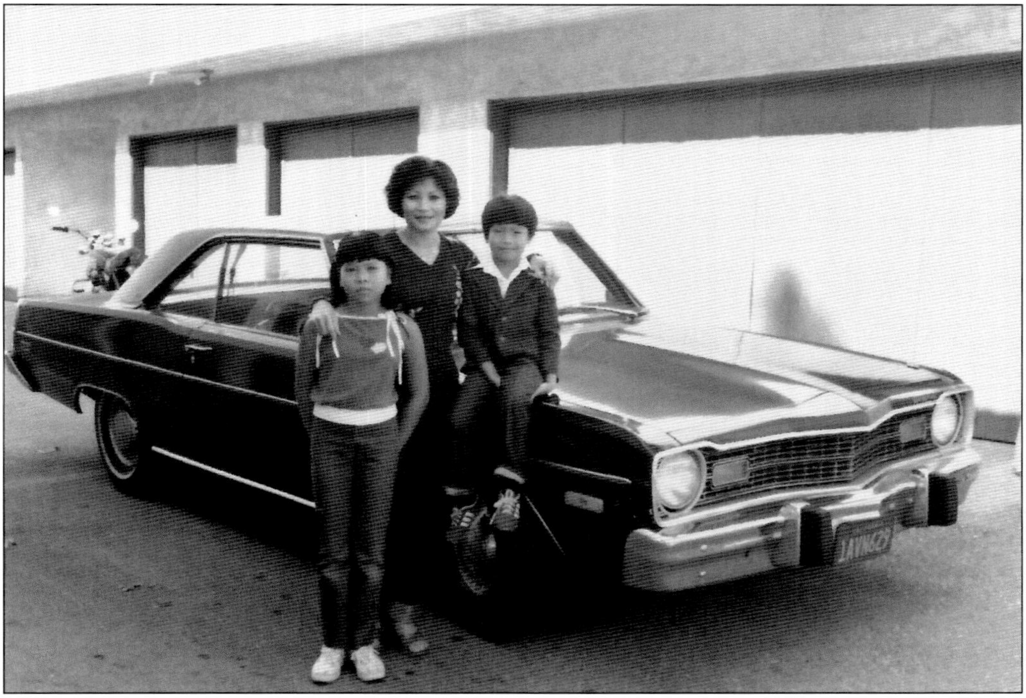

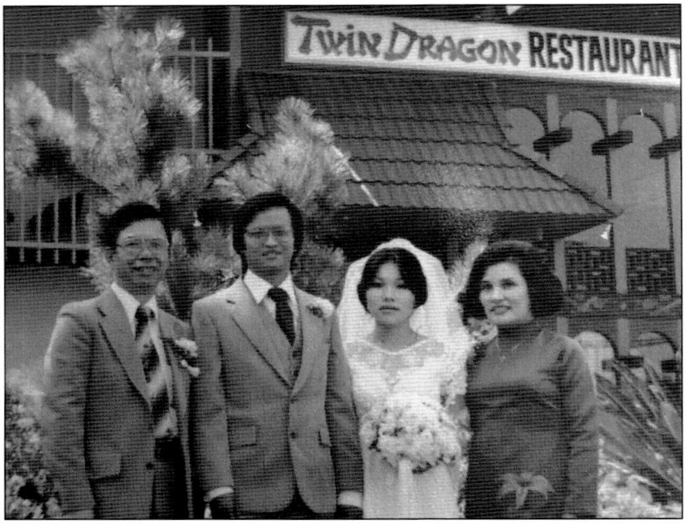

Nancy Nhung Phan and her husband, pictured here with her parents, held their wedding reception in 1981 at a Chinese restaurant in Westminster. Many Vietnamese wedding receptions are held in Chinese restaurants because they are affordable, and at the time there were no Vietnamese-owned restaurants spacious enough to accommodate large numbers of guests. (Courtesy of the UCI Vietnamese American Oral History Project, VAOHP0095.)

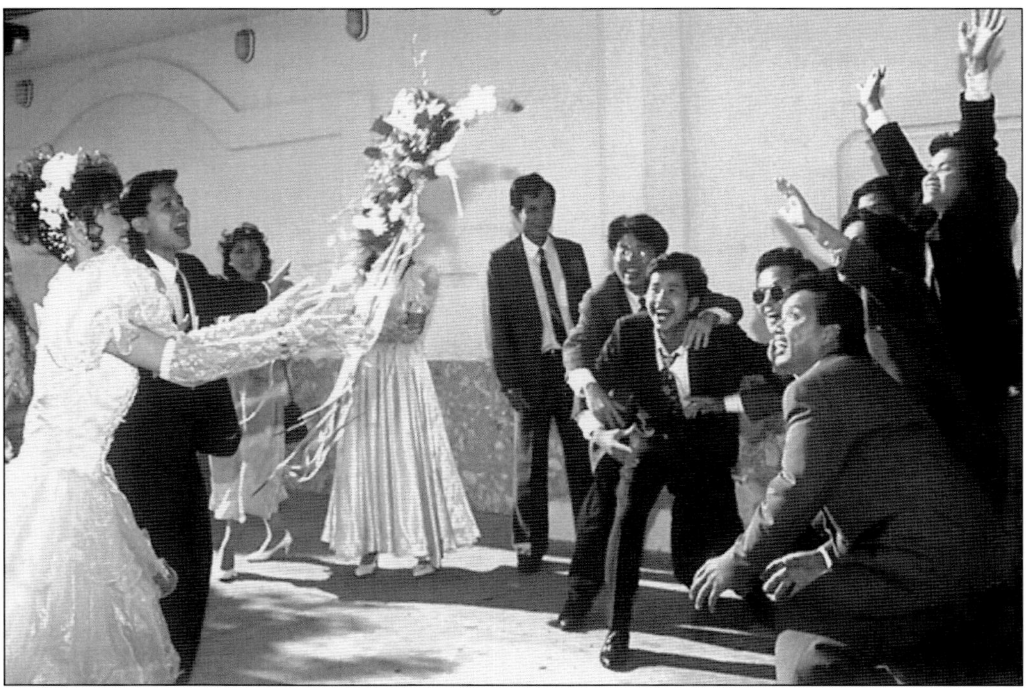

The Vietnamese American wedding often incorporates elements of Vietnamese, Chinese, and American traditions. This joyous image shows a bouquet toss from a bride to a group of spirited young men. (Courtesy of Nicholas Blair, from the collection of Jeffrey Brody and David DeVries, The Vietnamese: Self Portrait of a People.)

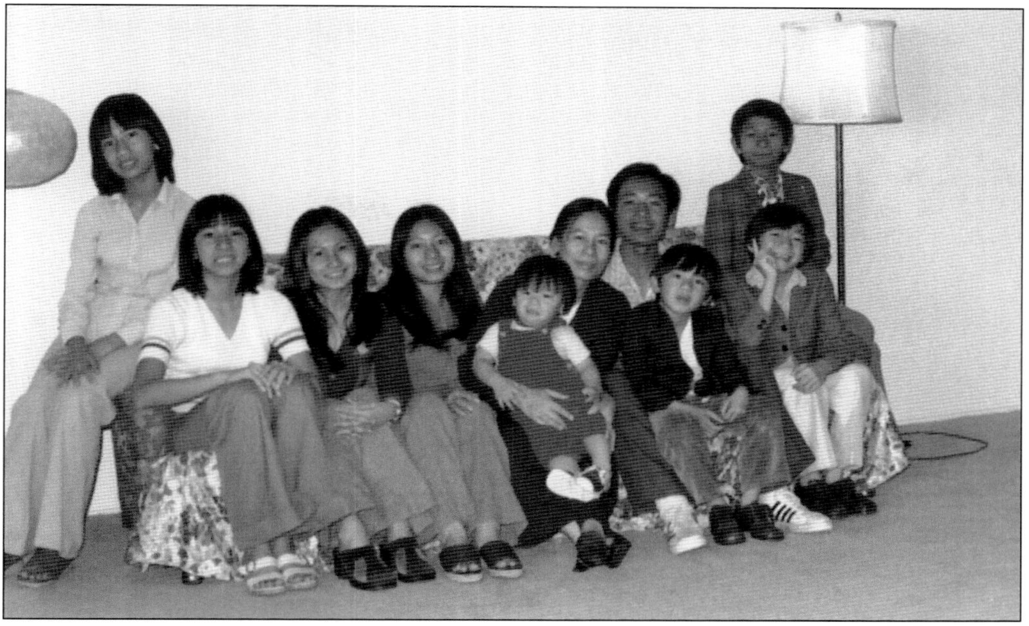

In 1975, while her husband was in a re-education camp, Nhan Thi Nguyen (sixth from left) brought her nine children, ages eight months to 18 years, to the United States and raised them as a single mother for 14 years. She worked as a seamstress in a clothing factory for 18 years to support her family. (Courtesy of the UCI Vietnamese American Oral History Project, VAOHP0143.)

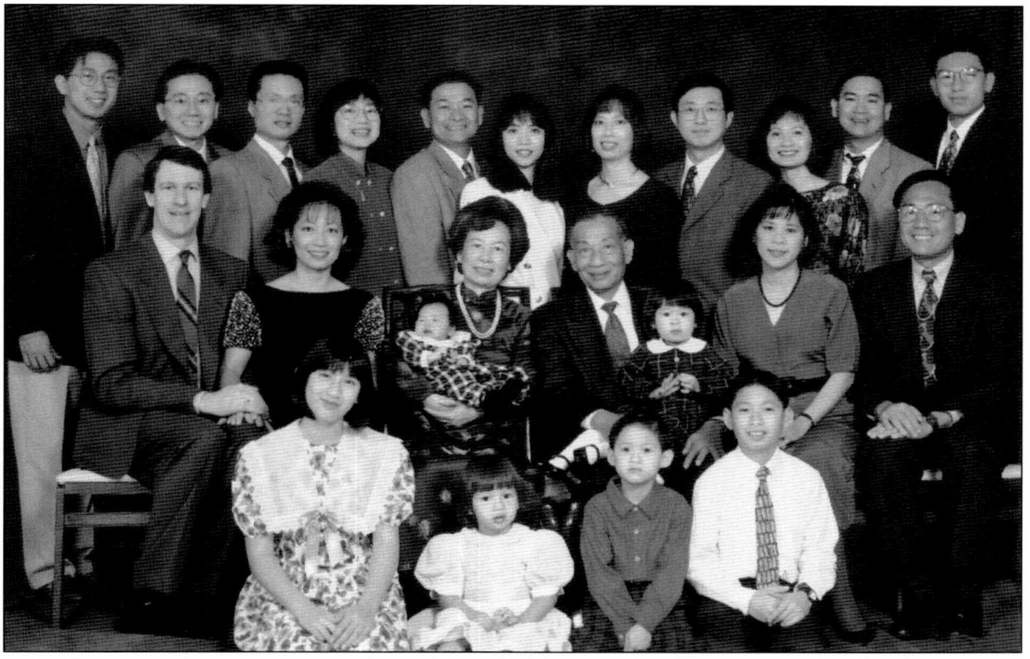

After 14 years of separation, in 1989 Nhan Thi Nguyen's husband, Duong Dinh Thu (seated, center), joined his family in the United States through the Orderly Departure Program. Here, they are reunited in Tustin with their in-laws and grandchildren. (Courtesy of the UCI Vietnamese American Oral History Project, VAOHP0143.)

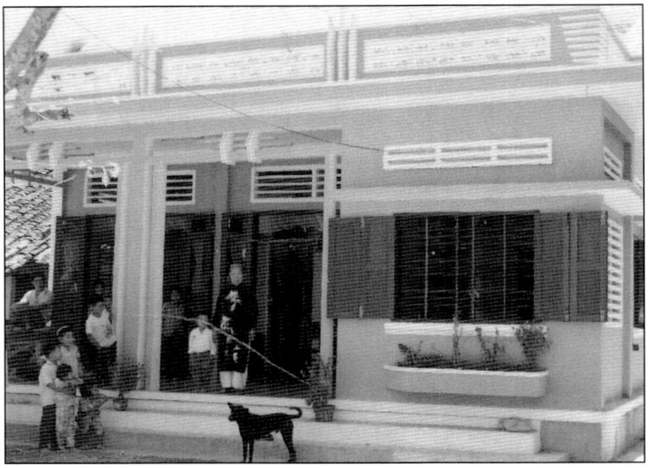

After Em Nguyen arrived in Orange County in 1990 and found employment in Westminster, she sent money home to her family in Ben Tre so that they could build this house in which they all live. Many refugees sent remittances to family members to pay for housing, food, and medical care as well as for luxury items such as air-conditioners, refrigerators, and motorcycles. (Courtesy of the UCI Vietnamese American Oral History Project, VAOHP0163.)

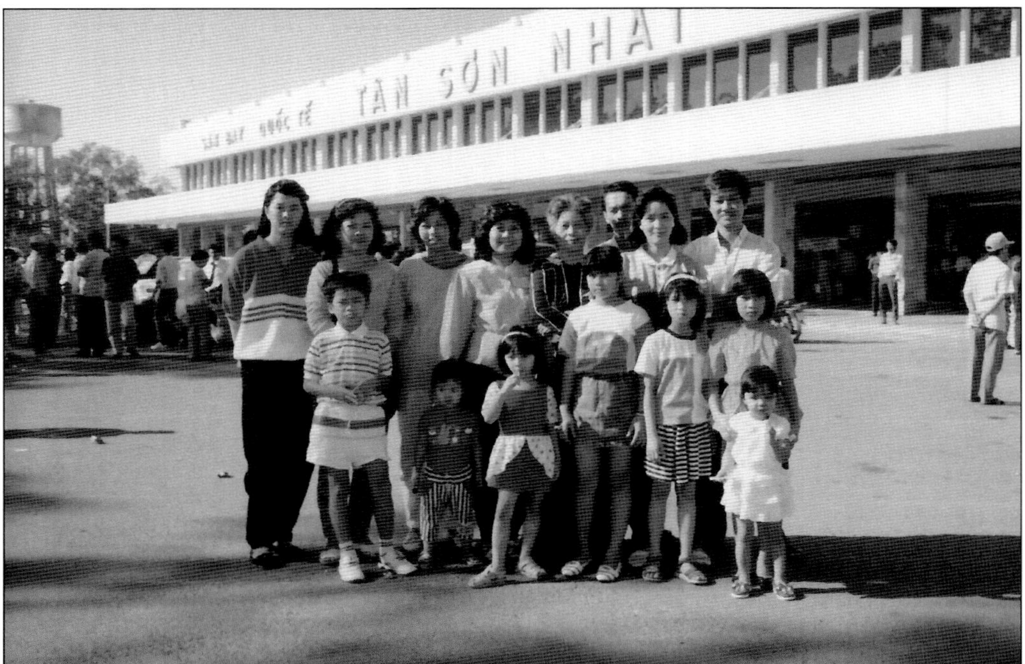

Van Bich Ha (second from left, back row) and her extended family are bidding farewell to Huong (fourth from left, back row) at Tan Son Nhat International Airport in the early 1990s. Since this photograph was taken, family members have dispersed to America and Australia, while others remain in Saigon. Vietnamese families often separate due to the uneven employment prospects and opportunities for immigration. After 1995, when the United States and Vietnam restored formal diplomatic relations, maintaining communication became significantly easier for many families. (Courtesy of Giana Nguyen Foster.)

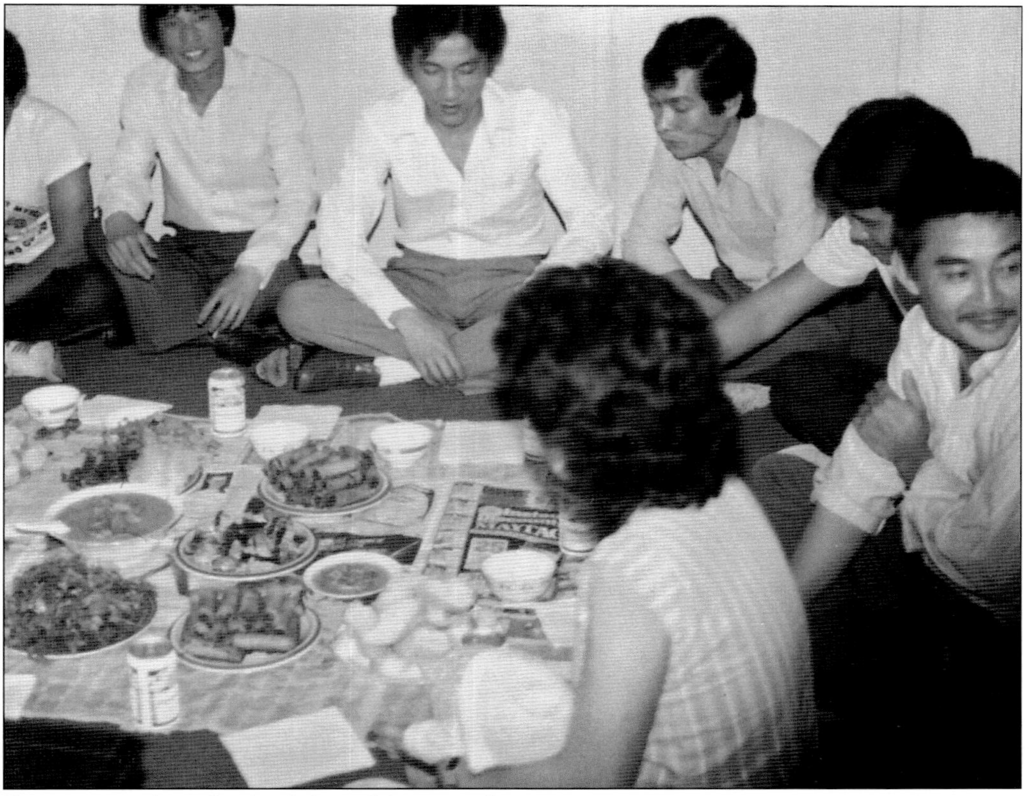

Occasions such as this birthday celebration often include specialty foods such as fried spring rolls and roasted duck that are shared communally. This particular celebration includes Orange County residents who traveled to San Diego for a reunion meal. (Courtesy of Jimmy Huynh.)

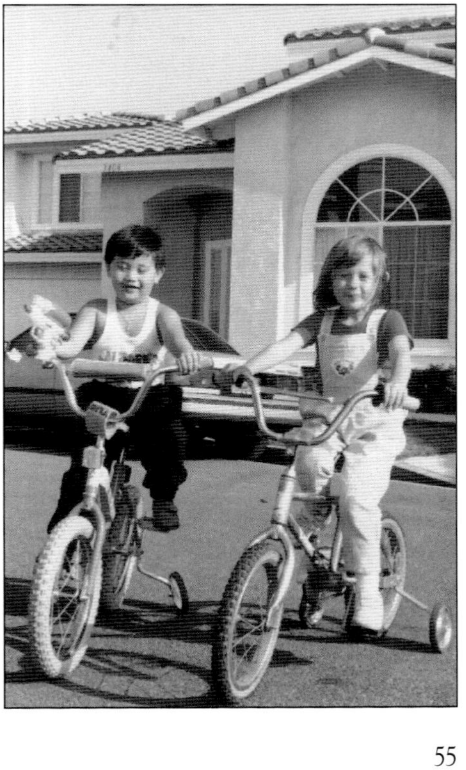

Jimmy Huynh rides his bike with a friend in one of the few gated communities in the Little Saigon region. As Vietnamese refugees became more economically mobile, they began to move out of rentals and become homeowners. A number have moved to more upscale parts of Orange County known for their lower crime rates and good public schools. (Courtesy of Jimmy Huynh.)

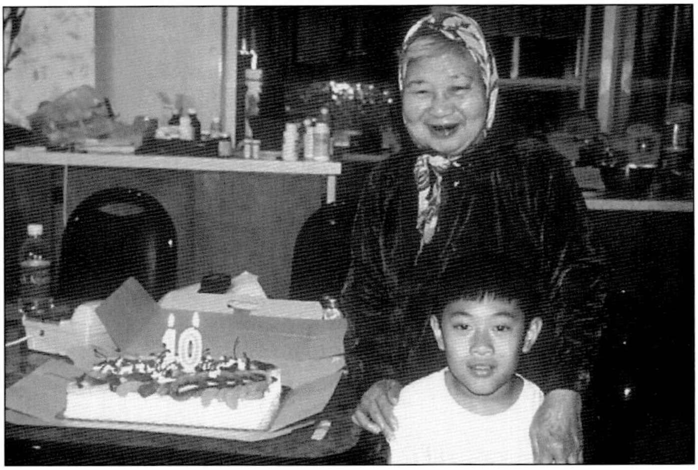

In a multi-generational household, an 89-year-old grandmother and her 10-year-old grandchild celebrate his birthday. Oftentimes, grandparents and other extended family members provide child care in households where parents have to work. (Courtesy of Hoai Thuy Quan and Phi Van Trung, from the collection of Jeffrey Brody and David DeVries, The Vietnamese: Self Portrait of a People.)

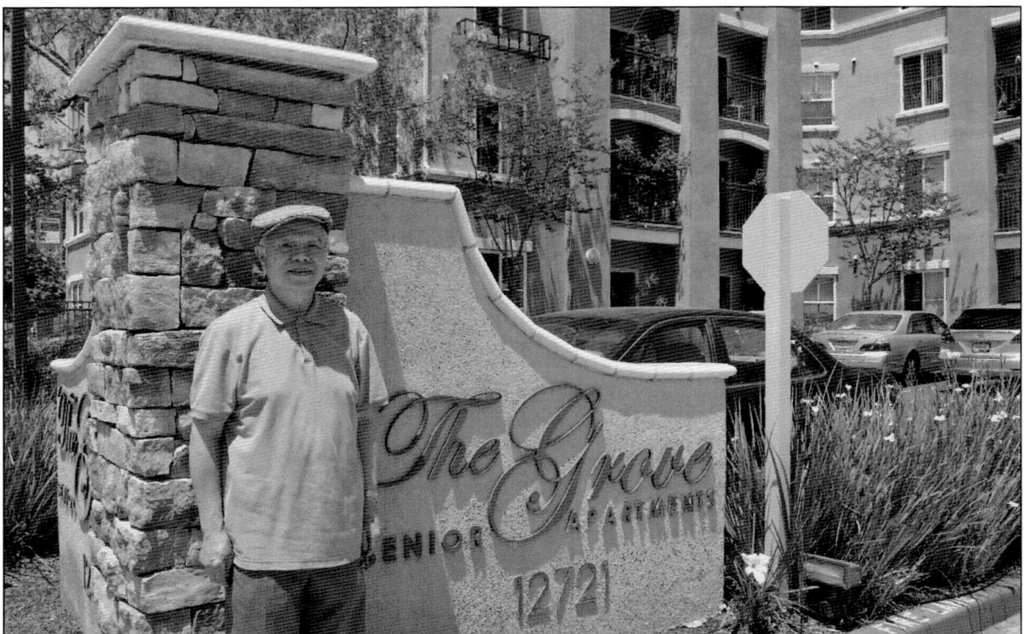

Anthony LeDuc was born in North Vietnam in 1940, moved to South Vietnam in 1954, and was a boat refugee who arrived in America in 1981. He is standing in front of his home, the Grove Senior Apartments, which provides activities and companionship with other Vietnamese seniors who may feel alienated or lost in American culture. In Vietnam, it is customary for adult children to live with and care for their elders, which is not always possible in America. (Courtesy of the UCI Vietnamese American Oral History Project, VAOHP0078.)

Five

EDUCATION

During the French colonial period in Vietnam, France built a limited number of schools and universities that were taught only in French. Education was accessible only to the privileged few, and most remained illiterate. After independence from the French in the 1950s, the educational system reintroduced Vietnamese language into schools, and literacy and enrollment in universities increased. The civil war disrupted schooling and further limited educational opportunities in the country.

Vietnamese who arrived in America in 1975 tend to be more educated than later cohorts of refugees. Some new arrivals were able to attend English-language classes and enroll in college courses, whereas others had to work immediately to support their families. Children adapted more quickly in America, while young adults struggled with the language barrier and often felt isolated from social life in American schools. The younger generation learned English quickly, and many forgot Vietnamese, prompting parents to send their children to temples, churches, and privately owned Vietnamese language schools with the hope that they will retain their mother tongue.

Vietnamese have made use of Orange County's educational options, including vocational training, community colleges, and public and private universities. While many in the earlier period focused on occupations in medicine, science, technology, business, and engineering fields, later generations can be found studying a wide range of majors, including the arts, humanities, and social sciences. Despite often being lumped together with other Asian Americans as "model minorities" (high academic achievers), Vietnamese American educational opportunities vary greatly, with a substantial proportion living in poverty and struggling scholastically.

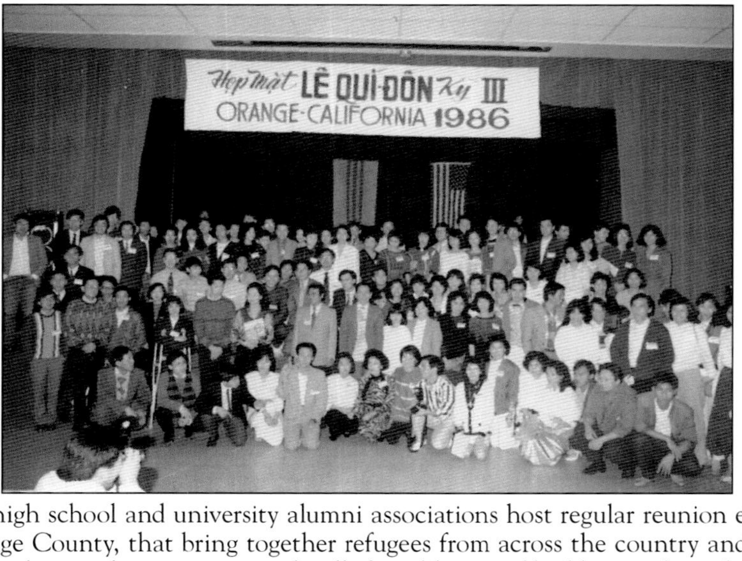

Vietnamese high school and university alumni associations host regular reunion events, many held in Orange County, that bring together refugees from across the country and around the world. It allows them to share memories, rekindle friendships, and build networks as they reestablish their lives. (Courtesy of the UCI Vietnamese American Oral History Project, VAOHP0211.)

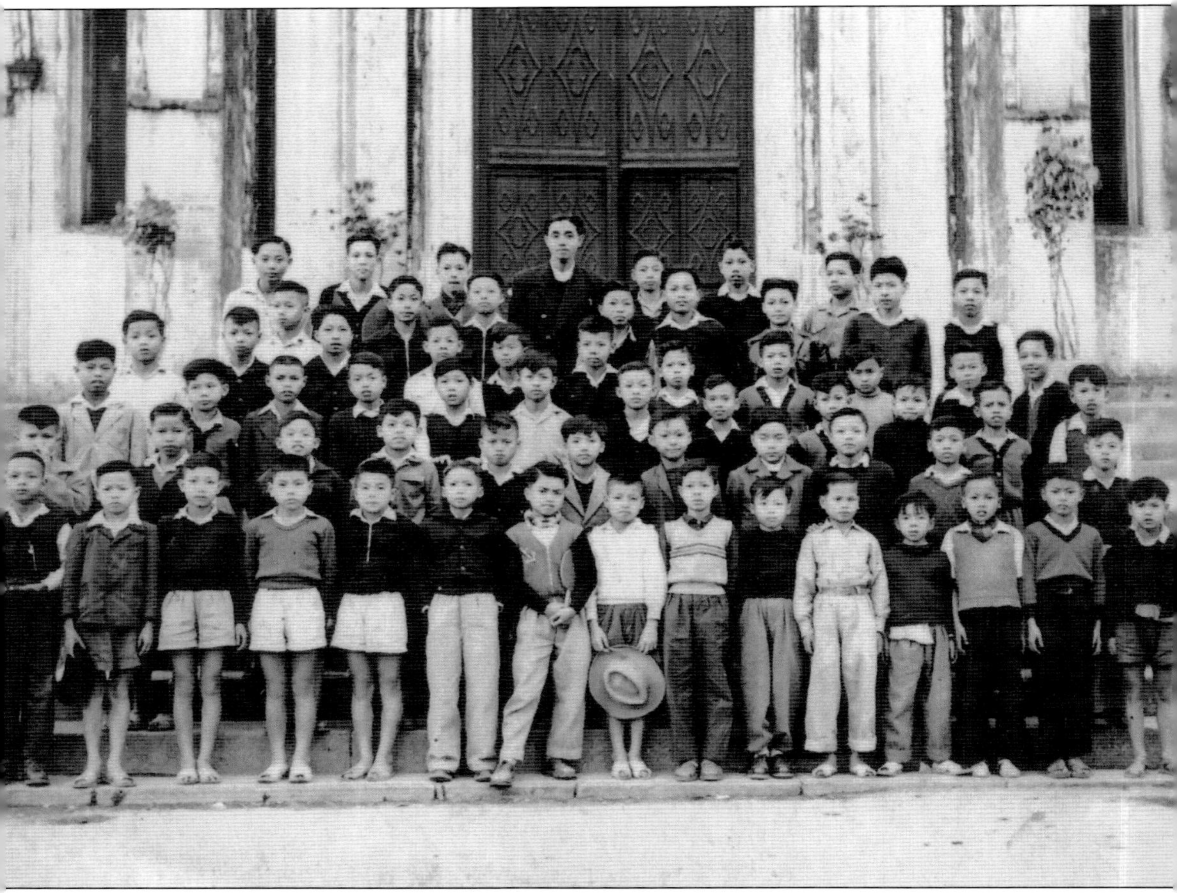

Quynh Nguyen is pictured here with his classmates from Dung Lac Primary School in Hanoi, Vietnam, in the 1940s. In 1954, when the country was partitioned, he moved to South Vietnam with his family. After leaving Vietnam as a refugee in the 1980s, he established a dental practice in Orange County. (Courtesy of Tu-Uyen Nguyen.)

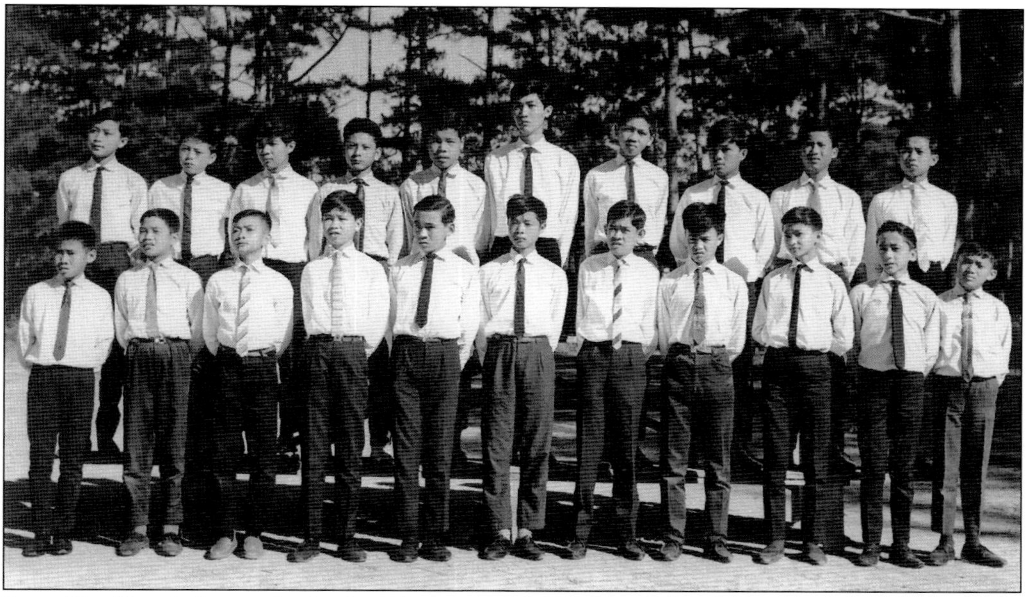

Steve Pho (fourth from right, back row) attended Da Lat Boarding School in 1964. Those who had some wealth would send their children to boarding schools or French schools, although some students attended on scholarships. Steve would later leave Vietnam in 1981 as a refugee and settle in Garden Grove. (Courtesy of the UCI Vietnamese American Oral History Project, VAOHP0164.)

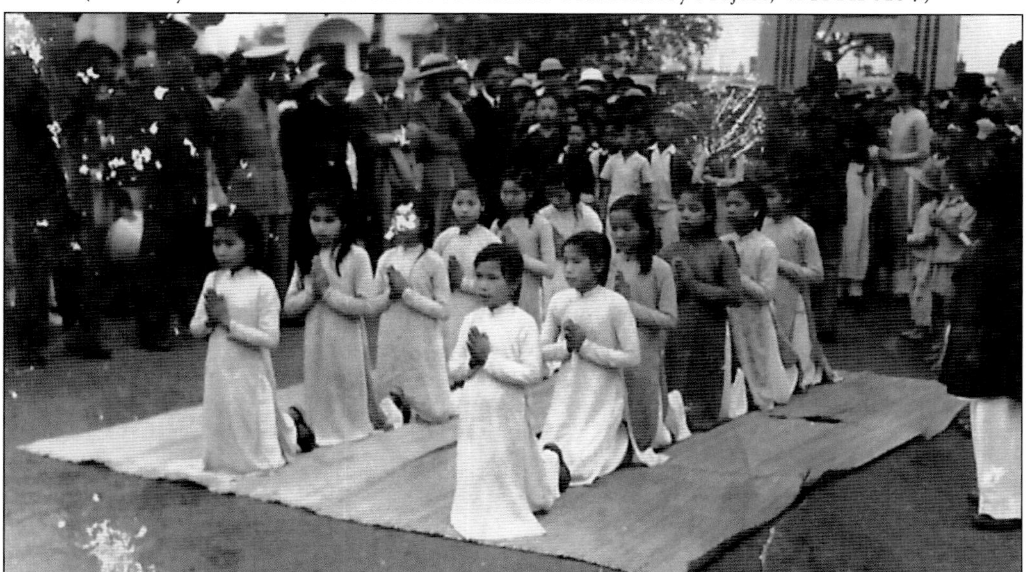

Dung Pham (second in left row) was a fifth-grader in the late 1940s at Bac Ninh Elementary School in North Vietnam. Students prayed in front of the Hai Ba Trung altar at a ceremony to honor Vietnam's heroines. Dung was born and raised in Thai Binh until she was 10 years old. She remembers, "In 1950, my family had to leave because of the war against the French spread to the area. We settled in Bac Ninh . . . we lived there until 1954, when the country was divided into two by the Geneva Agreement. We had to move again, to the South." (Courtesy of the UCI Vietnamese American Oral History Project, VAOHP0202.)

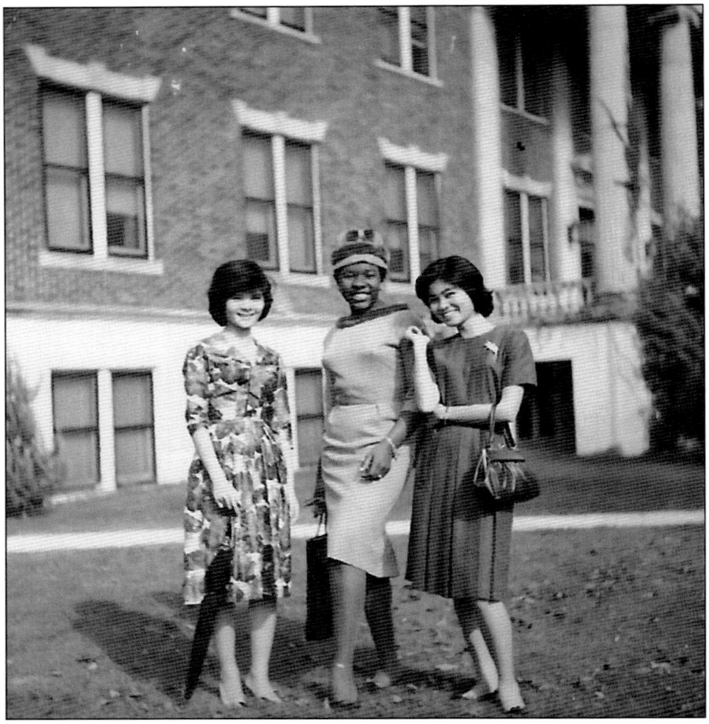

In December 1961, Dung Pham (right) poses with another Vietnamese nursing student and one of the first African American students at Texas Women's University in Denton, Texas. She explains, "I still remember that in those days, African Americans were called Negroes. On one field trip, when seeing 'White Females' and 'Colored Females' on restroom doors, I asked my white classmates which one I was supposed to use. They said the 'White Females' one." (Courtesy of the UCI Vietnamese American Oral History Project, VAOHP0202.)

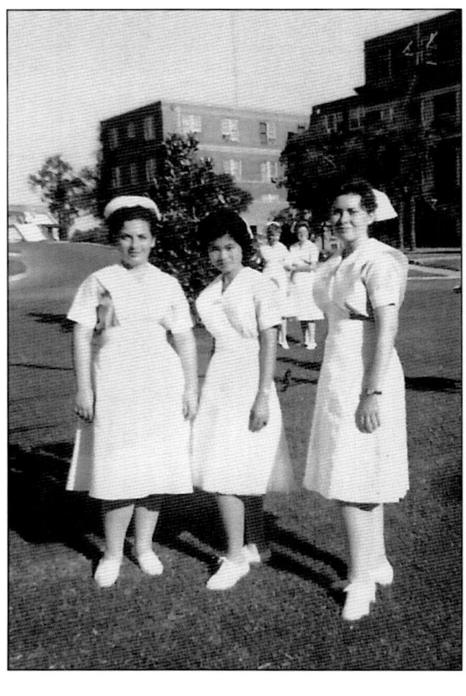

Dung Pham is waiting with her classmates for the bus to Parkland Memorial Hospital in Dallas, Texas, in August 1962. During her time as a nursing student at Texas Women's University, she recalls a memorable experience: "One day in November, 1963, while I was on the Surgical Ward on the second floor, President John F. Kennedy was assassinated and brought to the Emergency Room. When looking down through the windows, I saw crowds of police, news reporters, camera vans, etc. and crying people. I cried, too! Every day for the following week, we, as TWU students, brought a red rose to the bedside of wounded Texas Governor John Connally, still hospitalized after the shooting." She was among a handful of Vietnamese international students who came to America for their education. Many like her would return home to Vietnam, only to re-enter the United States again as refugees. In 1985, she settled in Orange County and worked as a nurse in a public school. (Courtesy of the UCI Vietnamese American Oral History Project, VAOHP0202.)

This photograph is from Fort Chaffee, Arkansas, where refugees were processed before being sponsored and resettled across the United States. Aid workers teach English to a group of refugee children in preparation for their new lives in America. (Courtesy of the UCI Libraries Southeast Asian Archive, MS-SEA025, B1:4.)

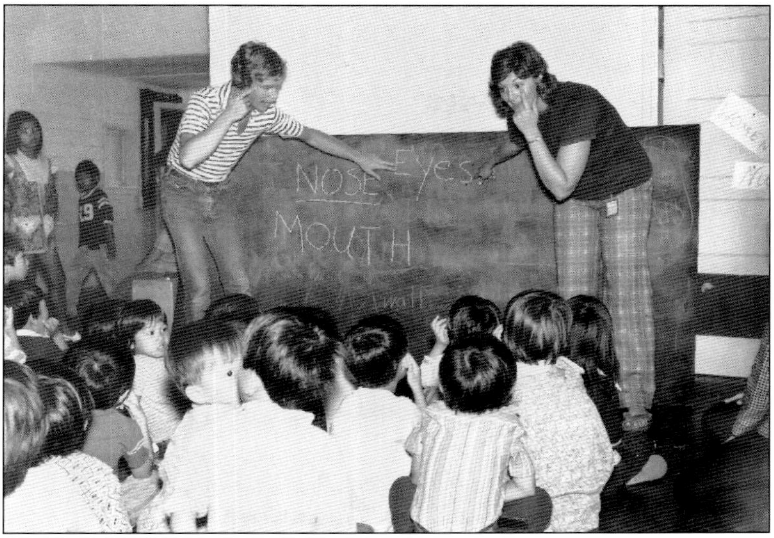

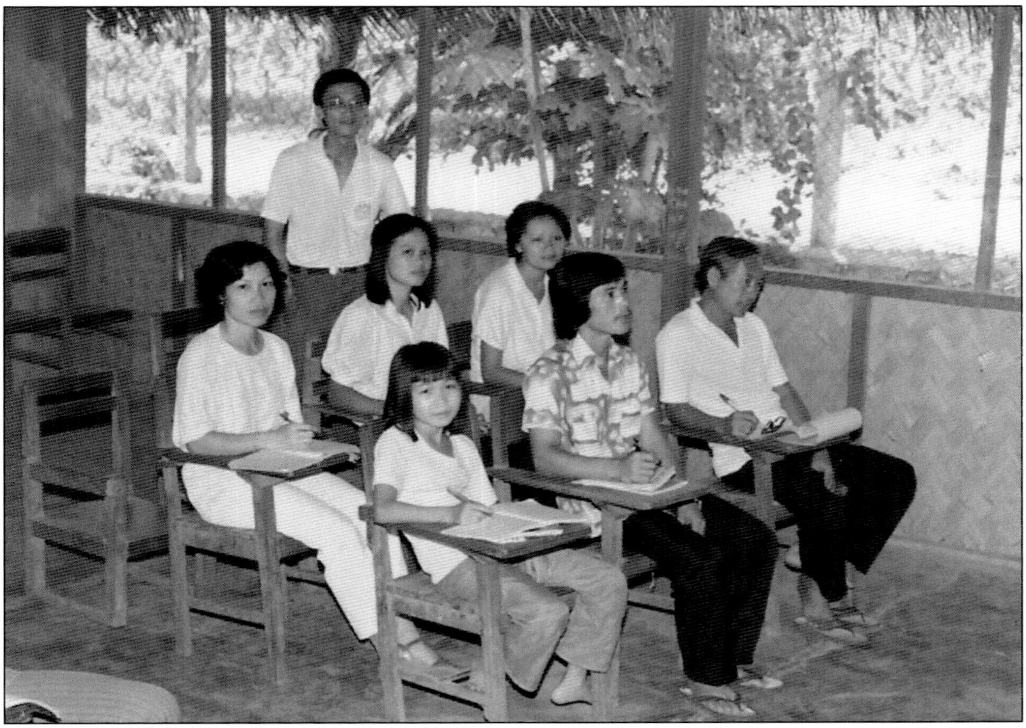

Tri C. Tran stands behind his students in the Palawan refugee camp in the Philippines in 1986. He taught German to Vietnamese refugees being resettled to Germany. He received his bachelors in Spanish linguistics from UC Irvine and his doctorate in romance linguistics and literature from UCLA. He currently teaches Vietnamese at UC Irvine as well as Spanish and Vietnamese at other colleges. (Courtesy of Tri C. Tran.)

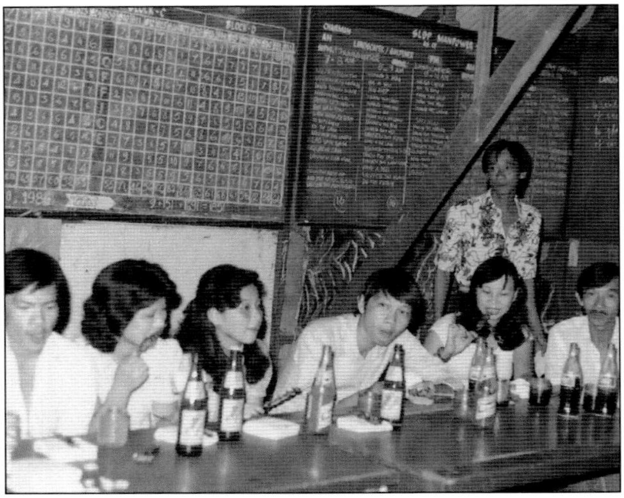

Steve Pho (seated, center) and other teachers and staff at the Bataan Refugee Camp taught English to other refugees in the camp. Those who spoke English found volunteer and paid jobs at the camps, helping to translate and assist other refugees. When they were sponsored to America, they found permanent employment working for local, state, or federal agencies, as well as for nonprofit organizations that were instrumental in resettling refugees. (Courtesy of the UCI Vietnamese American Oral History Project, VAOHP0164.)

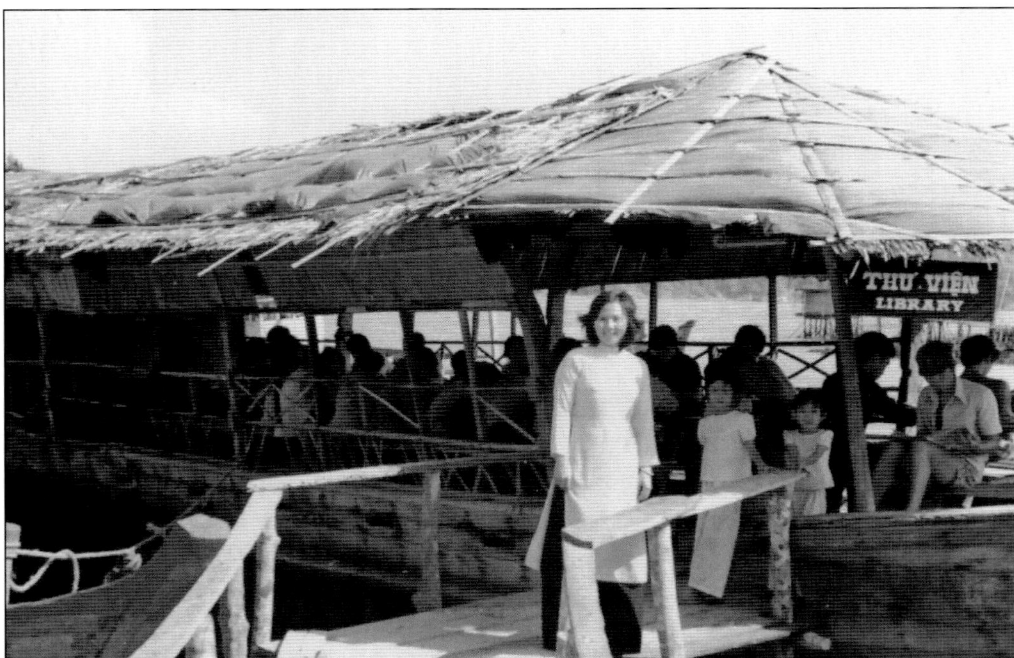

This boat, used by refugees to escape Vietnam, was repurposed into a library and meeting space at Leamsing, Thailand, and provided refugees with reading materials to pass the long days in the camp. The books were donated by Vietnamese who were already resettled in the United States, as well as by shops like Tu Quynh Bookstore in Westminster. *Nguoi Viet Daily News* and other print media in Orange County donated newspapers so that refugees were able to read about the Vietnamese American experience and news stories suppressed in their homeland. (Courtesy of Tran Quoc Bao.)

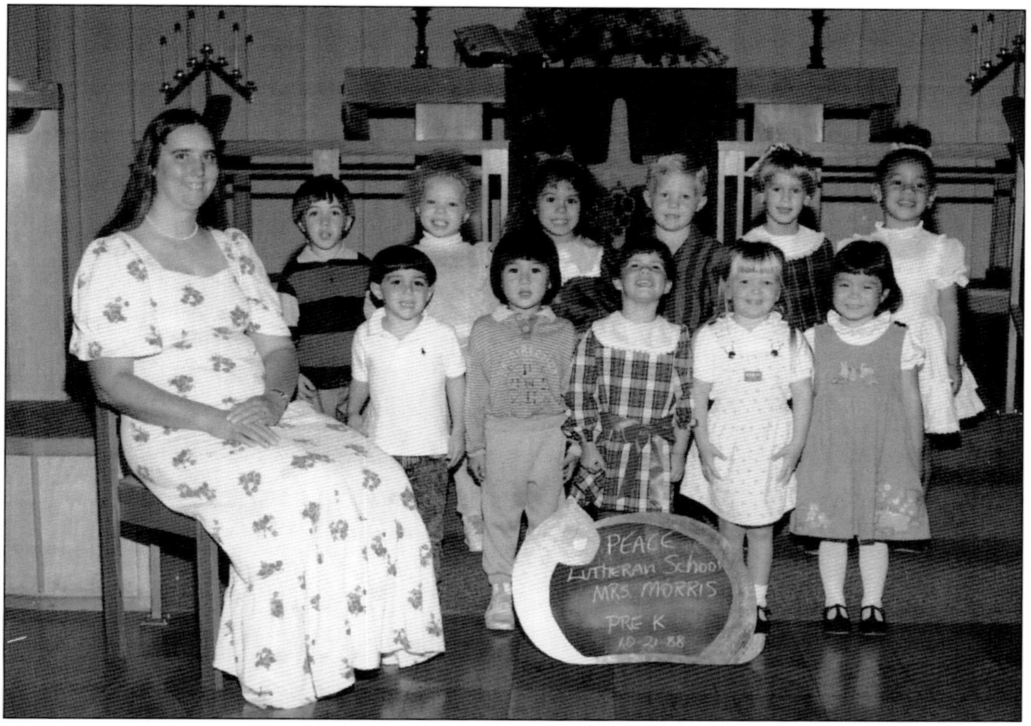

The Peace Lutheran School in Tustin is an example of the many faith-based and charitable institutions assisting Vietnamese refugees in Orange County. Child care and early childhood education allowed refugee parents to take classes or work outside the home. (Courtesy of the UCI Vietnamese American Oral History Project, VAOHP0209.)

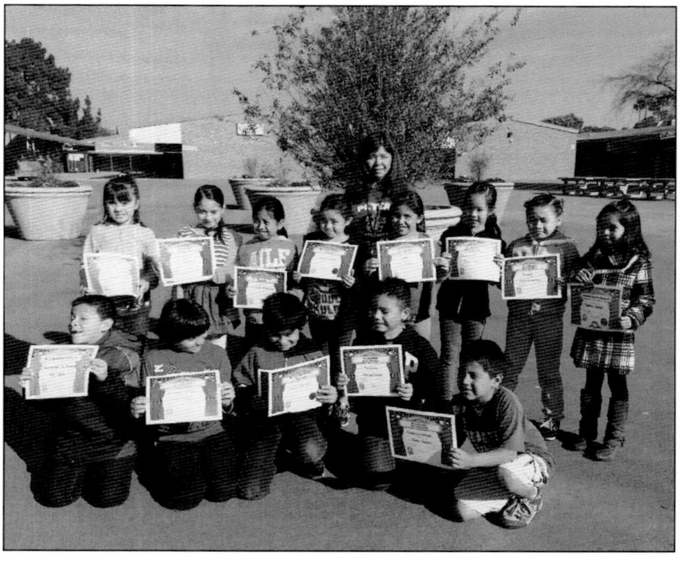

The Ocia A. Peters Elementary School in Garden Grove is one of the few elementary schools in the Garden Grove Unified District that offers a Gifted and Talented Education (GATE) program. Latinos and Asians, predominantly Vietnamese, are the majority population in a number of the K–12 grade schools in the Little Saigon area. Over the years, there have been racial tensions that have flared up between Latinos and Asians in the local high schools. (Courtesy of Thuy Vo Dang.)

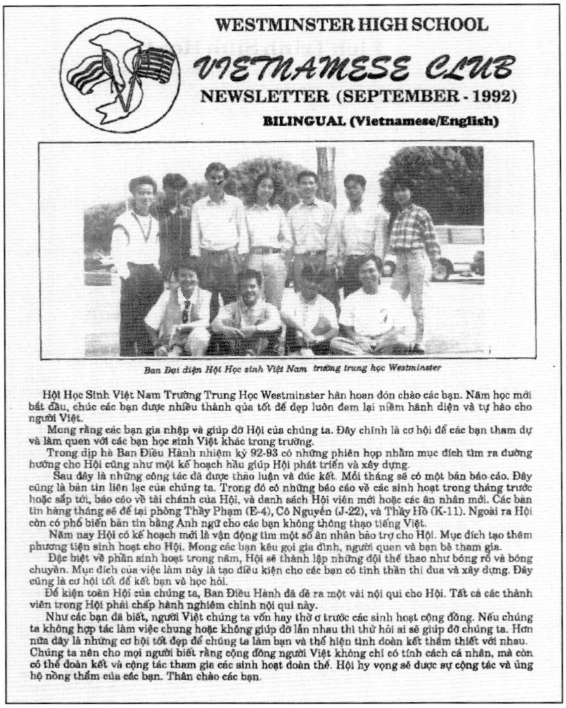

WESTMINSTER HIGH SCHOOL

VIETNAMESE CLUB

NEWSLETTER (SEPTEMBER - 1992)

BILINGUAL (Vietnamese/English)

Ban Đại diện Hội Học sinh Việt Nam trường trung học Westminster

Hội Học Sinh Việt Nam Trường Trung Học Westminster hân hoan đón chào các bạn. Năm học mới bắt đầu, chúc các bạn được nhiều thành qủa tốt đế đẹp luôn đem lại niềm hãnh diện và tự hào cho người Việt.

Mong rằng các bạn gia nhập và giúp dỡ Hội của chúng ta. Đây chính là cơ hội để các bạn tham dự và làm quen với các bạn học sinh Việt khác trong trường.

Trong dịp hè Ban Điều Hành nhiệm kỳ 92-93 có những phiên họp nhằm mục đích tìm ra đường hướng cho Hội cũng như một kế hoạch hầu giúp Hội phát triển và xây dựng.

Sau đây là những công tác đã được thảo luận và đúc kết. Mỗi tháng sẽ có một bản báo cáo. Đây cũng là bản tin liên lạc của chúng ta. Trong đó có những báo cáo về các sinh hoạt trong tháng trước hoặc sắp tới, báo cáo về tài chánh của Hội, và danh sách Hội viên mới hoặc các ân nhân mới. Các bản tin hàng tháng sẽ để tại phòng Thầy Phạm (E-4), Cô Nguyễn (J-22), và Thầy Hồ (K-11). Ngoài ra Hội còn có phổ biến bản tin bằng Anh ngữ cho các bạn không thông thạo tiếng Việt.

Năm nay Hội có kế hoạch mới là vận động tìm một số ân nhân bảo trợ cho Hội. Mục đích tạo thêm phương tiện sinh hoạt cho Hội. Mong các bạn kêu gọi gia đình, người quen và bạn bè tham gia.

Đặc biệt về phần sinh hoạt trong năm, Hội sẽ thành lập những đội thể thao như bóng rổ và bóng chuyền. Mục đích của việc làm này là tạo điều kiện cho các bạn có tinh thần thi đua và xây dựng. Đây cũng là cơ hội tốt để kết bạn và học hỏi.

Để kiện toàn Hội của chúng ta, Ban Điều Hành đã đề ra một vài nội qui cho Hội. Tất cả các thành viên trong Hội phải chấp hành nghiêm chỉnh nội qui này.

Như các bạn đã biết, người Việt chúng ta vốn hay thờ ơ trước các sinh hoạt cộng đồng. Nếu chúng ta không hợp tác làm việc chung hoặc không giúp đỡ lẫn nhau thì thử hỏi ai sẽ giúp đỡ chúng ta. Hơn nữa đây là những cơ hội tốt đẹp để chúng ta làm bạn và thể hiện tình đoàn kết thắm thiết với nhau. Chúng ta nên cho mọi người biết rằng cộng đồng người Việt không chỉ có tính cách cá nhân, mà còn có thể đoàn kết và cộng tác tham gia các sinh hoạt đoàn thể. Hội hy vọng sẽ được sự cộng tác và ủng hộ nồng thắm của các bạn. Thân chào các bạn.

With many refugees settling in Orange County, Vietnamese students started clubs or organizations, such as Vietnamese American High School Associations (VAHSA), to foster ethnic pride and friendships. They hold fundraisers to support their cultural and social events. In 1992, this group at Westminster High School produced a Vietnamese-language newsletter as an outlet for creative expression and to promote their upcoming activities. (Courtesy of the UCI Libraries Southeast Asian Archive, MS-SEA020.)

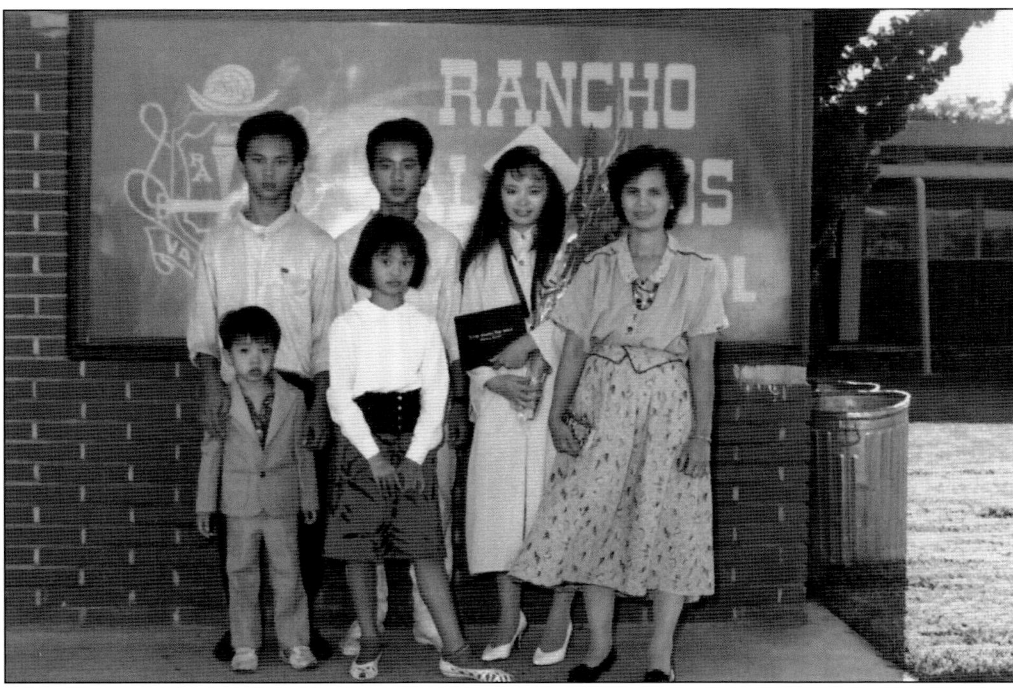

Hong Vo (center, with graduation gown) graduated from Garden Grove's Rancho Alamitos High School in 1988. She arrived in the United States with her family in 1984 with the mass migration of boat people from Vietnam. The eldest of nine children, she was the first in her family to attain a high school diploma in America. (Courtesy of Kelly Vo.)

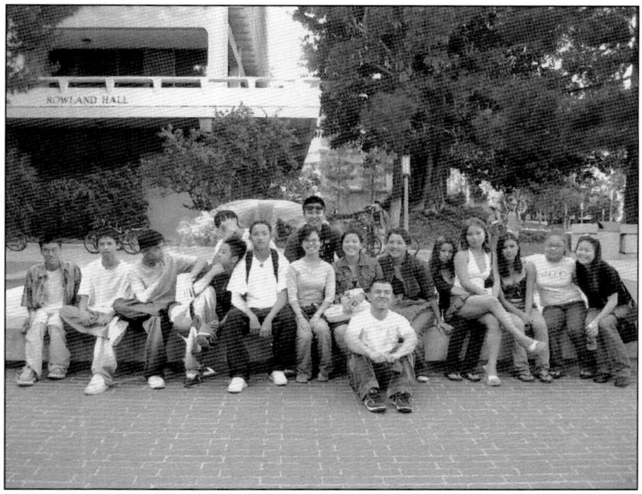

Started in 1996, Project MotiVATe (formerly Camp for Youth) is a nonprofit organization providing free mentoring and tutoring for Vietnamese youths in Orange County. This photograph shows college students organizing a UC Irvine campus visit for high school students in 2004. As children of refugee parents who face hardships adapting in a new county, Vietnamese American youths often struggle in school, face poverty, lack supervision, and are pressured to join gangs. (Courtesy of Quan Tran.)

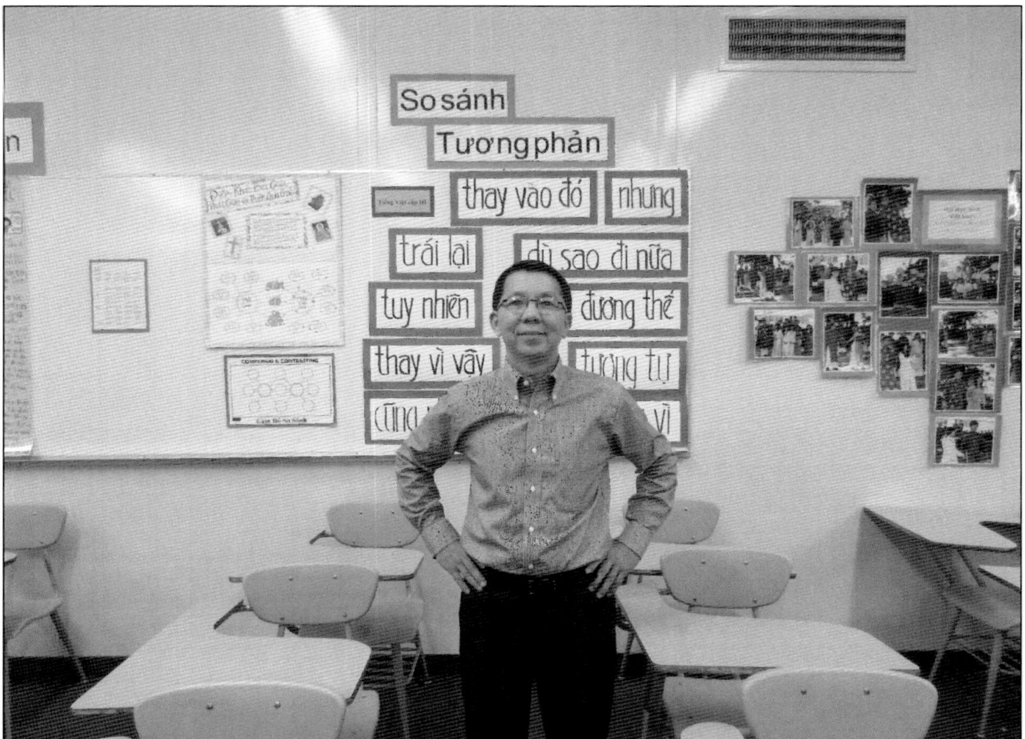

Dzung T. Bach is a Vietnamese language teacher at La Quinta High School in Westminster. Born in Hai Phong, North Vietnam, he and his family moved south in 1954, where he was in law school before enlisting as a first lieutenant in the army of South Vietnam. He was imprisoned in the re-education camps after the war and arrived in America through the Orderly Departure Program. In Vietnam, he spoke Vietnamese at home and French at school and learned English after he arrived in America. (Courtesy of the UCI Vietnamese American Oral History Project, VAOHP0022.)

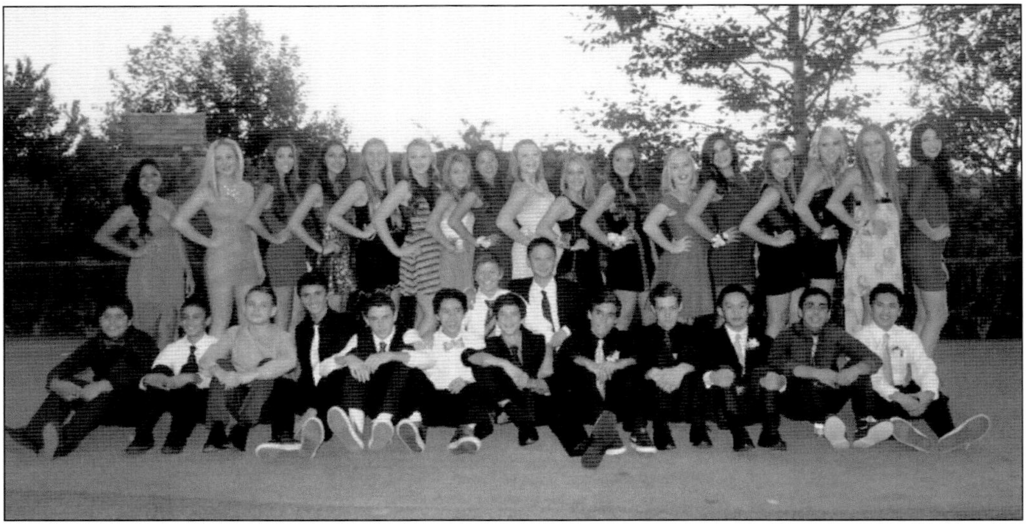

While early Vietnamese refugee students tended not to have the resources or were pressured to focus only on their education, second- and third-generation Vietnamese have more options to participate in school social activities. In this photograph, ninth-graders gather for dinner before attending the 2012 homecoming dance at University High School in Irvine. Three of the boys are Vietnamese Americans, and the group includes Anglo, Asian, Middle Eastern, Latino, and multiracial students. (Courtesy of Kian Vo Ross.)

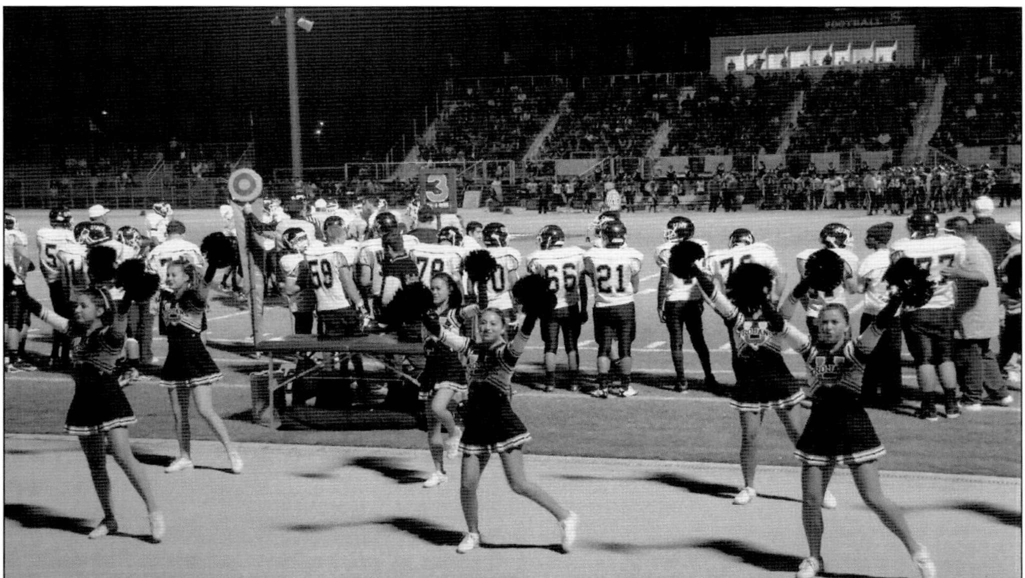

An increasing number of Vietnamese American students participate in campus extracurricular activities, from joining clubs to playing sports. This photograph shows a University High School football game in Irvine, a suburb close to Little Saigon, and includes two Vietnamese varsity cheerleaders, Aisha and Melissa (front center and back center, respectively). The team also includes Vietnamese football players. Irvine is known for its excellent public schools, which has attracted a growing number of Asian American families, including Vietnamese. (Courtesy of John Hiroshi Kamei.)

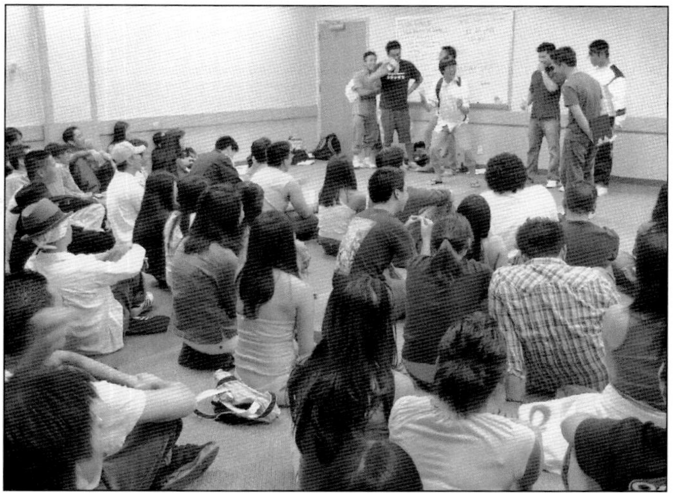

Vietnamese Student Associations (VSA) have been created at college campuses across the country, including this one that was started in 1979 at UC Irvine. Most VSAs organize annual Vietnamese Culture Nights and Black April commemorations, along with other cultural and social events. In some cases, they have advocated for Vietnamese language classes to be taught on college campuses as well. (Courtesy of Diana Nguyen.)

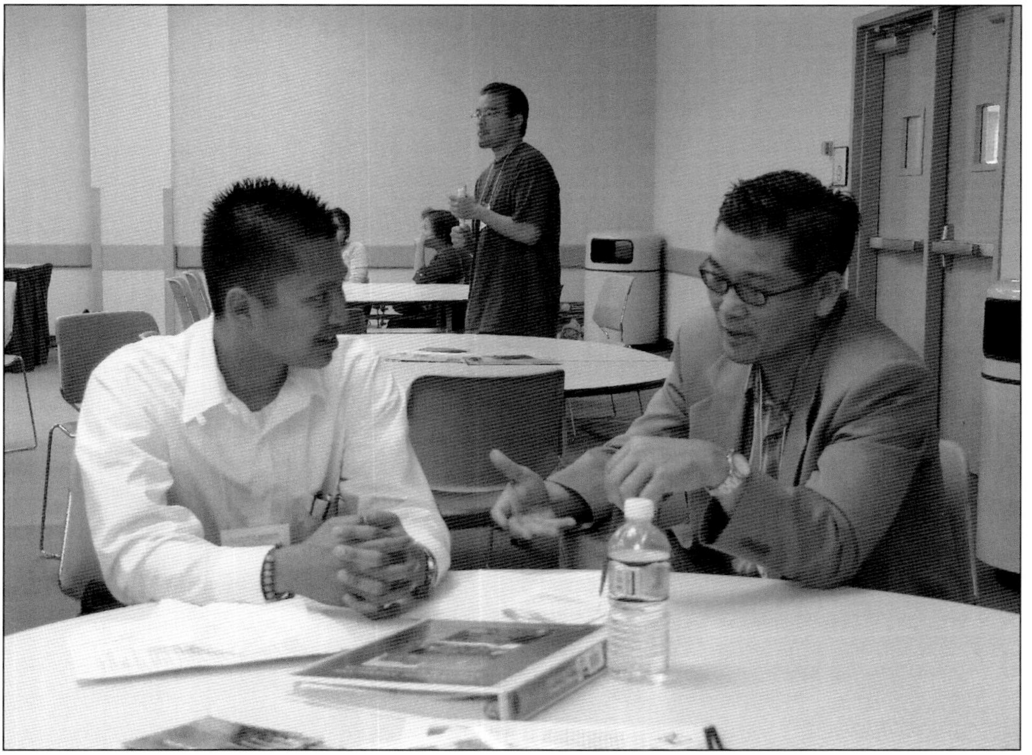

The Vietnamese American Coalition (VAC) is a student group that started in 1993 at UC Irvine. It is a socially and politically conscious organization that encourages awareness of Vietnamese American history and community involvement through conferences such as this one at UC Irvine in May 2004. At the event is Don Luong (left), then co-chair of VAC and now a middle school teacher, being mentored by VAC cofounder Michael Matsuda (right), an Anaheim Union High School superintendent. (Courtesy of Linda Trinh Vo.)

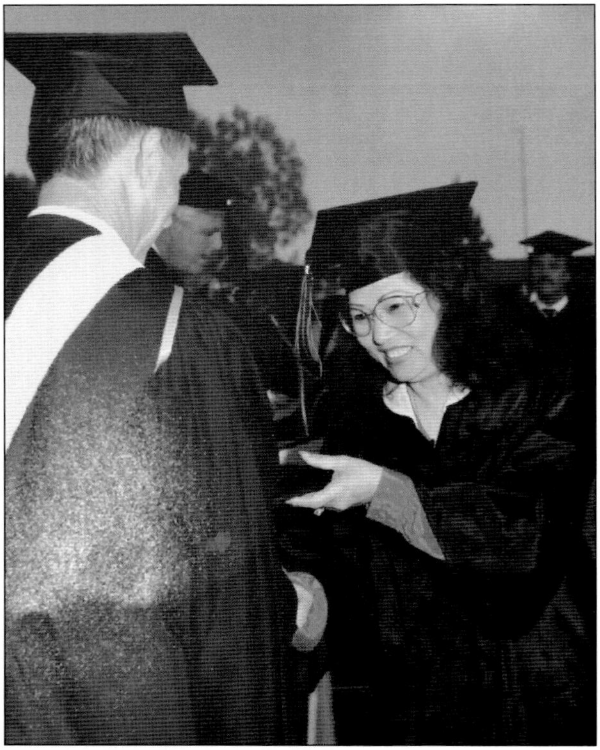

Ngoc-Hoa Lam graduated from Orange Coast Community College in 1993 and became an accountant with the State Board of Equalization. All four of her children earned doctorate degrees. For a vast number of Vietnamese refugees and immigrants, community colleges provide an accessible pathway to higher education. (Courtesy of the UCI Vietnamese American Oral History Project, VAOHP0104.)

Medical professions, such as physicians, pharmacists, nurses, and health-care workers, are popular among Vietnamese Americans. This photograph shows a booth offering free blood-pressure and glucose screenings at the annual Tet Festival in Garden Grove. It is hosted by the Vietnamese American Pharmacy Student Association of the University of Southern California, a predominately female group. (Courtesy of Linda Trinh Vo.)

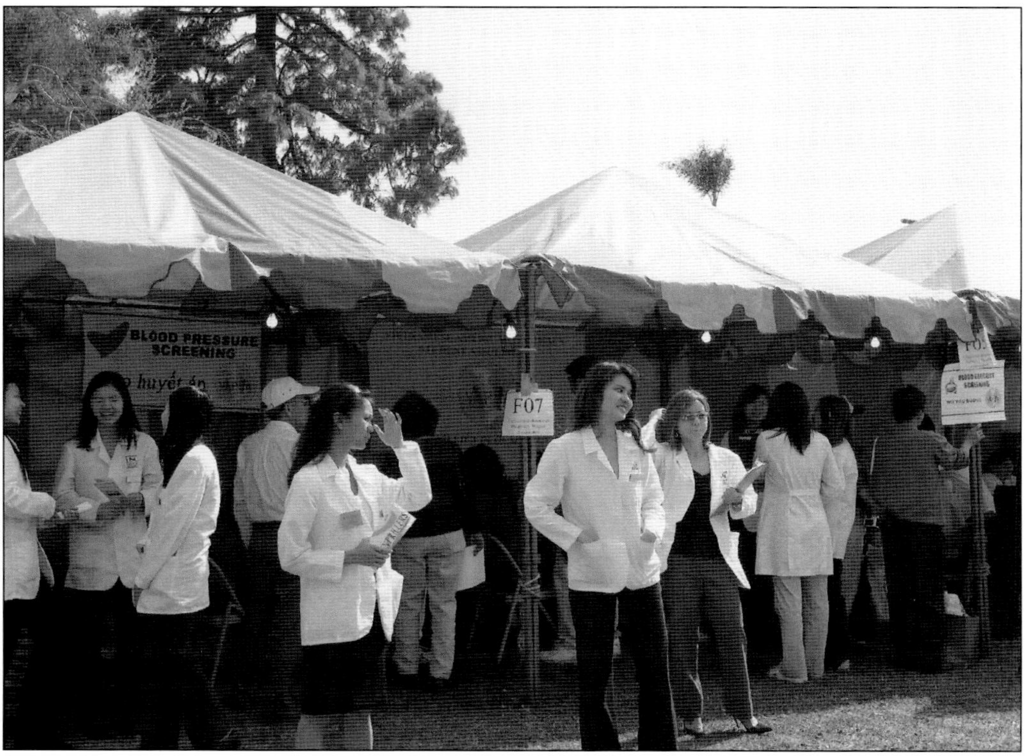

Jack Toan celebrates with his parents on graduation day at UC Irvine in 1994. He received his bachelor's degree in biology and would later return for his master's in business administration. He chairs the Vietnamese American Community Ambassadors, an alumni chapter, at his alma mater. UC Irvine has a Department of Asian American Studies that offers Vietnamese American Experience and Southeast Asian American Experience courses, and the campus also offers Vietnamese language classes. California State University, Fullerton (CSUF) also teaches similar courses, and Dr. Tam Nguyen, a graduate of both UC Irvine and CSUF, was president of CSUF's Alumni Association. (Courtesy of Jack Toan.)

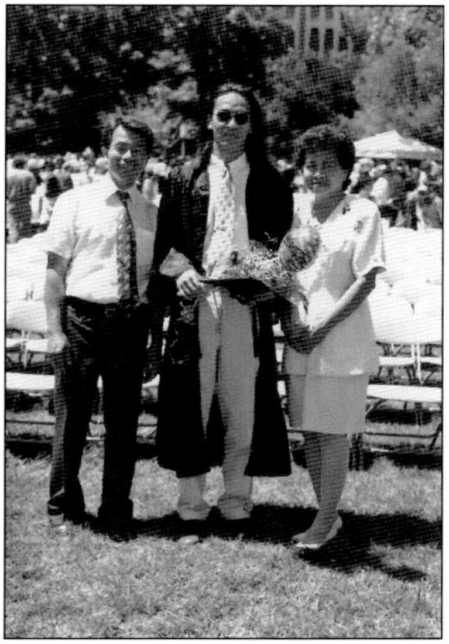

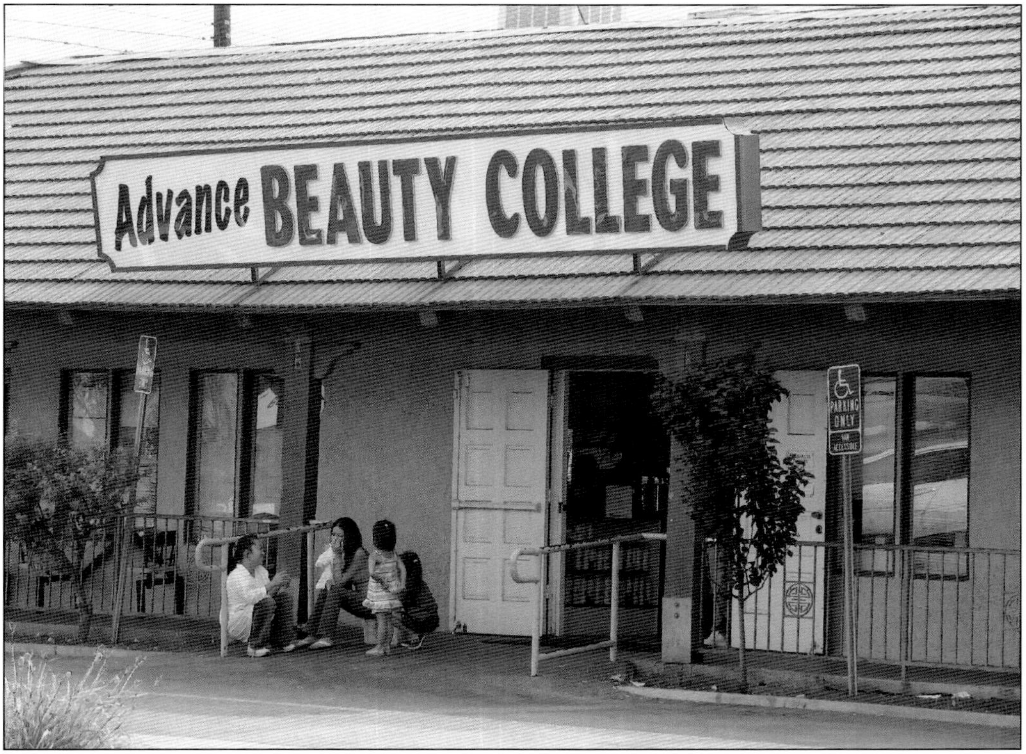

Founded in 1999 by Diem and Kien Nguyen and now run by their children, Linh and Tam, Advance Beauty College in Garden Grove offers training in Vietnamese. Diem was a navy commander in Vietnam and Kien owned a hair salon before they left as refugees. The photograph shows the Garden Grove location of their beauty college before it was remodeled in 2012, with a second location in Laguna Hills opening that same year. This school has graduated over 25,000 students, many who found work as licensed cosmetologists locally and across the nation. Vietnamese make up over 80 percent of California's licensed manicurists. (Courtesy of Linda Trinh Vo.)

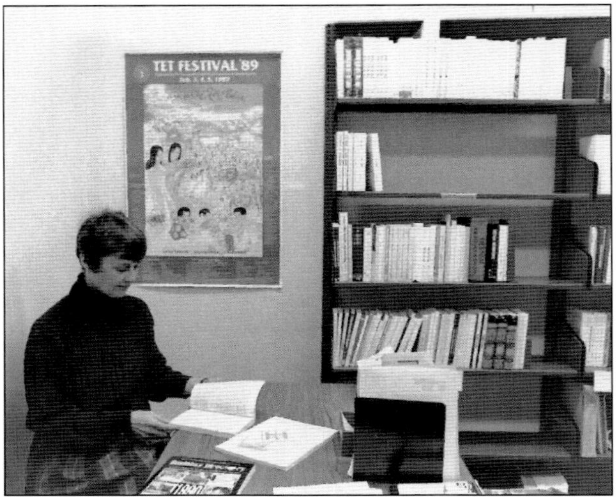

Anne Frank, who retired in 2007, is the founding librarian of the UC Irvine Libraries' Southeast Asian Archive, a nationally distinguished collection. With the impetus coming from members of the Southeast Asian American community in Orange County, such as Prof. Pham Cao Duong and Dr. Vu Dinh Minh, the archive was established in 1987 and documents Vietnamese, Cambodian, Hmong, and Laotians in the diaspora. Dr. Thuy Vo Dang continues to develop the collections. (Courtesy of the UCI Libraries Southeast Asian Archive, MS-SEA020.)

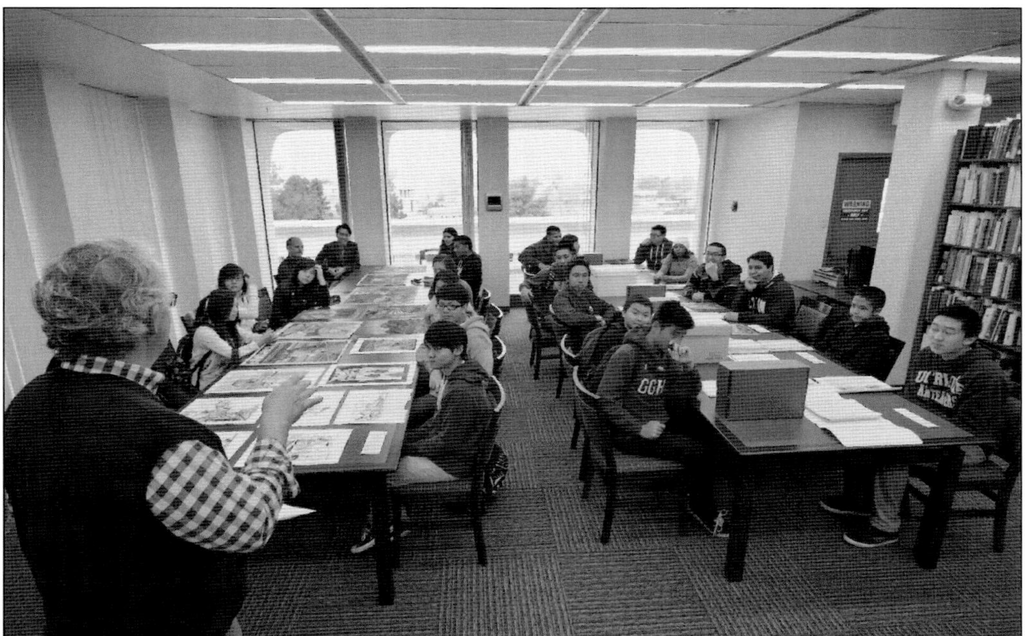

In 2012, Garden Grove High School offered the first-ever Vietnamese American History course. Taught by history teacher Katy Jue, the course became an annual offering and includes a field trip to the UC Irvine Southeast Asian Archive. Pictured are those students receiving instruction from librarian Steve MacLeod. Both Garden Grove and Westminster School Districts are in the process of implementing Vietnamese-English dual-language immersion programs. (Courtesy of UCI Libraries.)

Six

WORK

Vietnamese Americans are a socioeconomically diverse group who came in different periods, and while some are financially stable, others struggle economically. A number were well educated, had transferable skills, and knew some English; therefore, they adjusted more easily than those from rural areas with limited resources. Some found that their Vietnamese degrees, experiences, and language skills were valued in Little Saigon, allowing them to find jobs in the ethnic economy. Many later refugees labor in low-wage employment or the service sector, while some open small businesses. The Little Saigon community has many types of businesses, which allow individuals with a range of talents and skills to make a living. Profit margins are slim, and competition is fierce in this ethnic economy, so business owners often rely on the unpaid labor of their family. Many also find employment in local factories, the garment industries, and assembly work in the region. The Vietnamese have created economic niches, such as the nail salon industry, and dominate the field as nail technicians, shop owners, and suppliers. Increasingly, the second and third generations are finding employment in mainstream companies located outside of the Little Saigon area. The forms of employment that Vietnamese engage in vary greatly and will continue to become more diverse with future generations.

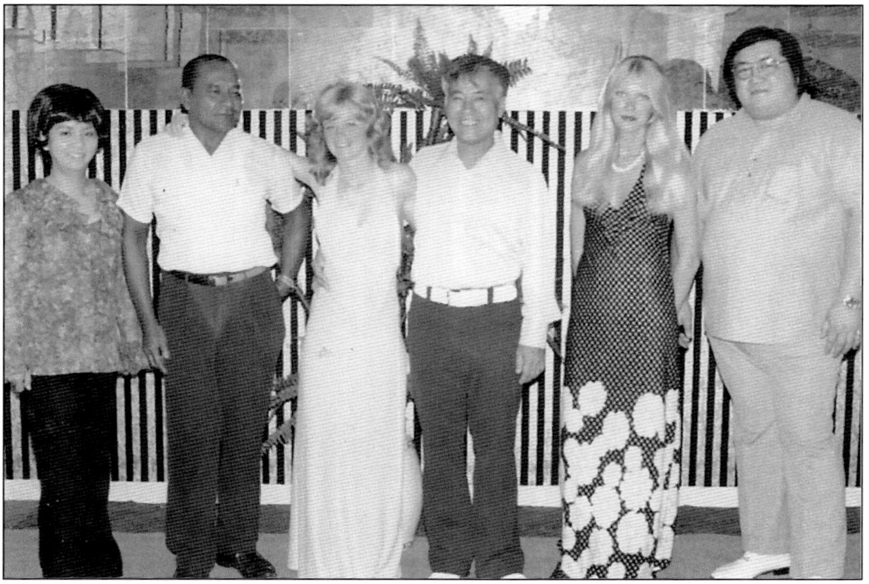

Han To (far left) married an American citizen who was a contractor working in Vietnam. After he passed away from illness, she left the country in 1975 with her son. Always the entrepreneur, she opened several bars in Guam while waiting to be sponsored to the United States, where she continued to open a variety of small businesses in Orange County to support her family. She is pictured here with her customers in one of her bars in Guam called Some Place Else. (Courtesy of Stephane Gauger.)

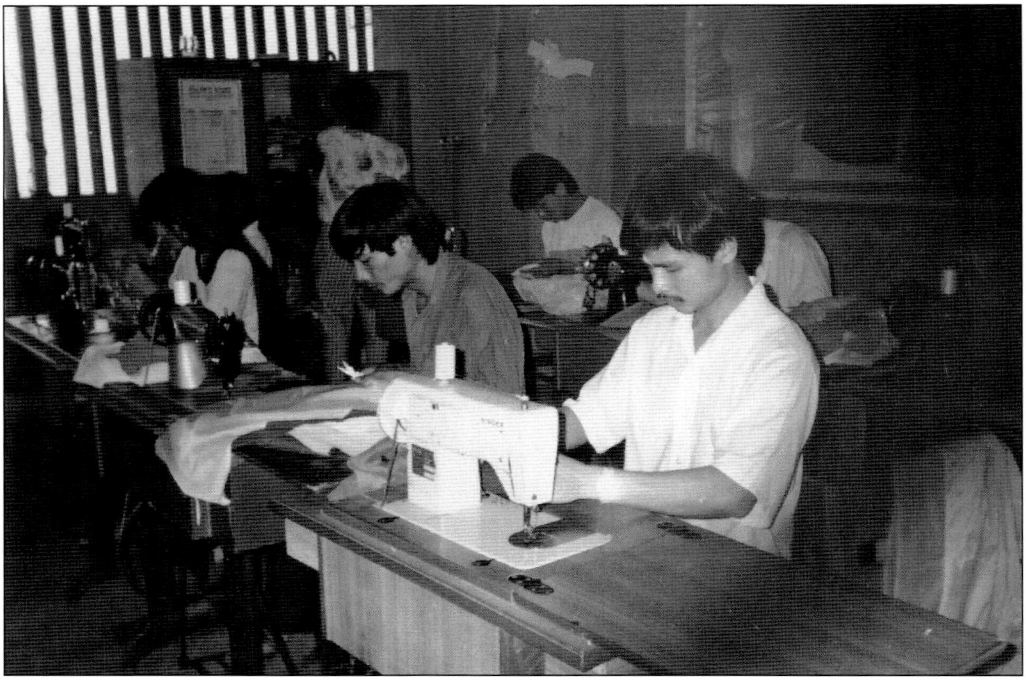

Refugees in the camps were taught basic occupational skills to prepare them for resettlement. Oftentimes, the skills taught were mismatched with the employment opportunities available to them once they arrived in America. Many former professionals found themselves doing manual labor; some stayed in these occupations, while others went back to school and found better paying jobs. Some female refugees had an easier time finding employment in the service sector, garment industry, and assembly work since stereotypes exist that they are docile and exploitable. (Courtesy of the UCI Libraries Southeast Asian Archive, MS-SEA016, B10:16.)

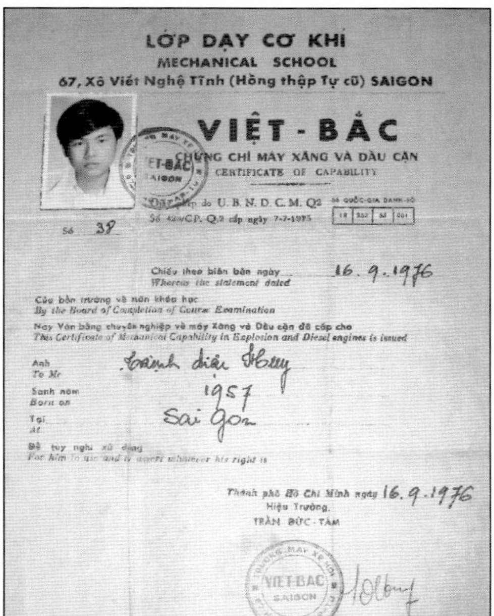

LỚP DẠY CƠ KHÍ
MECHANICAL SCHOOL
67, Xô Viết Nghệ Tĩnh (Hồng thập Tự cũ) SAIGON

VIỆT - BẮC
CHỨNG CHỈ MÁY XĂNG VÀ DẦU CẶN
CERTIFICATE OF CAPABILITY

Số 38

Chiếu theo biên bản ngày 16.9.1976
Whereas the statement dated

Của bản trường và nãn khóa học
By the Board of Completion of Course Examination

Nay Văn bằng chuyên nghiệp về máy Xăng và Dầu cặn đã cấp cho
This Certificate of Mechanical Capability in Explosion and Diesel engines is issued

Anh
To Mr

Sanh năm 1957
Born on

Tại Sài Gòn
At

Thành phố Hồ Chí Minh ngày 16.9.1976
Hiệu Trưởng.
TRẦN ĐỨC-TÂM

Some refugees were professionals who brought their degrees and certificates with them, hoping this would help them find employment in the United States. Oftentimes, their degrees were not recognized, regardless of their skills or years of experience. Some had to start over in school or switch professions altogether. (Courtesy of the UCI Vietnamese American Oral History Project, VAOHP0011.)

Since Little Saigon is a self-sufficient community, clients can purchase homes, furniture, and cars from Vietnamese-speaking salespeople or businesses. Many mainstream financial, insurance, and real estate offices also hire bicultural and bilingual employees who can cater to the community. This Century 21 advertisement for Vietnamese real estate agents was published in the *1987 Vietnamese Business Directory*. (Courtesy of the UCI Libraries Southeast Asian Archive.)

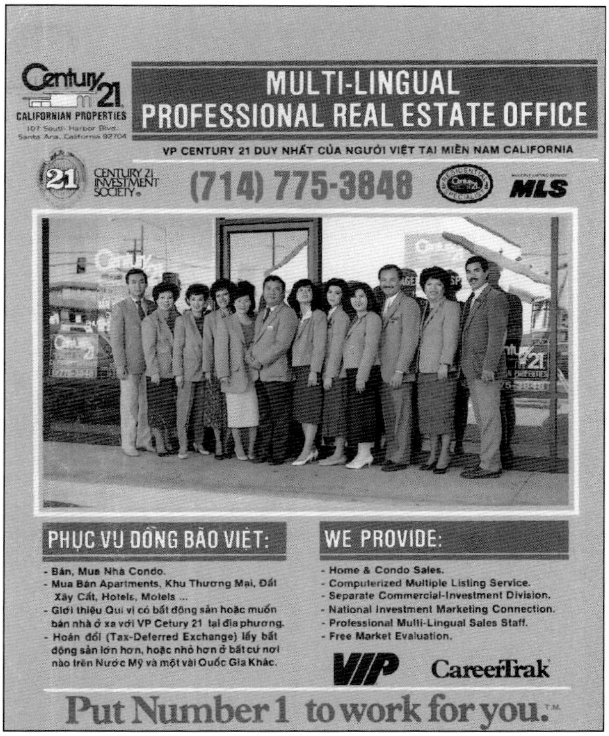

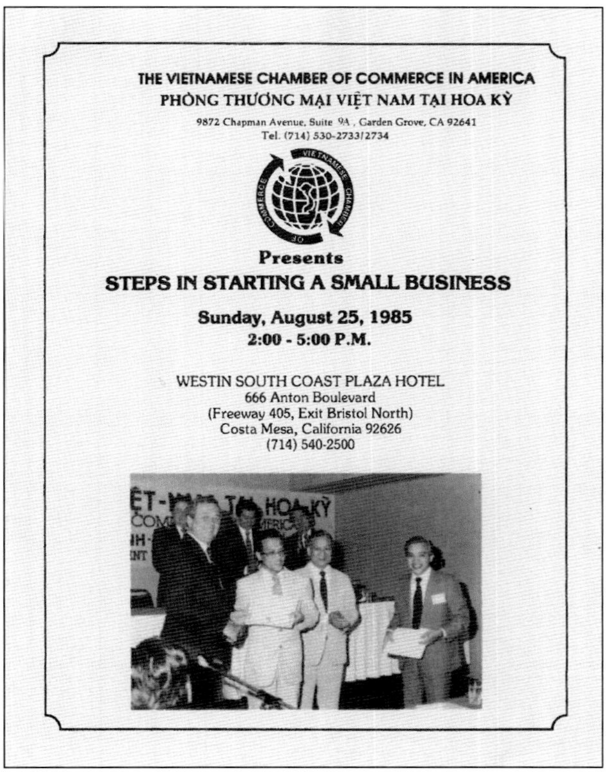

The Vietnamese American Chamber of Commerce (VACOC), established in Orange County in 1985, is the first and largest of its kind, with over 1,500 members. Dr. Pham Dang Long Co was its longest-serving president. Its 1985 newsletter included information on how to start a business. (Courtesy of the UCI Libraries Southeast Asian Archive, MS-SEA004, B10:1.)

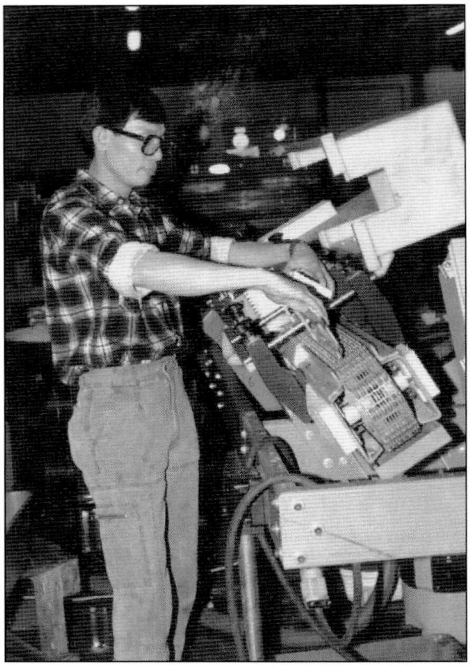

This photograph, taken in 1985, shows Do Hoang Vo working as a machine operator in a Huntington Beach company that manufactured metal parts for computers. A number of refugees, especially those with limited language skills, found unskilled or semi-skilled work in the local industries of Southern California. (Courtesy of Jimmy Huynh.)

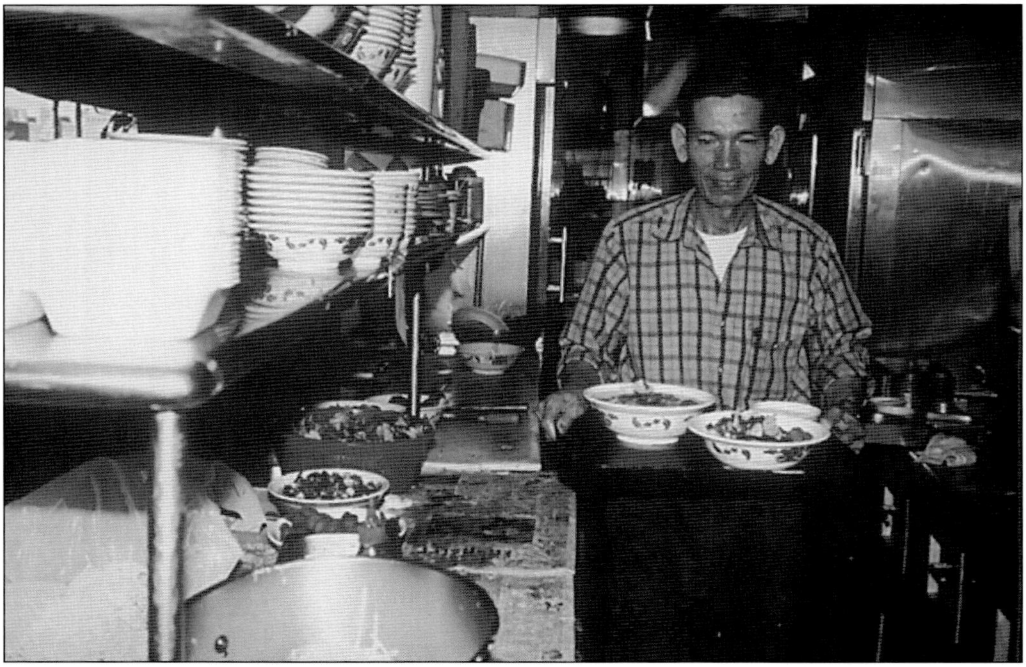

Many Vietnamese with an education or professional work experience could not transfer their skills easily in America and had to start in blue-collar jobs. Restaurant work was one area where men and women could quickly earn a wage since their language skills were an asset. Server David Banh balances steaming bowls of noodles at Mi La Cay restaurant. (Courtesy of Hoai Thuy Quan/Phi Van Trung, from the collection of Jeffrey Brody and David DeVries, The Vietnamese: Self Portrait of a People.)

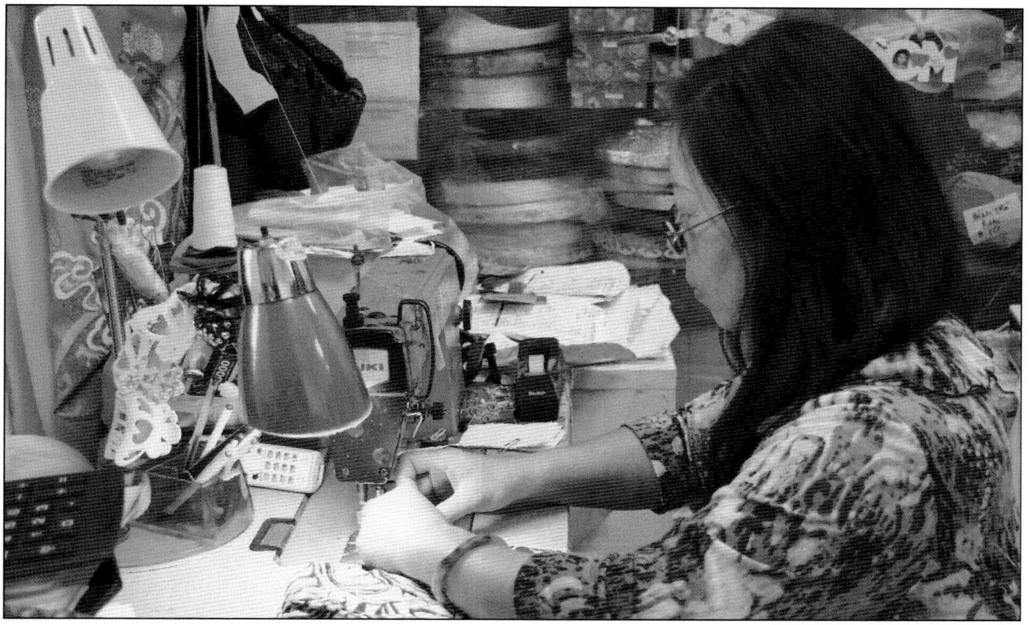

Kathy Nguyen, owner of Thuy's Bridal and Florist in Garden Grove, sews wedding dresses in front of a display case of traditional Vietnamese headdresses for special occasions called *khan dong*. While skilled workers are able to find employment in more specialized work, other refugee women toil in the garment factories or for subcontractors in Orange and Los Angeles Counties, with some women and their families doing piecemeal work in their homes. (Courtesy of Kim Chu and Uyen Huynh.)

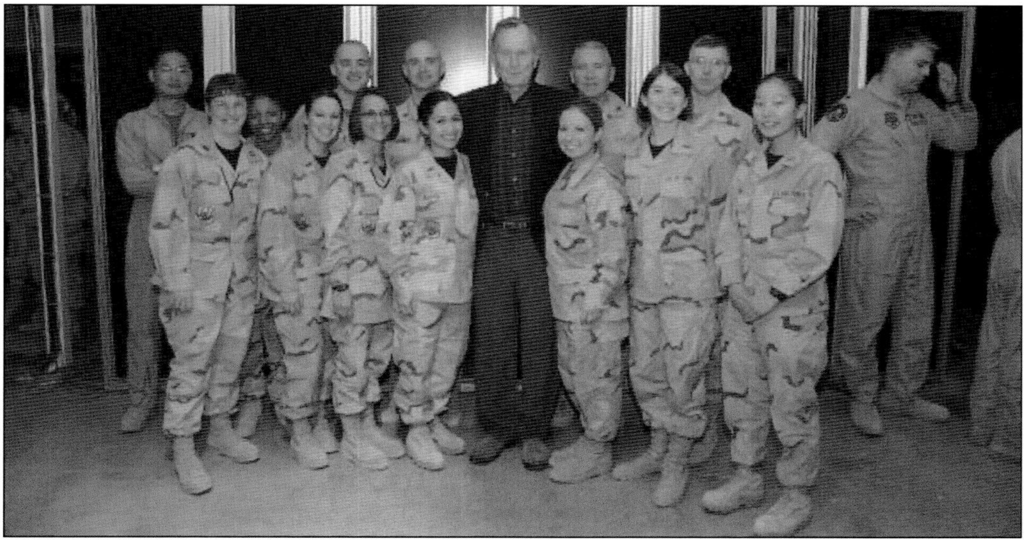

Nicole Nguyen, born in Santa Ana and raised in Garden Grove, graduated from the Air Force Academy in 2004 and became an intelligence officer for Middle Eastern operations. She left the military in 2011 after seven years of service. Here she is shown (fourth from left, front row) in uniform with former President George H. W. Bush in Qatar in 2006. Younger generations of Vietnamese Americans are recruited to serve in various branches of the military. (Courtesy of the UCI Vietnamese American Oral History Project, VAOHP0046.)

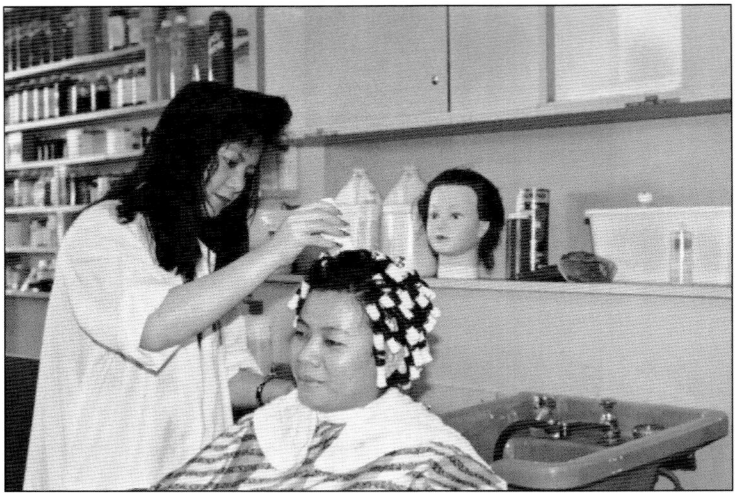

In 1990, beautician Mary Hoang Long works on a customer's hair in her beauty shop in Garden Grove. She stayed at home, raising her children for 15 years, before going back to work when her children were older to help pay for their college education. (Courtesy of the UCI Vietnamese American Oral History Project, VAOHP0101.)

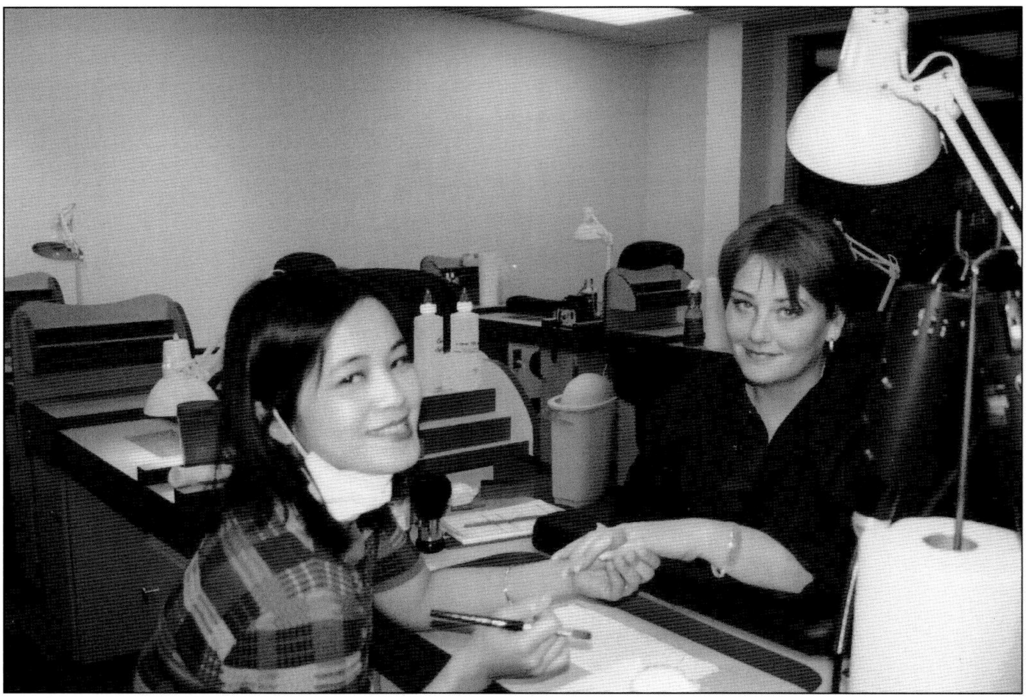

In the 1990s, due to more refugees opening salons and lowering prices, some Vietnamese nail salon owners in Orange County moved to other states where there was less competition. Yet, they often returned to Orange County to stock up on supplies and Vietnamese groceries, as well as visit relatives. This photograph depicts a nail salon called Nail FX in upstate New York. The Vietnamese owners moved there to open this business but returned after five years because it was too cold and isolated. (Courtesy of Tram Le.)

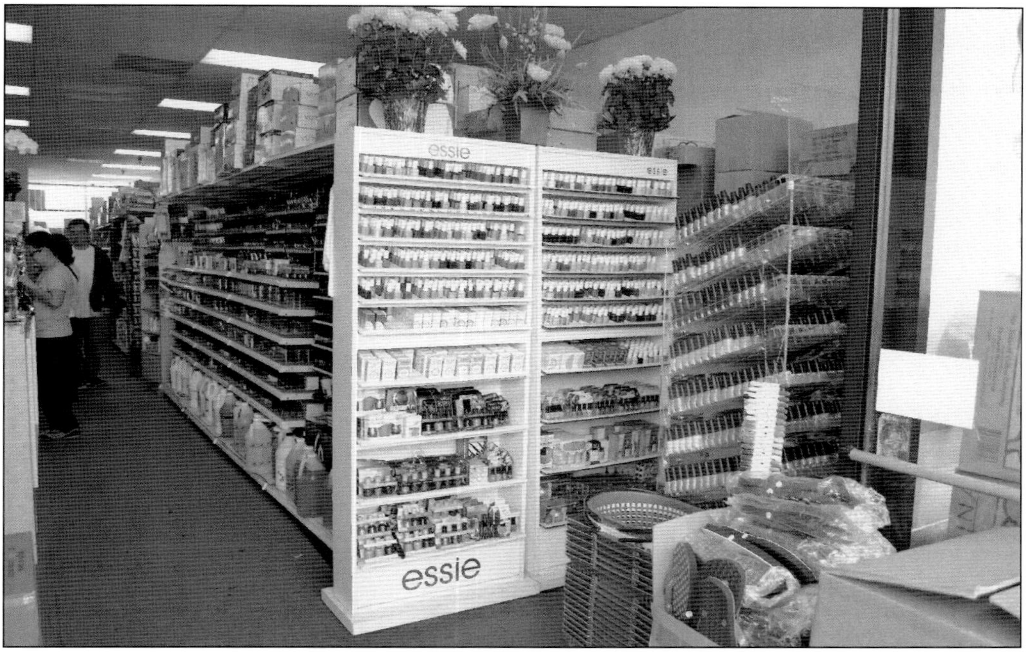

This is one of many nail supply stores concentrated in Orange County where local and out-of-state salon owners buy supplies at wholesale prices. These stores are often open to the public and also sell a wide range of cosmetic and hair products. (Courtesy of Helen Lee.)

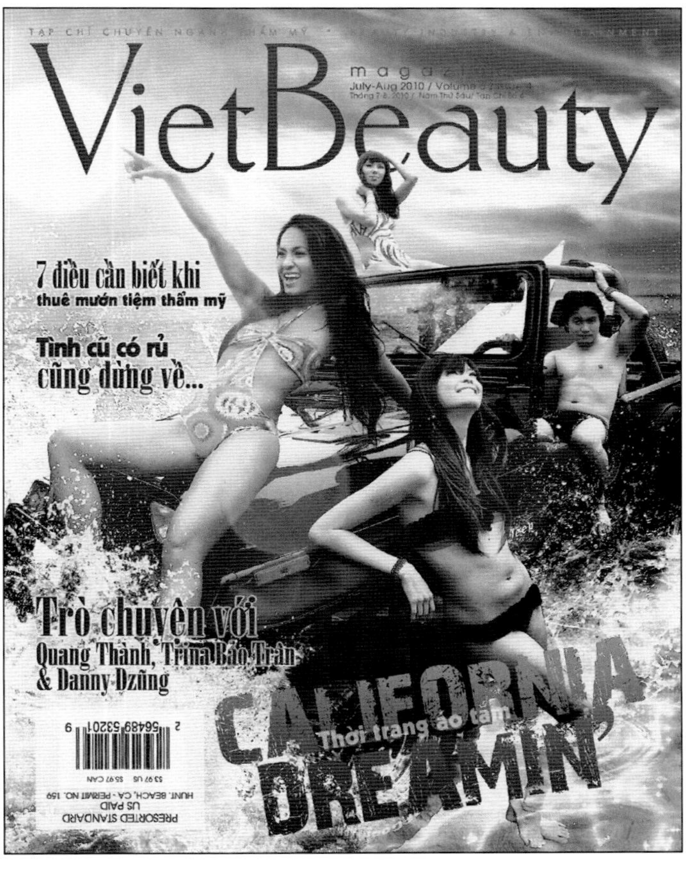

In addition to nail salons, a robust beauty industry provides employment for local Vietnamese. *VietSALON* and *VietBeauty* are two popular Vietnamese-language magazines that include information on the latest nail, beauty, and fashion trends. This July-August 2010 issue of *VietBeauty* has the theme "California Dreamin' " and features a spread on the latest swimsuit collection. (Courtesy of Quang Nguyen.)

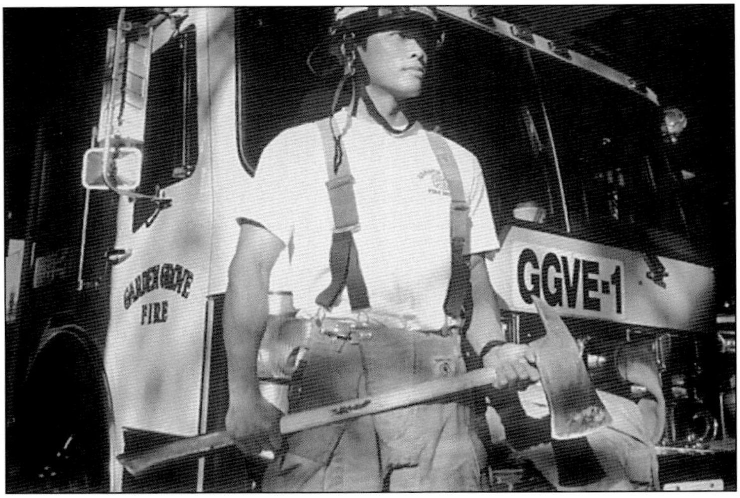

Son Nguyen is a decorated fireman from the Garden Grove Fire Department and the city's first Vietnamese American firefighter on a 94-member force. In 1994, he joined the department, following his childhood dream. (Courtesy of Nicholas Blair, from the collection of Jeffrey Brody and David DeVries, The Vietnamese: Self Portrait of a People.)

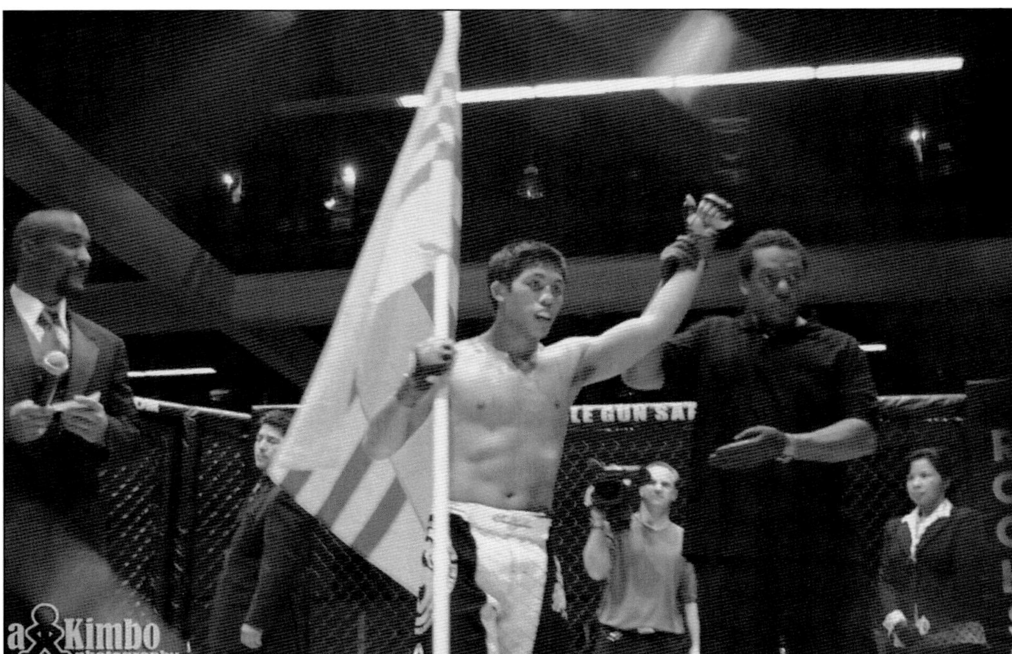

Born in Fountain Valley, Nam Phan is a Vietnamese American professional mixed martial artist. On February 16, 2008, at the Gladiator Challenge in the Los Angeles Convention Center, Nam defeated Saad Awad 52 seconds into round two. He is proudly carrying the South Vietnamese flag. In 2008, Nam opened up a mixed martial arts academy in Garden Grove. There are numerous martial arts schools in Orange County, many of them Vietnamese owned. (Courtesy of Kimberly Phan.)

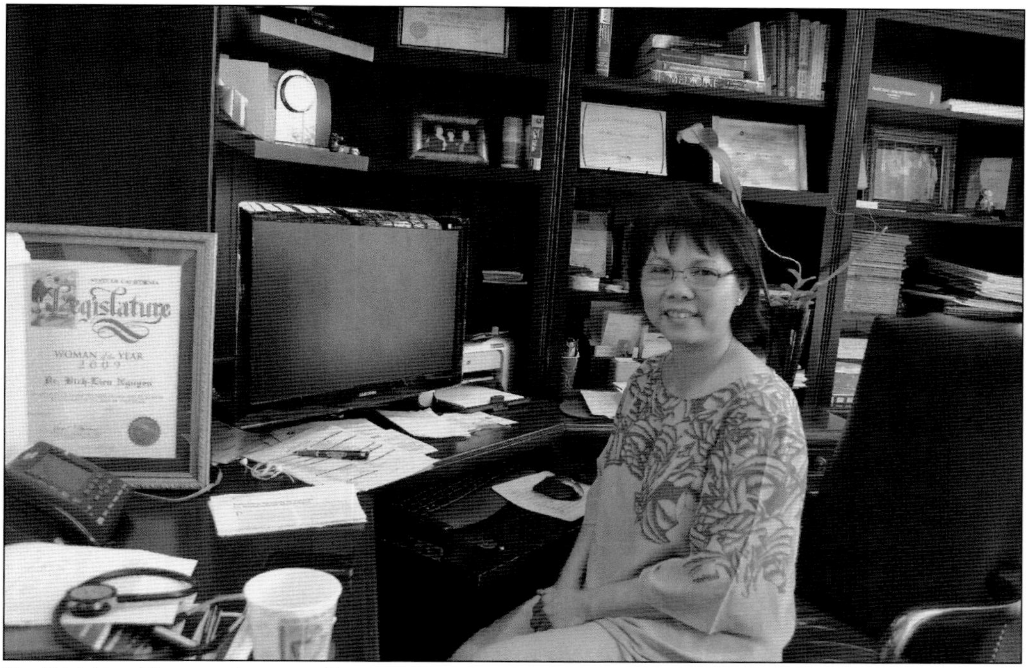

Dr. Bichlien Nguyen, born in Saigon, Vietnam, cared for her mother who had cancer, inspiring her to become a doctor. Her family escaped in 1975 aboard a US Navy ship that took them to Guam. They resettled in Albuquerque, New Mexico, where they were sponsored by a Lutheran church. Formerly a pharmacy student in Vietnam, she resumed her studies and went to medical school at UC Irvine, becoming an oncologist and co-founding the Vietnamese American Cancer Foundation in 2002. (Courtesy of the UCI Vietnamese American Oral History Project, VAOHP0081.)

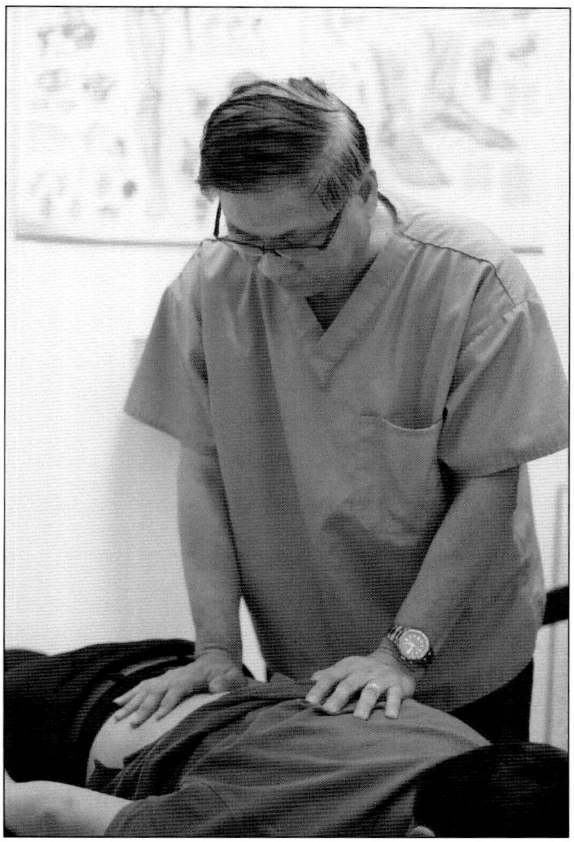

Traditional health practices continue to be popular within the Vietnamese community. Dr. Tuan Nguyen is realigning his patient's spine in his Garden Grove practice. Chiropractic care, cupping therapy, and acupuncture are some of the holistic healing practices preferred by many first-generation Vietnamese. (Courtesy of Kathy Nguyen and An Luu.)

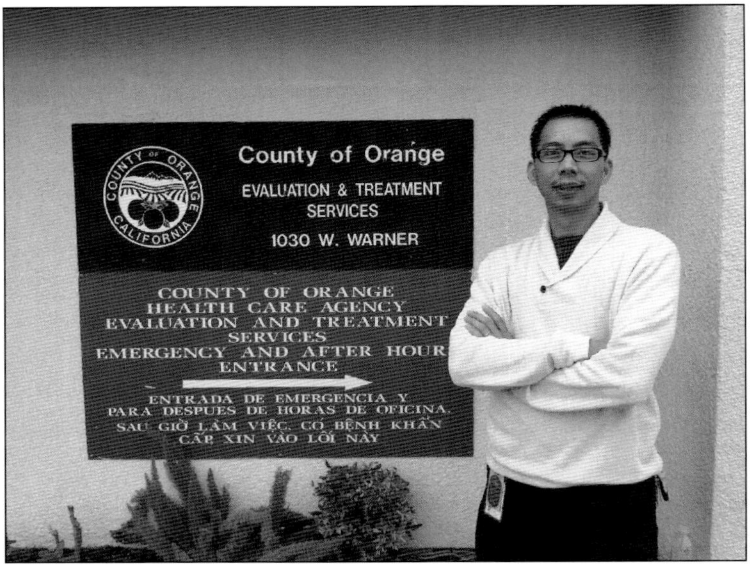

Paul Chi Hoang works for the Orange County Health Care Agencies as part of the Psychiatric Emergency Response team. He partners with the Garden Grove Police Department to respond to mental health emergencies and also works part-time at a community clinic providing therapy. (Courtesy of the UCI Vietnamese American Oral History Project, VAOHP0097.)

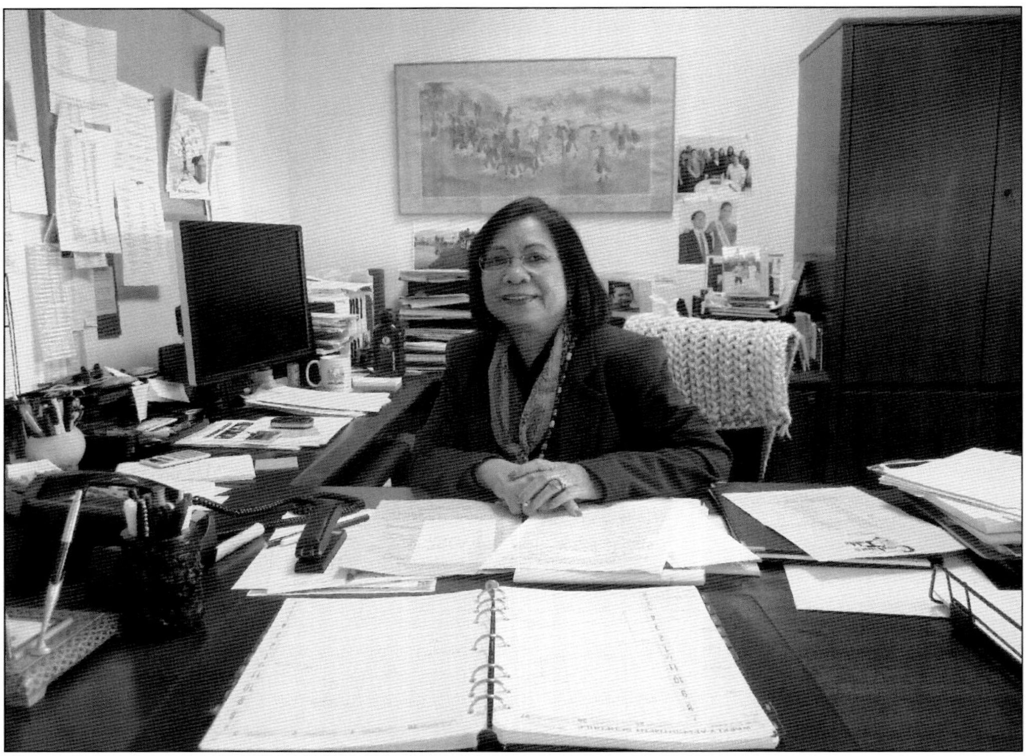

Dr. Hue Pham, dean of Counseling and Special Services Program at Orange Coast College in Costa Mesa, hosts local Vietnamese radio and television programs, where she provides educational advice. Coming from a farming family in Thai Binh, Vietnam, she moved from the North to the South in 1954. She came to the United States as an international student before 1975, attended school in Michigan, and then went to Texas for her doctorate degree. (Courtesy of the UCI Vietnamese American Oral History Project, VAOHP0118.)

Seven

Religion

Although Buddhism and Catholicism are the major religions in Vietnam, there are a variety of other religious practices. The Vietnamese practice of Buddhism blends Mahayana Buddhism, Confucianism, and Taoism into Tam Giao (three religions). The religion with the second highest following is Catholicism, which was introduced to Vietnam by missionaries as early as the 1750s. Cao Dai, a more recent religious movement, started in the Mekong Delta in the 1920s and combines Buddhism, Confucianism, Taoism, Christianity, and Islam. Regardless of what denomination a family follows, the majority simultaneously practices ancestral worship by maintaining an altar honoring deceased relatives they believe watch over them.

Many escaped Vietnam seeking religious freedom. After coming to America, Christian-based churches sponsored many refugees who then felt obligated or pressured to convert and continue practicing their new faiths, while others returned to their former religious practices. Vietnamese Americans have created religious centers where services are held in Vietnamese, allowing them to find comfort connecting with co-ethnics and maintaining their cultural traditions. While some religious groups have youth divisions to attract new members, the challenge will be sustaining these religious communities for future generations.

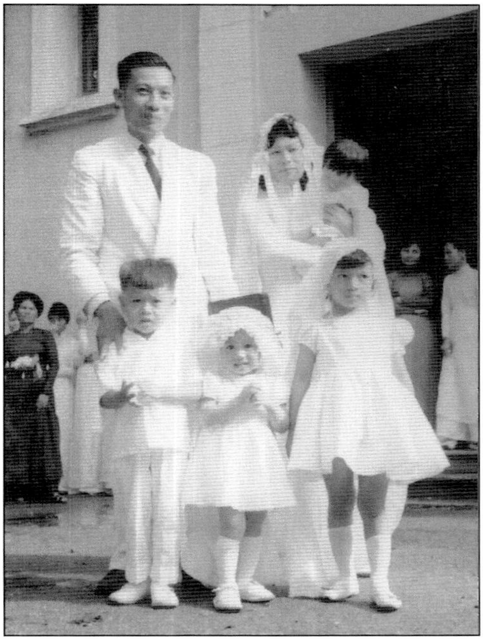

Nhan Nguyen is seen with her husband and children after her daughter's First Holy Communion in Vietnam. She arrived in the United States as a refugee with her nine children in 1975. Her husband was finally able to rejoin the family 14 years later. (Courtesy of the UCI Vietnamese American Oral History Project, VAOHP0143.)

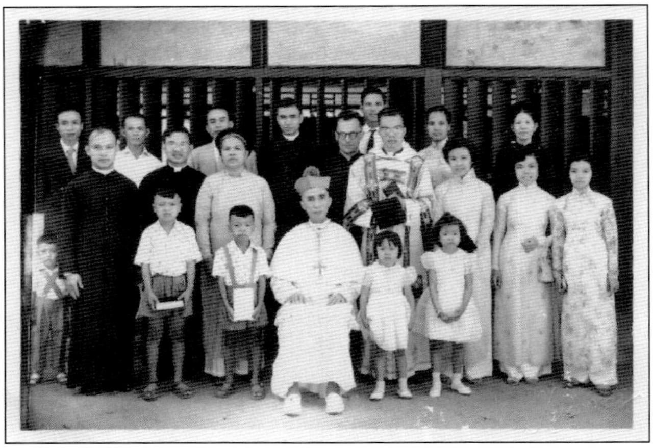

This photograph was taken in 1960 after the Sous-Diaconat, or ordination, of Joseph Tran Phuc Hanh (second row, with ornate robe) in Saigon. Bishop Thaddee Anselme Le Huu Tu (front row, center, seated) presided over the marriage of Joseph's older sister and new brother-in-law. A number of their relatives would come to the United States as refugees and continue practicing Catholicism. (Courtesy of the UCI Vietnamese American Oral History Project, VAOHP0038.)

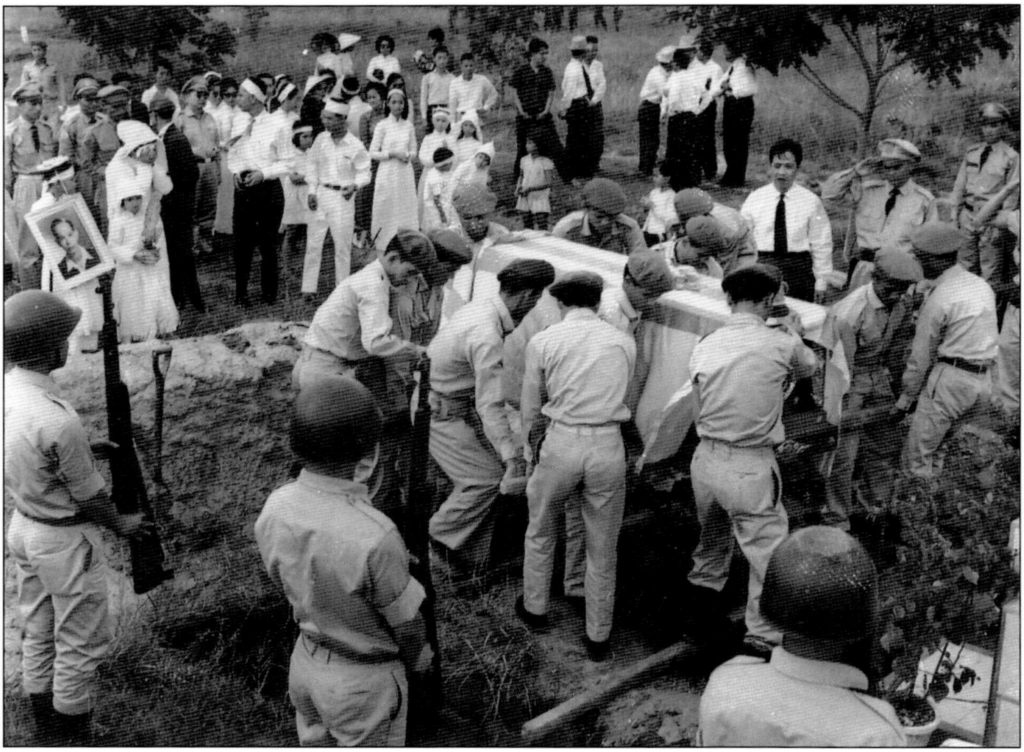

This is a funeral ceremony for Capt. Pho Thinh Trinh on July 18, 1962, at the Republic Institute for Health and Veteran Cemetery in Saigon. He died on July 15 in Kontum when the H-21 plane he was flying crashed. His wife, eight children, other family members wear mourning clothes, and his oldest son carrying his portrait watch while soldiers lower his coffin. His surviving family members later came to the United States as boat people refugees. (Courtesy of the UCI Vietnamese American Oral History Project, VAOHP0164.)

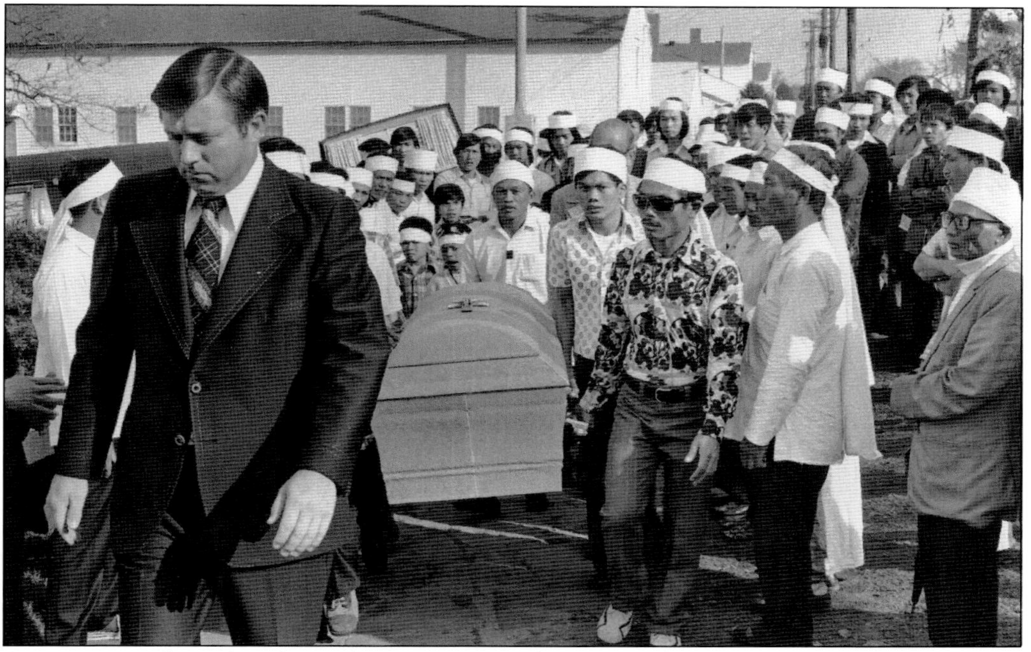

A Vietnamese funeral tradition that continues to this day involves the surviving family members wearing white gauze turbans for the funeral. This image shows a funeral procession at Fort Chaffee refugee camp in the mid-1970s. (Courtesy of the UCI Libraries Southeast Asian Archive, MS-SEA025, Box1:6.)

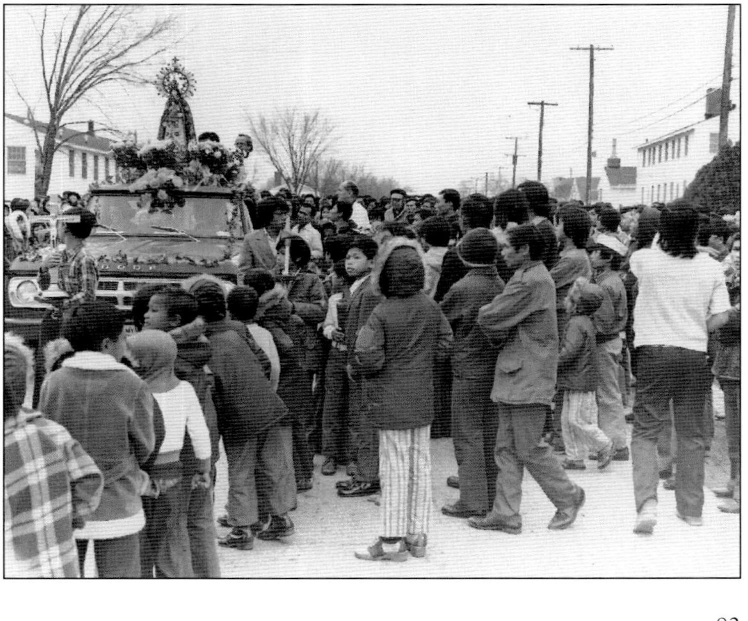

Vietnamese Catholics celebrate the May Crowning for the Virgin Mary in 1975 at the refugee camp in Fort Chaffee. (Courtesy of the UCI Libraries Southeast Asian Archive, MS-SEA025, B1:6.)

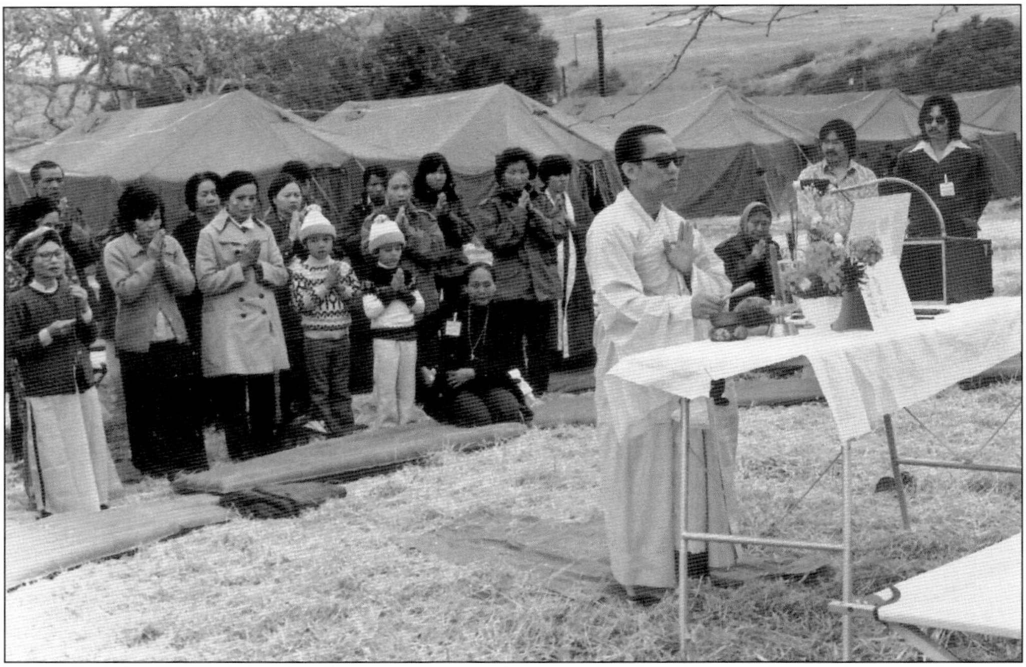

Buddhists hold services at the Camp Pendleton refugee camp, setting up makeshift altars and using blowup mattresses as cushions for kneeling. (Official Marine Corps photograph.)

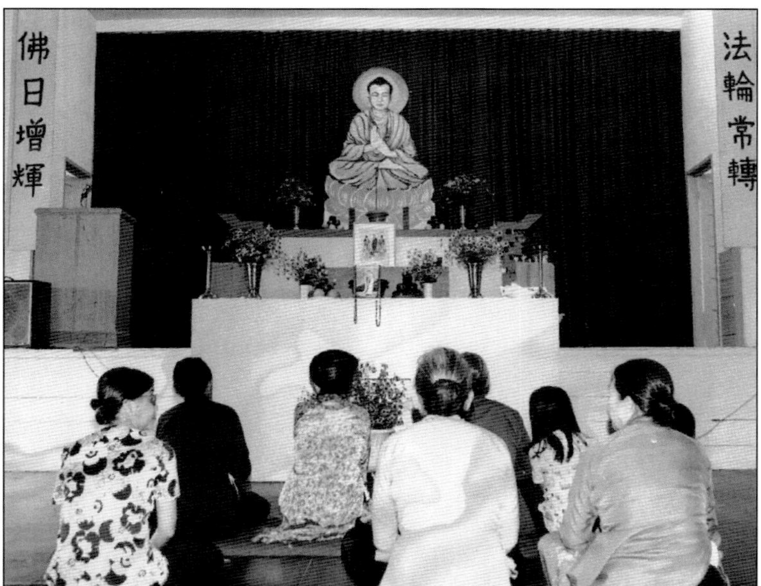

Religious services provide a sanctuary from the challenges of the refugee camps, such as this one in Fort Chaffee. Vietnamese elders continued practicing their religion, in this case Buddhism, and constructed elaborate altars for worship. (Courtesy of the UCI Libraries Southeast Asian Archive, MS-SEA025, Box1:6.)

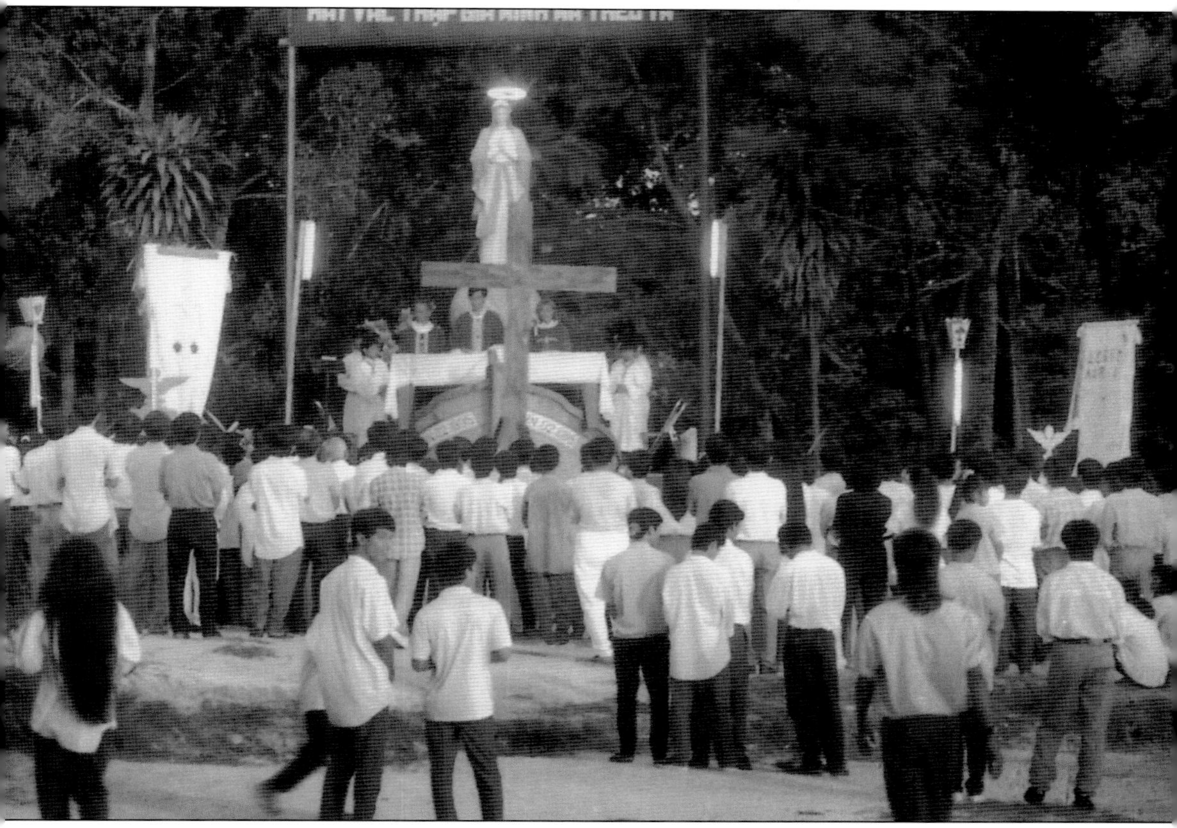

Refugees at the Galang refugee camp made a Catholic altar from a boat used to carry them to the island. In 1954, when Vietnam was divided, many Catholics fled from North Vietnam to South Vietnam, and they were forced to flee again after 1975 for fear of religious persecution from the communist government. (Courtesy of Tho Nguyen.)

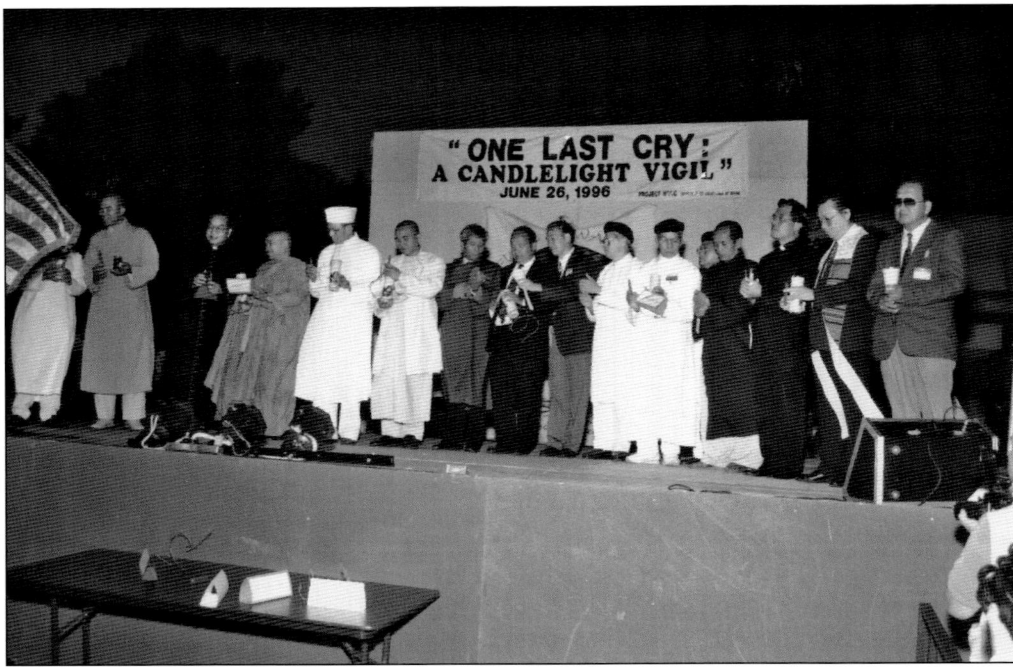

In 1996, religious leaders of various denominations gather in Orange County to express their solidarity with a candlelight vigil protesting the repatriation of Vietnamese refugees. Overseas Vietnamese continue to advocate for religious freedom in their homeland. (Courtesy of the UCI Libraries Southeast Asian Archive, MS-SEA016, Box9:6.)

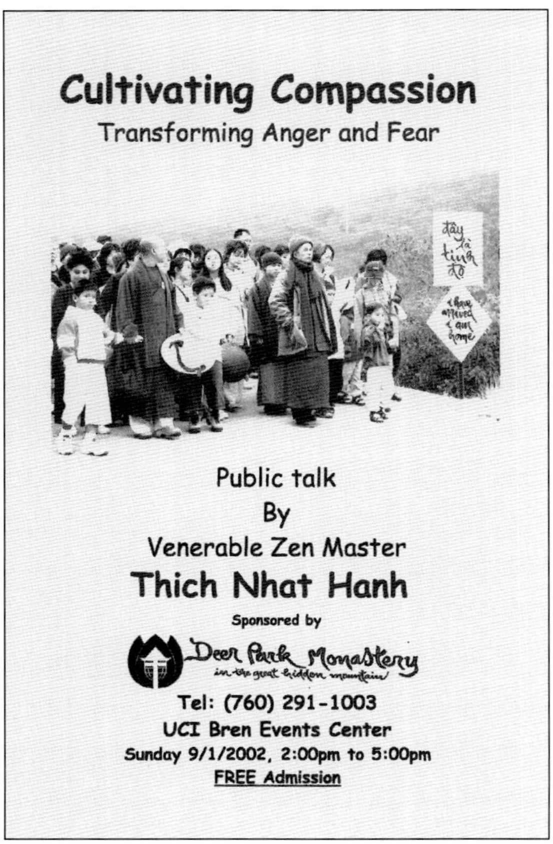

A flyer advertises a presentation at UC Irvine with Master Thich Nhat Hanh, one of the prominent Vietnamese Zen Buddhist monks. Although he lived in Plum Village Monastery, he traveled internationally to teach mindfulness and peaceful activism. (Courtesy of the UCI Libraries Southeast Asian Archive, MS-SEA020.)

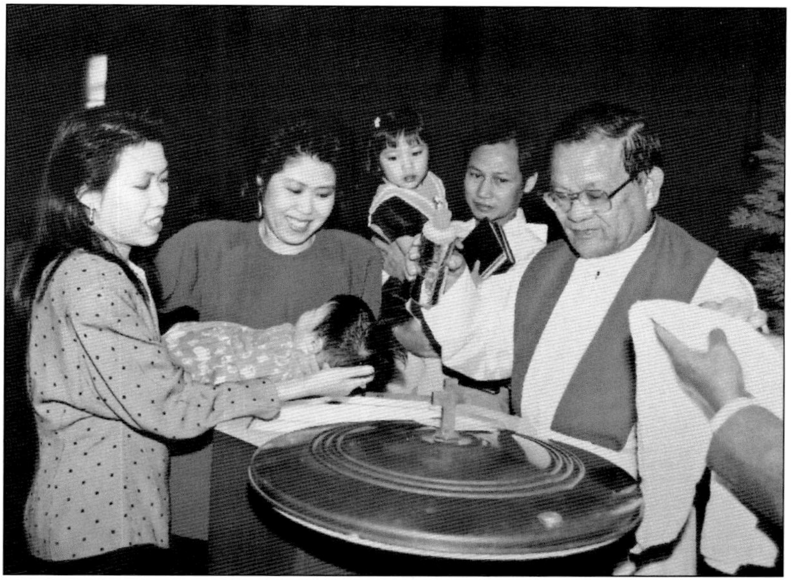

In 1992, Fr. Tran Phuc baptized Jennifer Duong, who is being held by her aunt and godmother, at St. John the Baptist Catholic church in Costa Mesa. Pictured here from left to right are Thu Tran, Jennifer Duong, Thuy Tran, Tiffany Duong, Long Duong, and Fr. Tran Phuc Long. (Courtesy of Jennifer Duong and Vivian Lau.)

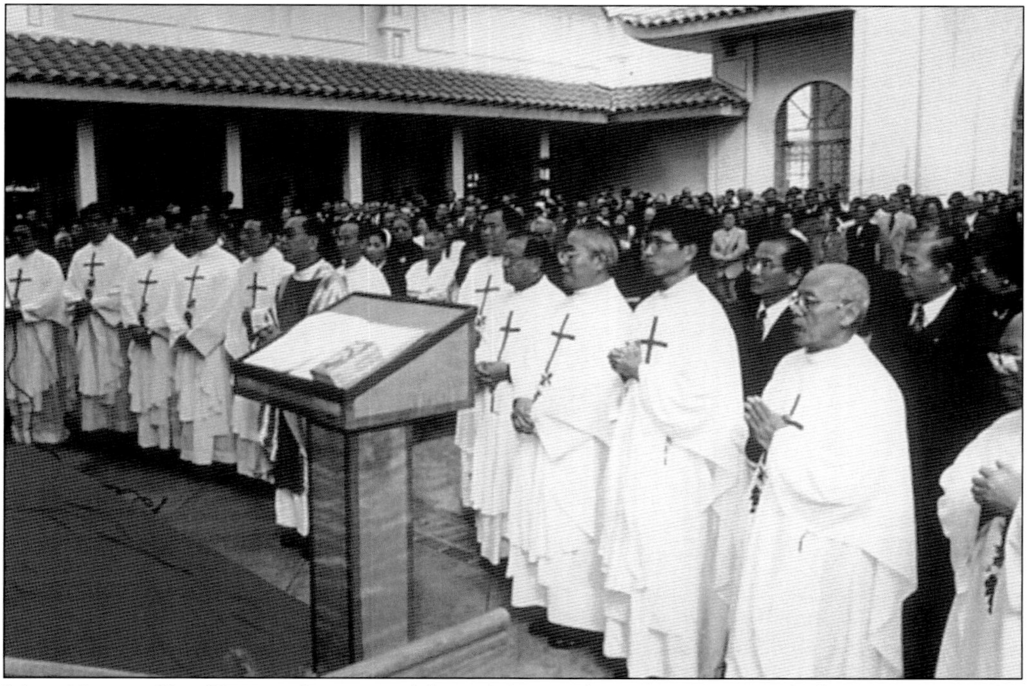

Msgr. Nguyen Duc Tien and priests celebrate Mass at the Vietnamese Catholic Center in Santa Ana in 1999, a project that took 10 years and $5 million to build. As Vietnamese became more established, their increased financial contributions have encouraged the Catholic Church to be more responsive to their needs. (Courtesy of Minh Le from the collection of Jeffrey Brody and David DeVries, The Vietnamese: Self Portrait of a People.)

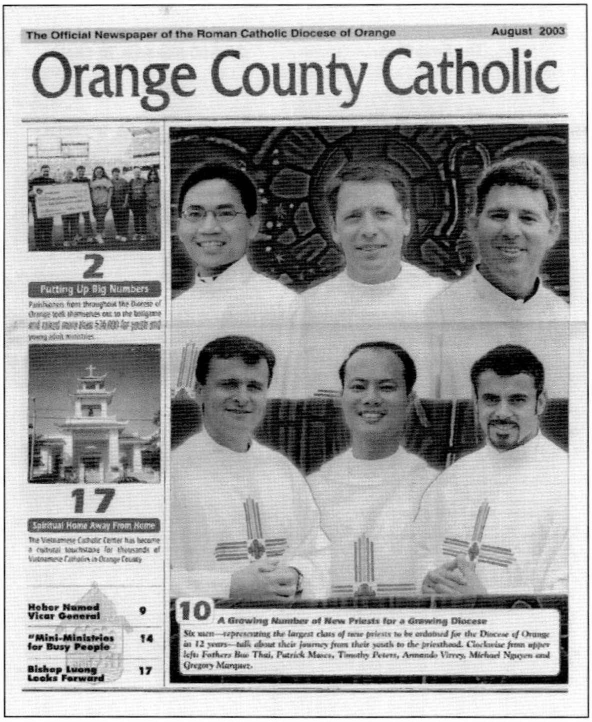

The Official Newspaper of the Roman Catholic Diocese of Orange August 2003

Orange County Catholic

2

Putting Up Big Numbers

Parishioners from throughout the Diocese of Orange took themselves out to the ballgame and raised more than $26,000 for youth and young adult ministries.

17

Spiritual Home Away From Home

The Vietnamese Catholic Center has become a cultural touchstone for thousands of Vietnamese Catholics in Orange County

Hoher Named Vicar General 9

"Mini-Ministries for Busy People 14

Bishop Luong Looks Forward 17

10 A Growing Number of New Priests for a Growing Diocese

Six men—representing the largest class of new priests to be ordained for the Diocese of Orange in 12 years—talk about their journey from their youth to the priesthood. Clockwise from upper left: Fathers Bao Thai, Patrick Moses, Timothy Peters, Armando Virrey, Michael Nguyen and Gregory Marquez.

This August 2003 newspaper of the Roman Catholic Diocese of Orange County features Frs. Bao Thai and Michael Nguyen. As the parish became more diverse, the need for more Vietnamese-speaking priests to conduct Mass for Vietnamese parishioners have increased. The new Lady of Lavang Parish in Santa Ana, the first in Orange County with a Vietnamese name, opened in 2006 and has two clergy who were born in Vietnam and one who was born in Mexico, providing services in Spanish, Vietnamese, and English. (Courtesy of the UCI Libraries Southeast Asian Archive, MS-SEA020.)

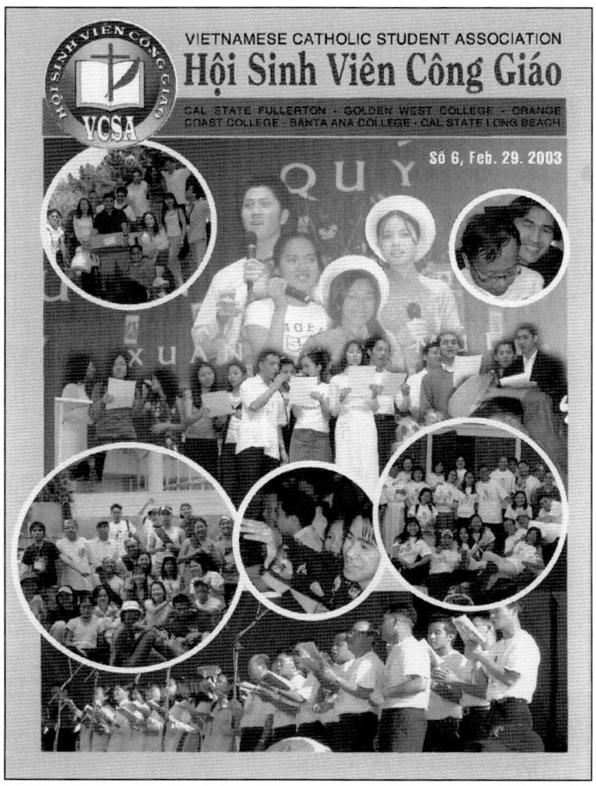

This is a 2003 magazine cover for the Vietnamese Catholic Student Association, which organizes Catholic youths from different colleges. They also offer educational scholarships to Vietnamese college students in Orange County. (Courtesy of the UCI Libraries Southeast Asian Archive, MS-SEA020.)

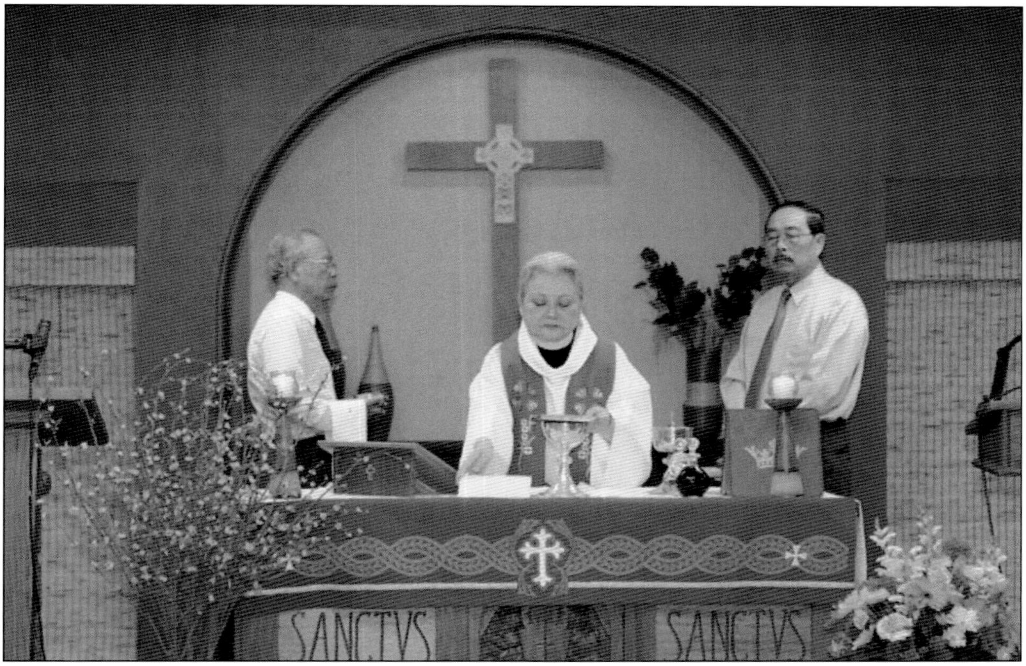

Rev. Minh-Hanh Nguyen was born in Saigon, and after arriving in the United States she worked as a vocational rehabilitator for persons with disabilities. She later attended Pacific Lutheran Theological Seminary and was ordained in the Evangelical Lutheran Church in 1999. She is the associate vicar of St. Anselm Episcopal Church in Garden Grove, where she provides services in English and Vietnamese. (Courtesy of the UCI Vietnamese American Oral History Project, VAOHP0042.)

Len dong is a Vietnamese spiritual practice where deities communicate with believers through mediums. It often involves music, song, dance, and elaborate costumes as evident in this image of a len dong event in Orange County in 1999. (Courtesy of Hoai Thuy Quan and Phi Van Trung, from the collection of Jeffrey Brody and David DeVries, The Vietnamese: Self Portrait of a People.)

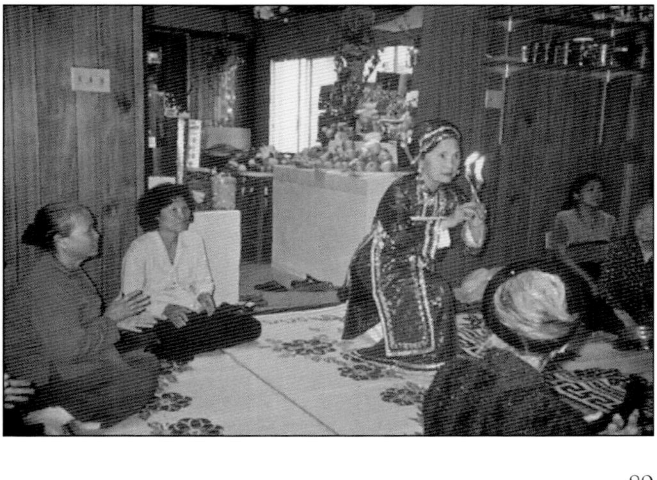

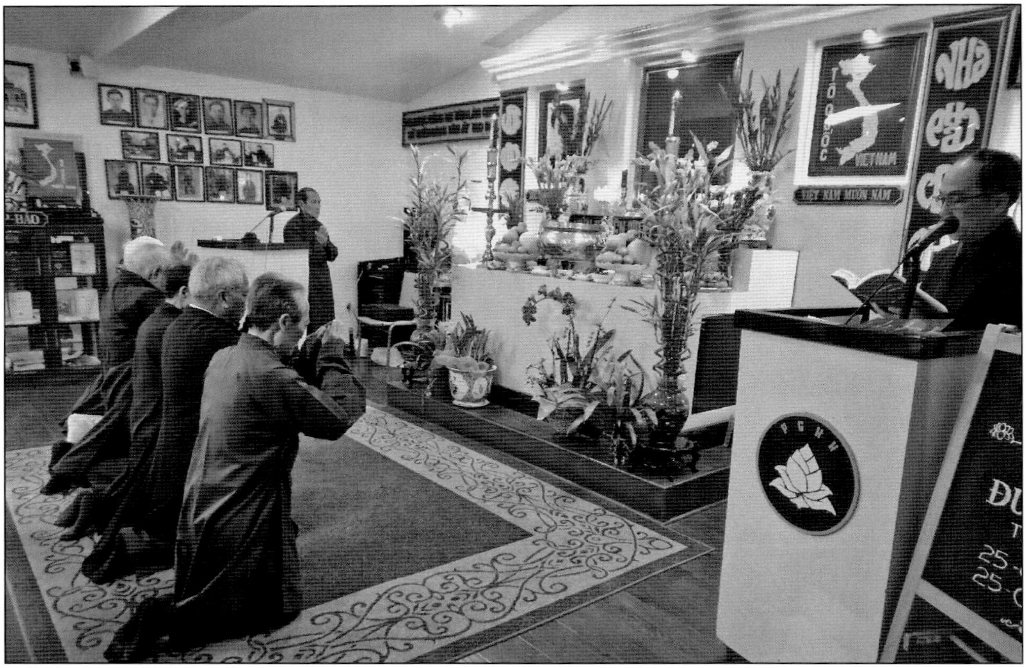

Founded in 1939 by Huynh Phu So, Hoahaoism is a religious tradition that emphasizes the practice of Buddhism in the home instead of spending money to build elaborate temples for worship. The largest number of Hoahaoists living outside of Vietnam is in Santa Ana. On April 7, 2013, approximately 200 people attended this remembrance of Master Tho Nan. (Courtesy of Nguyen Van Liem/*Viet Tide*.)

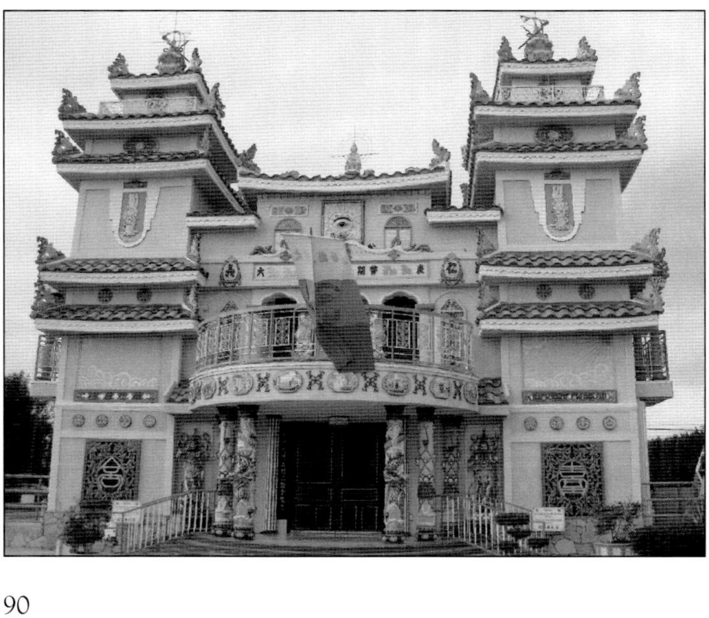

This is the front entrance of the Cao Dai Temple in Garden Grove, a smaller but no less ornate copy of the original temple, known as the Holy See in the Tay Ninh Province in Vietnam. Although there are about 20 small Cao Dai temples in California, most of them are remodeled detached garages, former churches, or converted homes. This is the first one built specifically as a temple. (Courtesy of Jennifer Duong and Vivian Lau.)

Since ancestral worship is customary in Vietnam, many practice it regardless of their religious beliefs. In the United States, many Catholic families also have a space on their home altar for honoring their deceased family members, such as this one in Nhan Thi Nguyen's home in Tustin. (Courtesy of the UCI Vietnamese American Oral History Project, VAOHP0143.)

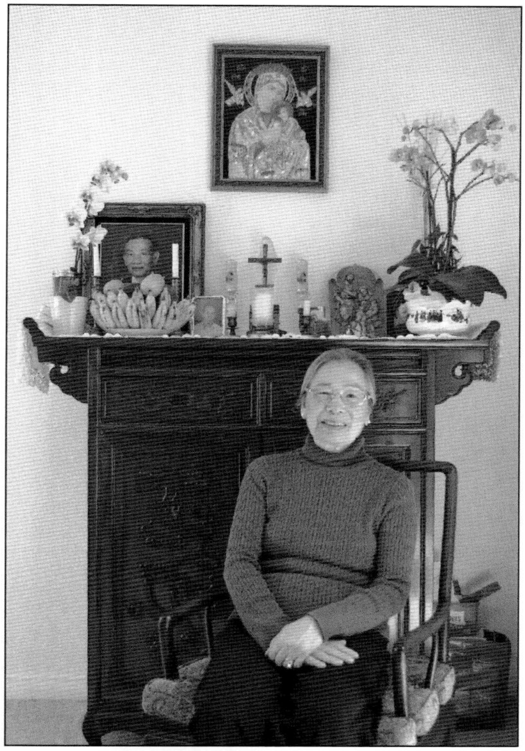

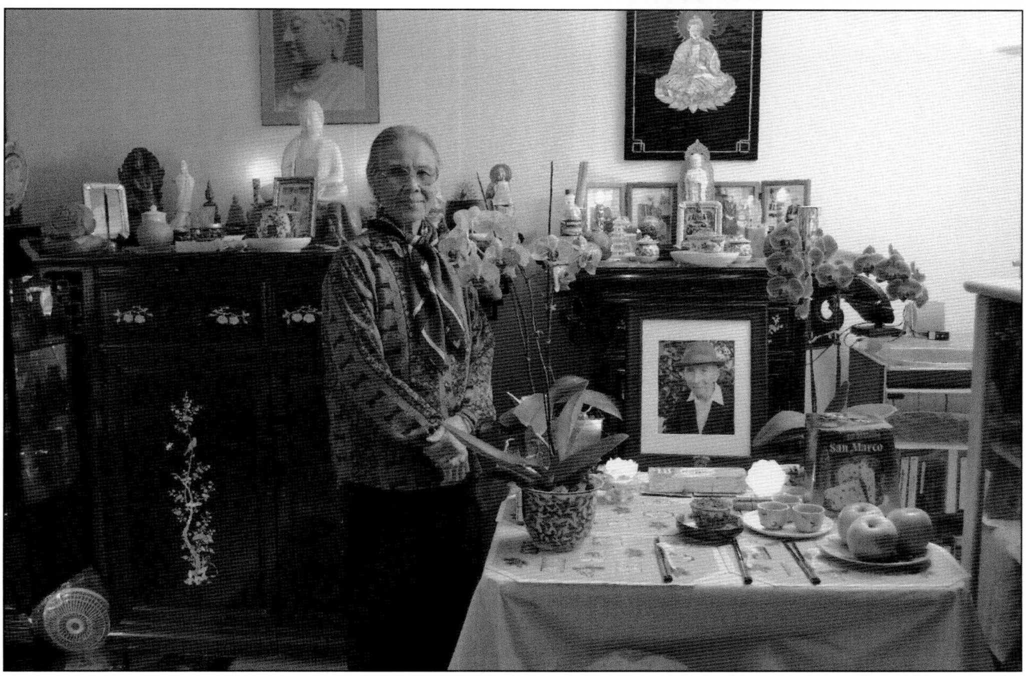

Westminster resident MoLan Tran Doan is shown in front of her Buddhist altar, which also honors her deceased husband as part of ancestral worship. (Courtesy of the UCI Vietnamese American Oral History Project, VAOHP0106.)

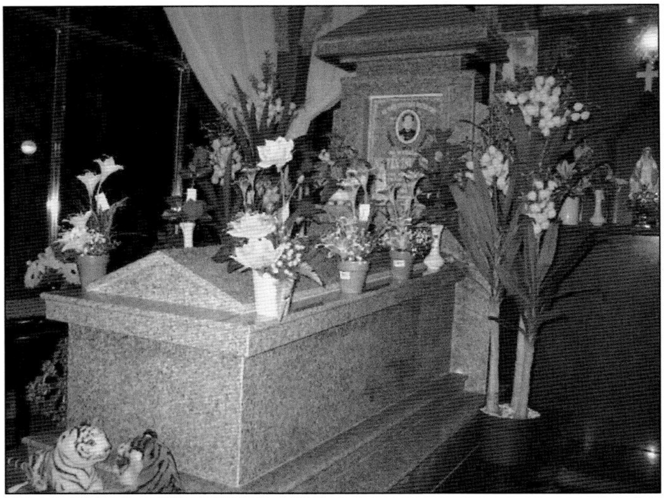

An elaborate and costly tombstone made of marble and enshrined in a glass enclosure in front of a family home was built with remittance money sent back to Vietnam. Many family members who settled in the United States send money to their families to help with living expenses, as well as to fulfill filial piety to parents and other relatives left behind. Others send money to help build churches or temples and support religious practices in Vietnam. (Courtesy of Linda Trinh Vo.)

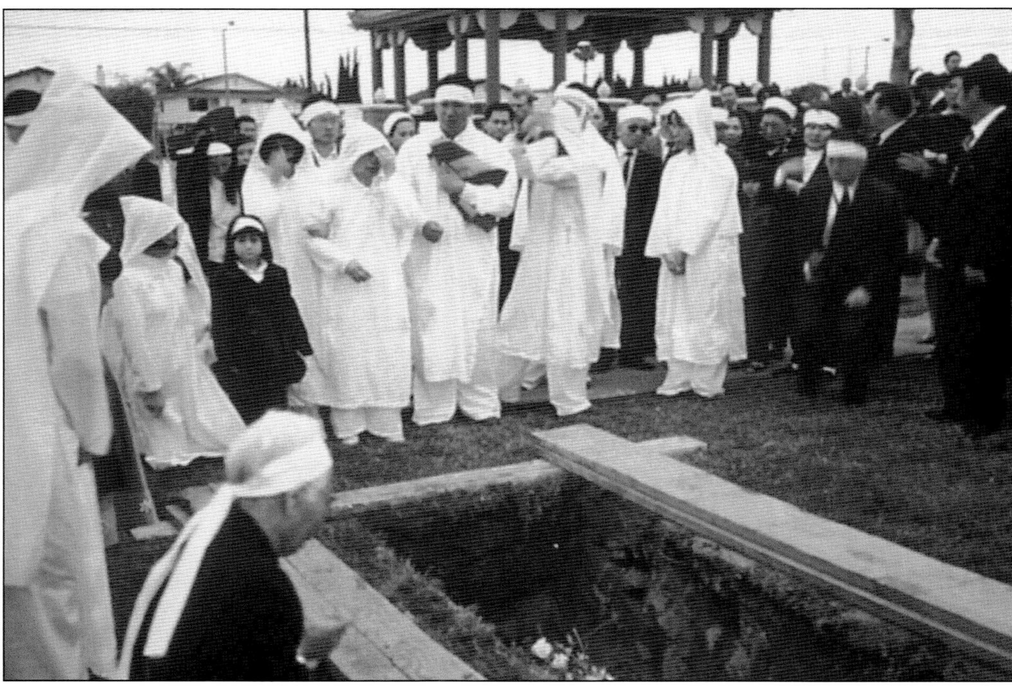

In Westminster Memorial Park, Vietnamese can bury family members in a plot of land known as the Garden of Peaceful Eternity, or "Asian Garden." It features the Vietnam Monument of Freedom dedicated to Vietnamese veterans who died during the war. Associated with this cemetery, Peek Funeral Home in Westminster accommodates Buddhist burial traditions that allow for shrines and the burning of incense. (Courtesy of Theresa Phung, from the collection of Jeffrey Brody and David DeVries, The Vietnamese: Self Portrait of a People.)

This is an ancestral altar in a Buddhist temple honoring family members who have passed away. Many families leave their loved ones' ashes and photographs at a temple so that monks can burn incense and bring peace to the departed as part of the monks' daily ritual. (Courtesy of Nhu-Ngoc Ong, from the collection of Jeffrey Brody and David DeVries, The Vietnamese: Self Portrait of a People.)

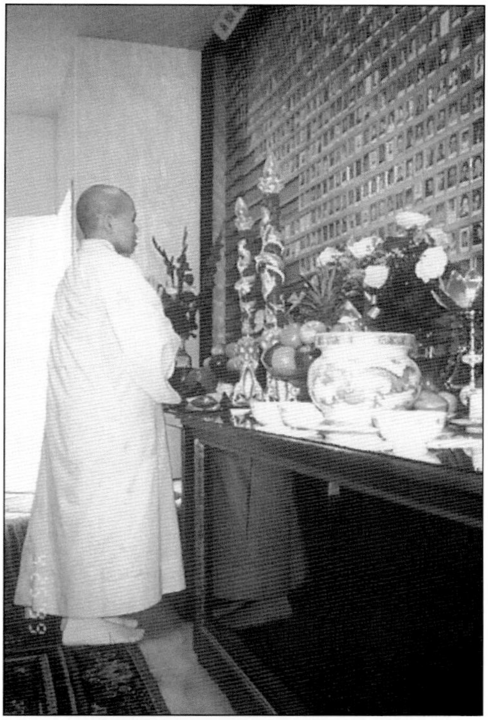

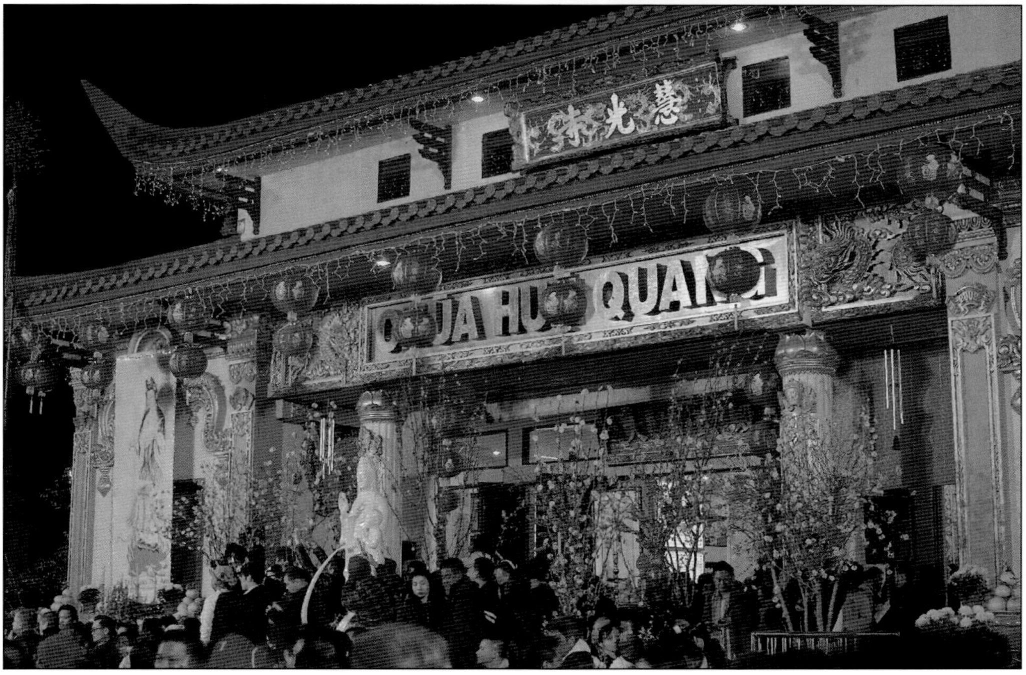

Hue Quang Temple in Santa Ana is noted for its Tet Festival (or Vietnamese Lunar New Year) events with concerts, firecrackers, and lion dancing performances. On important holy days, Buddhist temples often offer complimentary vegetarian food to the public in addition to group chanting and prayer. (Courtesy of Brian Dang.)

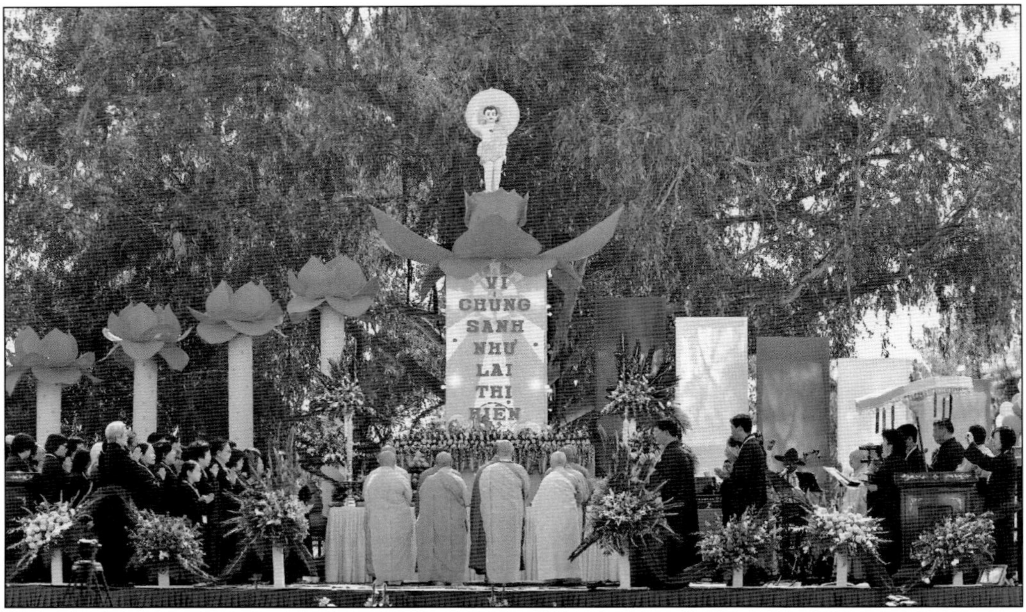

About 2,000 people attended this ceremony for Buddha's birthday, organized by the Unified Buddhist Church of Southern California on May 11 and 12, 2013, at Mile Square Regional Park in Fountain Valley. During these two days, people burned incense to pray for world peace along with democracy and human rights in Tibet and Vietnam. (Courtesy of Nguyen Van Liem/*Viet Tide*.)

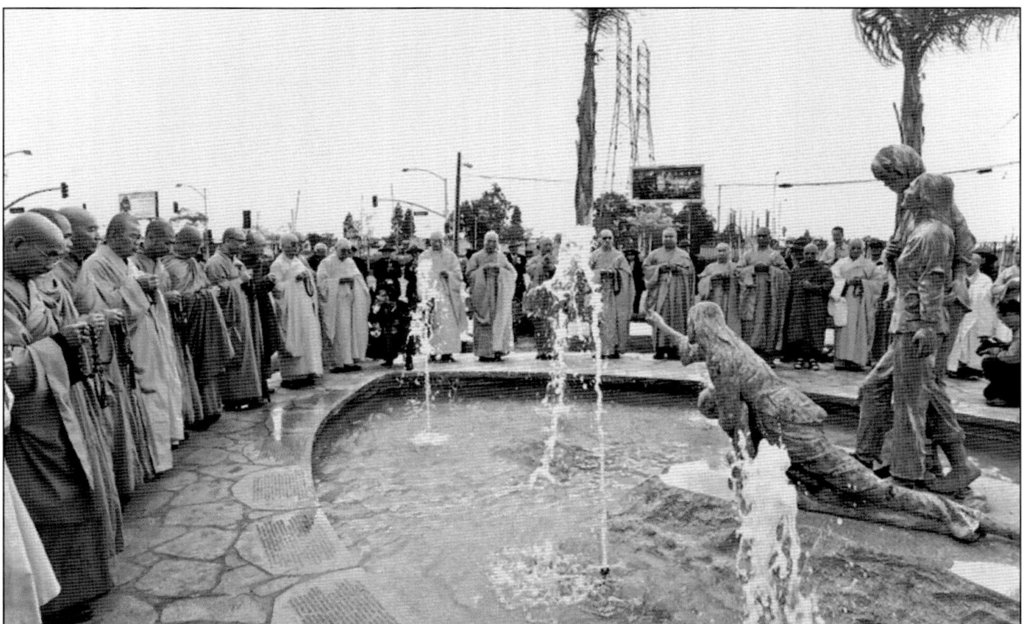

In 2013, Buddhist monks encircle the Vietnamese Boat People Monument, installed in the Westminster Memorial Park in 2009, as part of the Black April commemoration of the Fall of Saigon. (Courtesy of Nguyen Van Liem/*Viet Tide*.)

Eight

Civic Engagement

Vietnamese Americans have formed numerous social, cultural, religious, economic, and political organizations in Orange County. Some organizations focus on homeland issues, while others cater to the resettlement needs of refugees and immigrants. These organizations provide support and a network for employment and charitable services. The Vietnamese continue to gain momentum in electoral politics through fundraising, voter registration, and voting into office Vietnamese candidates. By 2008, there were close to a dozen elected Vietnamese officials in Orange County, including three out of five members of the Westminster City Council and three members of the Garden Grove Unified School District Board of Education. Vietnamese Americans continue to gain leadership positions, and this is expected to increase as they become more established and influential in Orange County.

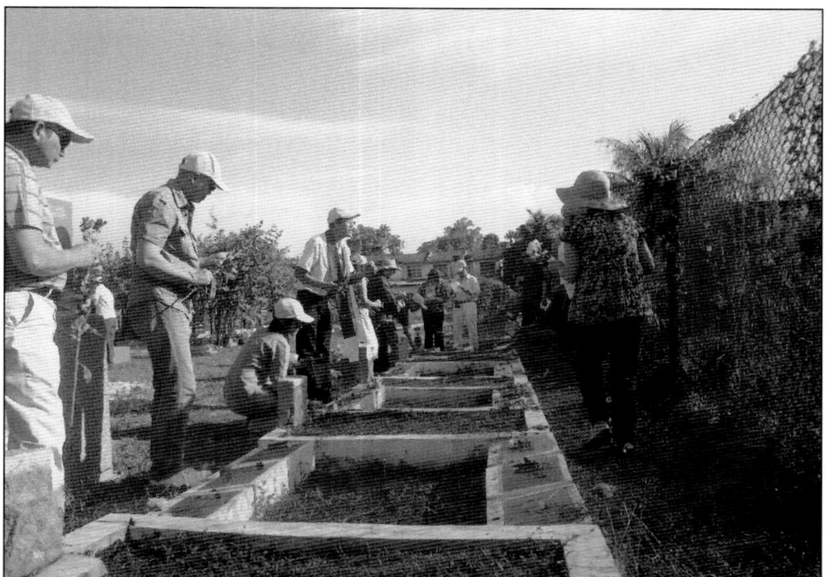

After Vietnamese refugees resettled, many found ways to commemorate and heal from their difficult journeys. The Vietnamese Boat People Grave Yard in Kota Bharu Panji Christian Cemetery in Kelantan, Malaysia, is an official boat refugee memorial site recognized by overseas Vietnamese. In 2007, donations, including efforts from Orange County–based Little Saigon Radio and *Viet Tide Newspaper*, helped fund the renovation of these mostly unmarked graves and the construction of a granite memorial wall. Shown are resettled refugees, some who lost loved ones during their escapes, participating in the "Return to the Shore of Freedom" trip organized by the Australia-based Archive of Vietnamese Boat People in 2011. They prayed for the souls of the deceased in an interfaith ceremony presided by a Buddhist monk and a Catholic priest, both of whom were refugees who had passed through Malaysia. (Courtesy of Quan Tran.)

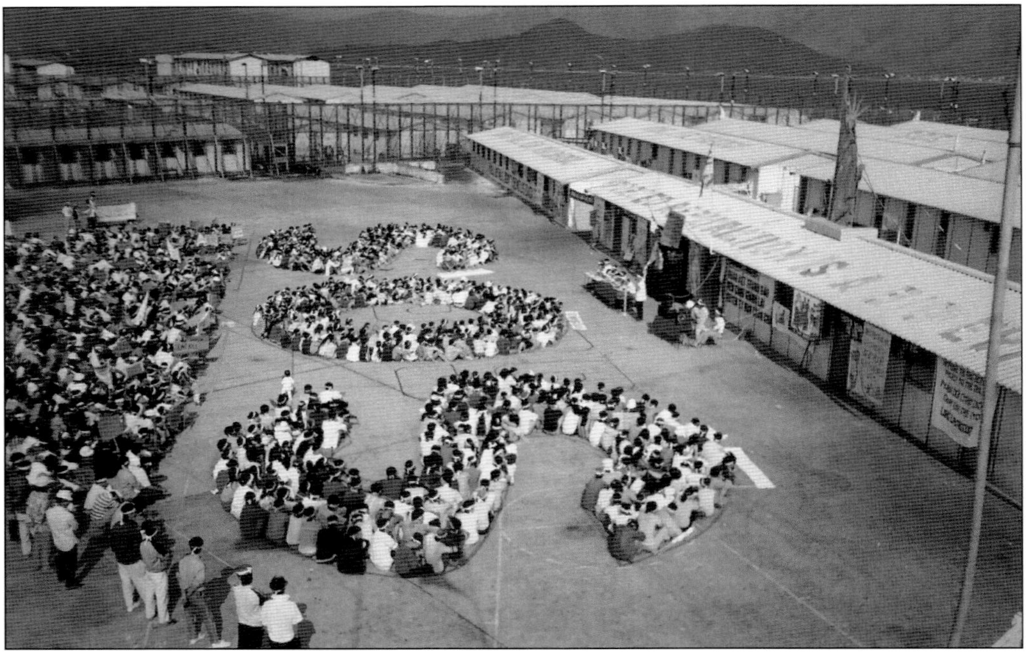

In the late 1980s, countries of first asylum were overburdened with large numbers of refugees, and host countries became less willing to permanently resettle them. Governments began repatriating refugees, sending them back to Vietnam, especially when the United Nations High Commissioner for Refugees (UNHCR) terminated funding, claiming that they were not political refugees fleeing persecution but rather seeking economic opportunities. In protest, refugees staged hunger strikes, committed suicide, escaped, rioted, and set fire to the camps. Here, refugees at Whitehead Detention Centre in Hong Kong have organized a protest forming an "SOS" signal to bring worldwide attention to their plight. (Courtesy of the UCI Libraries Southeast Asian Archive, MS-SEA016.)

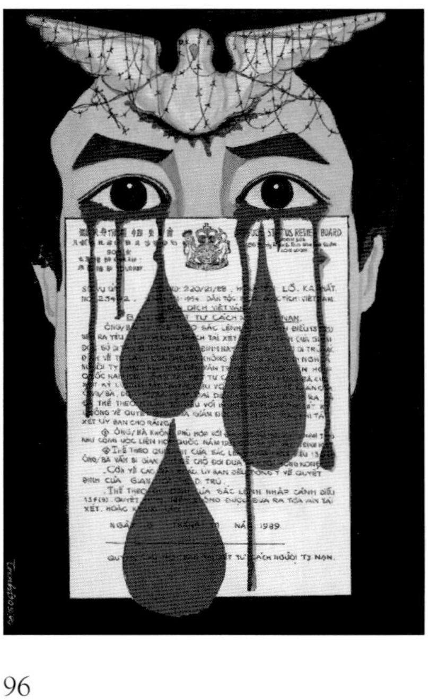

Art created by refugees in the camps during the 1980s and 1990s often expressed political turmoil. This painting depicts a meticulously hand-copied rejection letter sent from the Refugee Status Review Board to a Vietnamese refugee. Created in 1990 by refugee artist Trinh Do, this painting was later brought to the United States by Vietnamese Americans to bring visibility to the repatriation of refugees. It is housed in UC Irvine Libraries Southeast Asian Archive with over 400 other original works of art brought from the camps. (Courtesy of the UCI Libraries Southeast Asian Archive, MS-SEA016.)

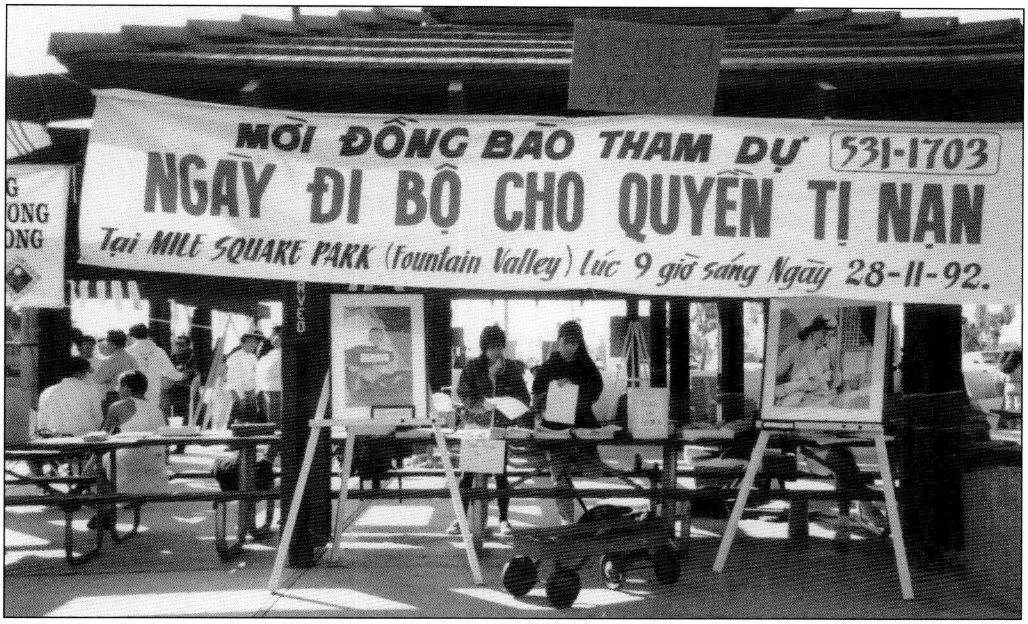

In the 1980s and 1990s, college students and community leaders advocated for refugee rights. Events such as this walkathon in 1992 raised awareness about the forced repatriation of refugees in Southeast Asia. This fundraising event at Mile Square Regional Park in Fountain Valley was open to all community members and included informational booths along with artwork from the camps. (Courtesy of the UCI Libraries Southeast Asian Archive, MS-SEA016, B11:5.)

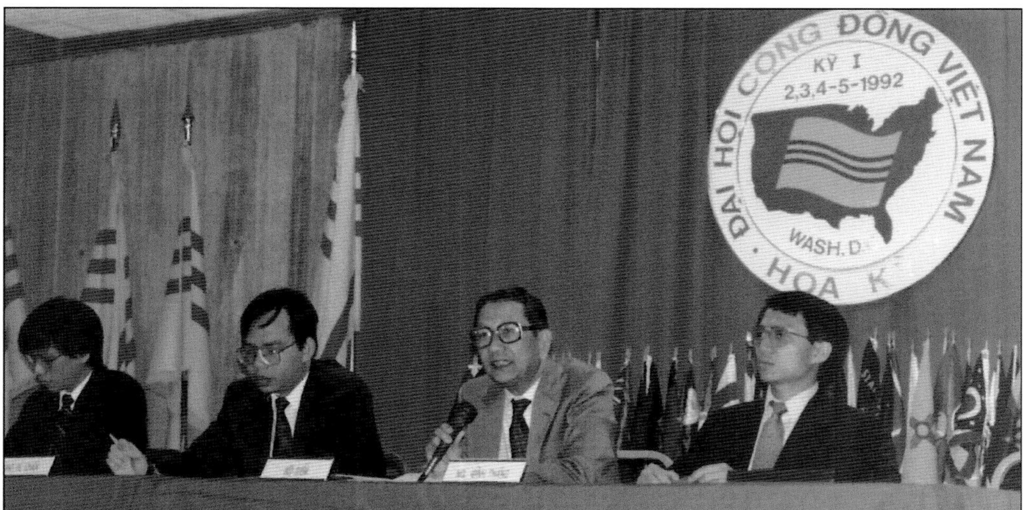

In 1992, the first National Summit for Vietnamese American Leaders took place in Washington, DC. Pictured on the right is Dr. Thang Nguyen, president and chief executive officer of Boat People SOS, a nonprofit human services agency founded in 1980 to advocate for boat people at sea. The co-founders were Phan Lac Tiep and Prof. Xuong Nguyen-Huu. The organization later focused on human-rights issues and relocated its headquarters to Virginia to be closer to the nation's capital but has branches across the nation, including Orange County. (Courtesy of Tran Kim Lan.)

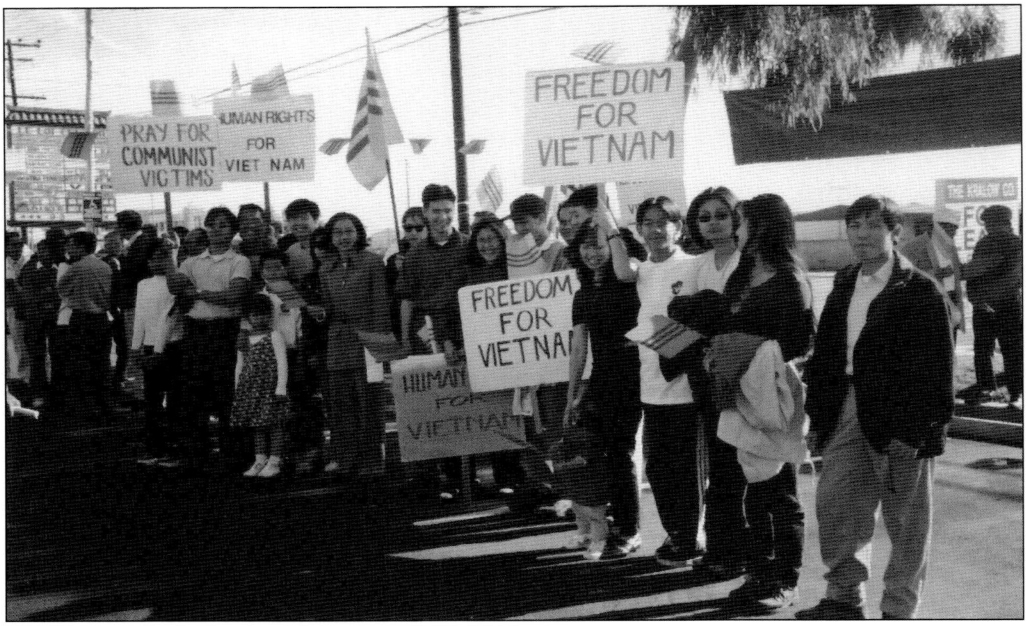

Vietnamese Americans mobilize on issues related to human rights in their homeland and over the years have used direct action, such as staging this protest. Activists continue to lobby elected officials at the local, state, and national levels to place economic sanctions and political pressure on Vietnam to improve their human rights and religious freedom policies. (Courtesy of the UCI Libraries Southeast Asian Archive, MS-SEA022, B1:10.)

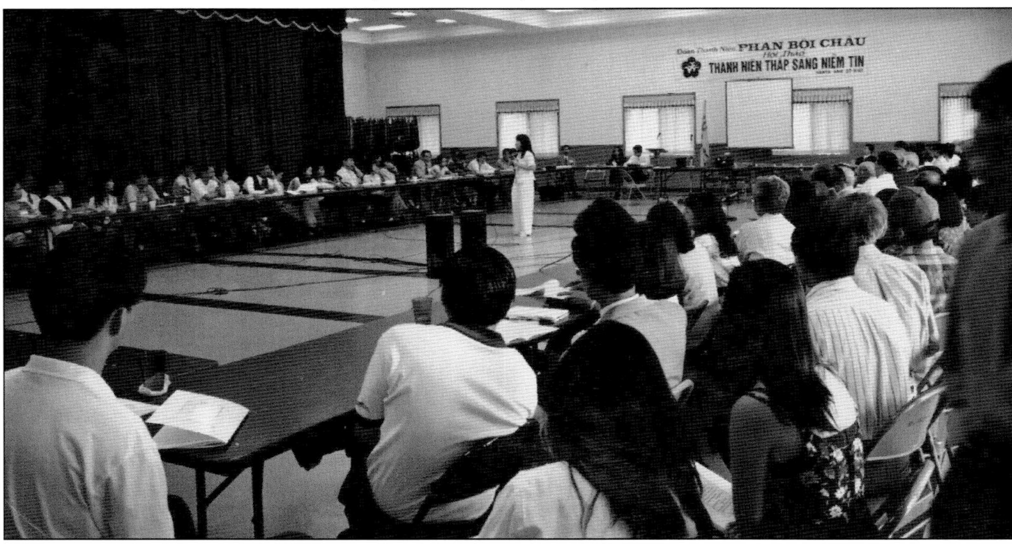

Doan Thanh Nien Phan Boi Chau (Youth for Democracy of Southern California) organized a conference for "Youth Spotlighting the Faith" in 1997 in Santa Ana. The organization's name is derived from the late Phan Boi Chau, a pioneer of 20th century Vietnamese nationalism and a role model for generations of Vietnamese leaders. Some Vietnamese American youth identify with their ethnicity and cultural heritage through organized activities such as summer camps, conferences, and social gatherings. (Courtesy of the UCI Libraries Southeast Asian Archive, MS-SEA022, B1:10.)

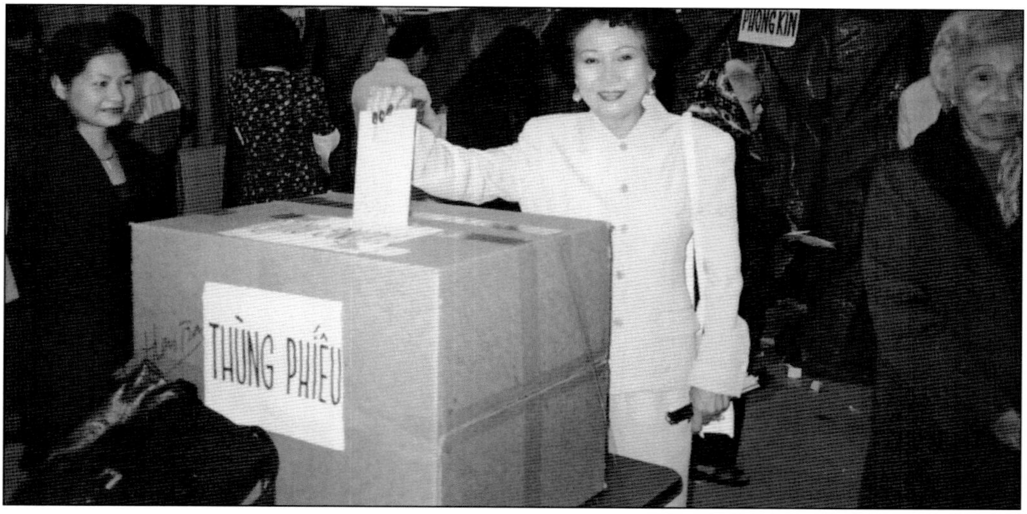

Vietnamese American organizations often hold their own elections to select official community leaders such as the Vietnamese community president. A number of them held leadership positions in Vietnam prior to immigrating to the United States. First-generation Vietnamese organizations are typically led by men, but women labored intensively behind the scenes to make many of the events and programs possible. Here, Tran Kim Lan is voting in an organizational election in Westminster in 1989. (Courtesy of Tran Kim Lan.)

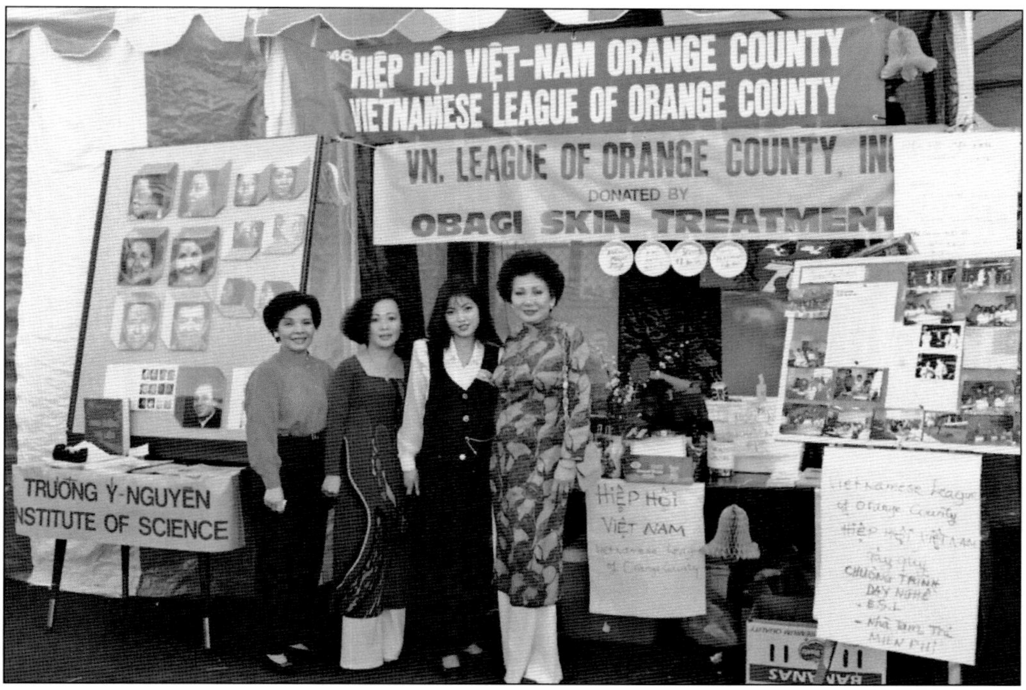

Given the cultural and linguistic barriers, Vietnamese Americans often form their own ethnic organizations, including ones that replicate mainstream organizations or re-create ones from their homeland. Organizations such as the one pictured help refugees rebuild lives and maintain networks while also providing charitable services for their community. (Courtesy of Tran Kim Lan.)

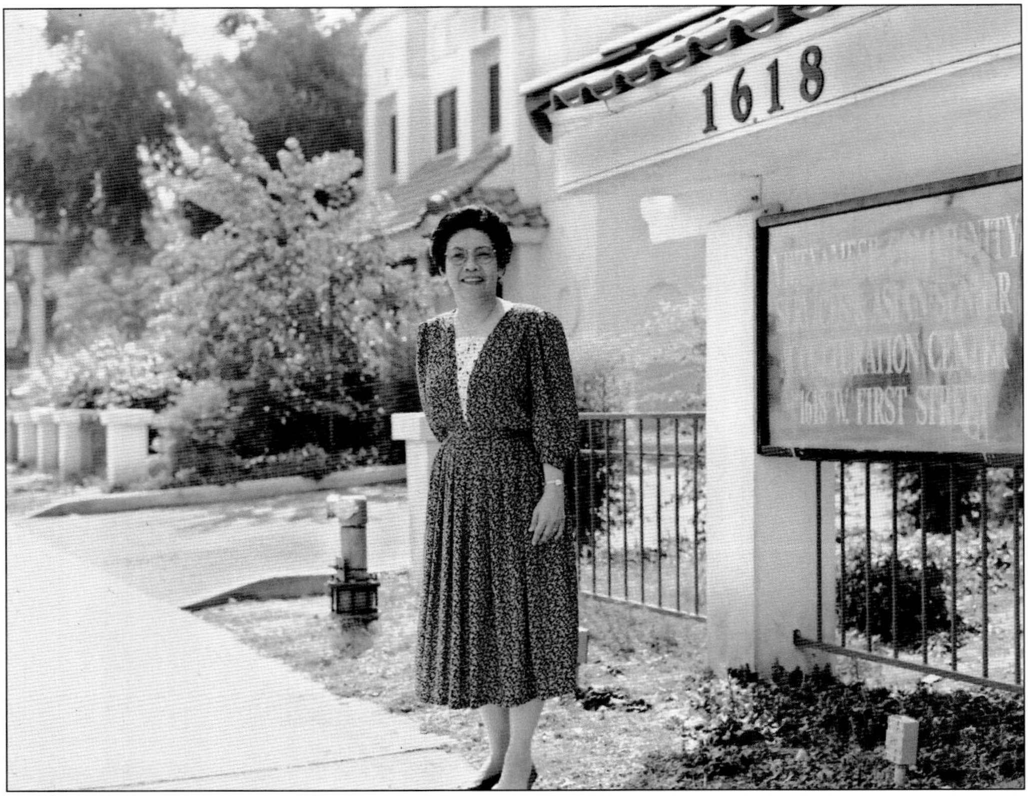

In 1979, Mai Cong founded the Vietnamese Community of Orange County, Inc., a nonprofit refugee resettlement support agency. Headquartered in Santa Ana with offices in Westminster and Garden Grove, the organization provides English and citizenship classes as well as senior, mental health, and early childhood services. (Courtesy of the Santa Ana History Room.)

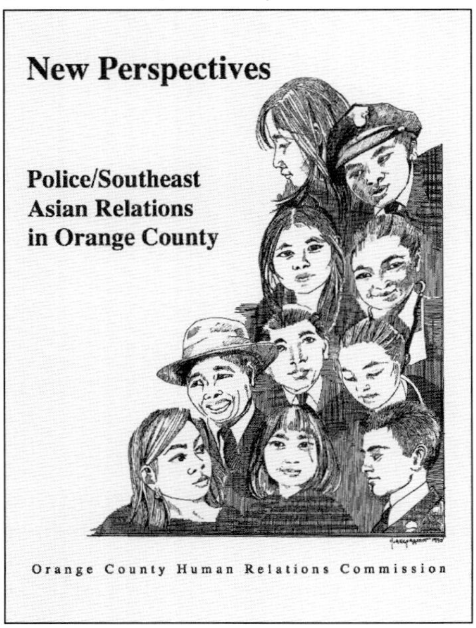

Local police agencies had to accommodate the increased numbers of new refugees and immigrants in the county, and this January 1991 report by the Orange County Human Relations Commission was intended to improve relations between officers and the community. Vietnamese may distrust law enforcement officers based on their experiences with police officials in their homeland and, because of linguistic barriers, may be reluctant to report crimes. Over the years, there have been complaints about the lack of bilingual officers, harassment of youth, and cultural insensitivity. (Courtesy of the UCI Libraries Southeast Asian Archive, MS-SEA020.)

This is an early AIDS awareness and education poster from the 1990s targeting the Vietnamese American community. It reinforced the message by using local and national Vietnamese American leaders and role models from the entertainment, media, medical, nonprofit, and sports professions. (Courtesy of the UCI Libraries Southeast Asian Archive.)

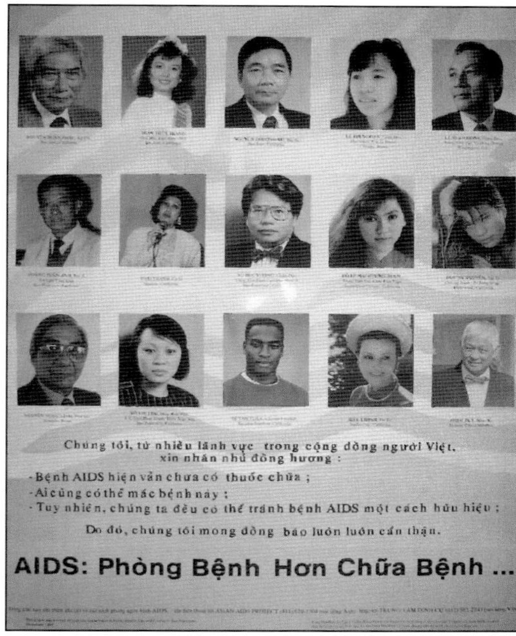

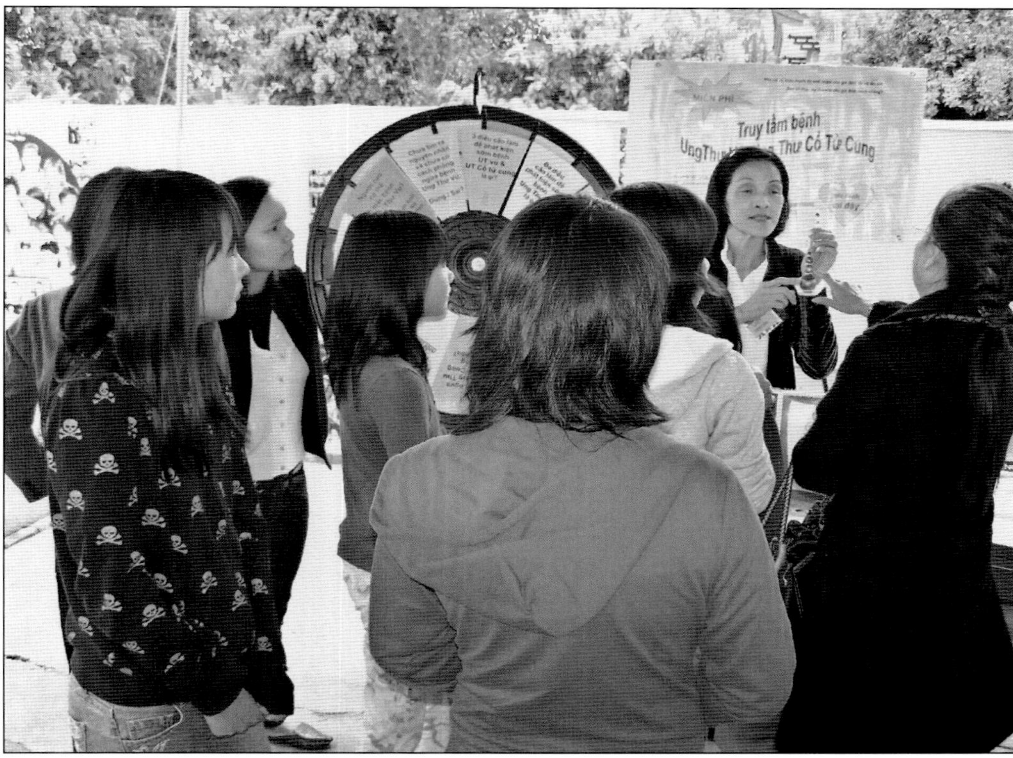

Health educator Lucy Huynh and program coordinator Duyen Tran from the Orange County Asian Pacific Islander Community Alliance (OCAPICA) educate community members about breast and cervical health at the Hue Quang Temple in Garden Grove in 2011. (Courtesy of Lucy Huynh.)

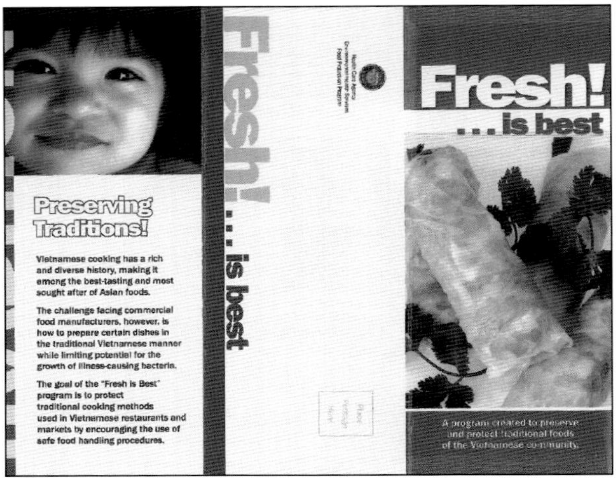

Some traditional Vietnamese foods such as *banh bao*, *banh cuon*, and *xoi* are best eaten at room temperature, so markets, cafés, and restaurants in Little Saigon do not refrigerate certain delicacies, a custom they have had to defend against mainstream health codes. In 2005, the Orange County Health Care Agency started a "Fresh is Best" program to educate manufacturers and consumers about preserving traditional food practices while also protecting public safety. (Courtesy of the UCI Libraries Southeast Asian Archive, MS-SEA020.)

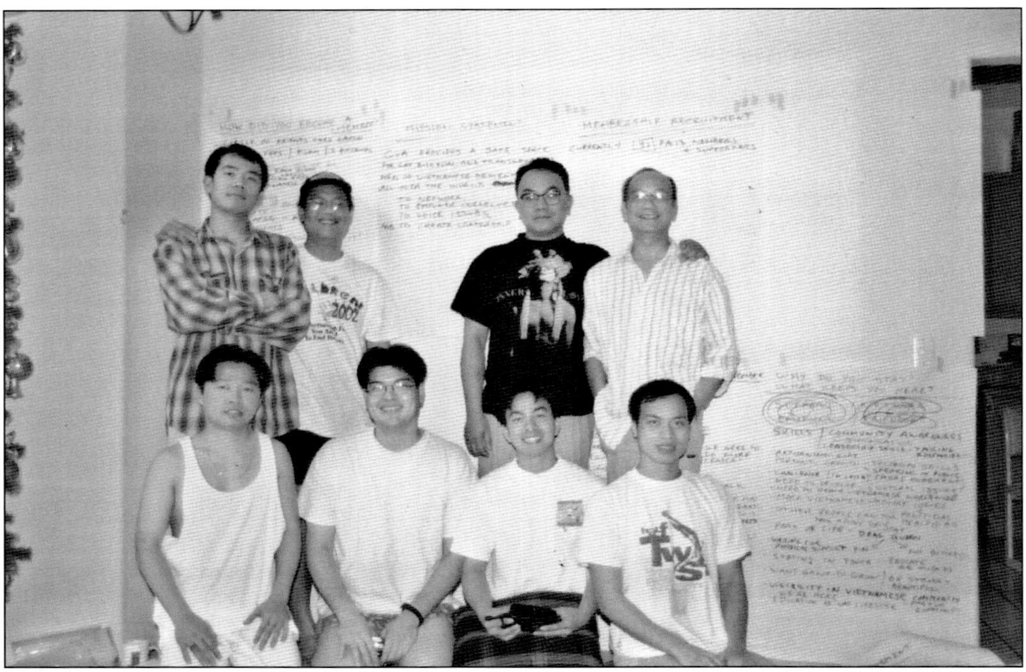

The Gay Vietnamese Alliance (GVA) was founded in 1994 to provide a safe space for gay, bisexual, and transgender men of Vietnamese descent from all over the world. This photograph was taken in Laguna Niguel in 1995. Tuan Le (back row, second from the left) was the first president and is shown here with the founding members of the group. There was also an organization called O-moi, a support group for lesbian, female bisexual, and female-to-male transgendered people of Vietnamese descent. (Courtesy of the UCI Vietnamese American Oral History Project, VAOHP0208.)

Founded in 1992, Social Assistance Program for Vietnam (SAP-VN), a nonprofit humanitarian organization based in Orange County, organizes an annual free mobile health-care program, such as this one in 2011, which provides medical surgeries and dental care to villagers throughout Vietnam. During this mission in the Phan Ri Thanh commune of ethnic minorities, volunteers are registering patients for care. (Courtesy of Social Assistance Program for Vietnam.)

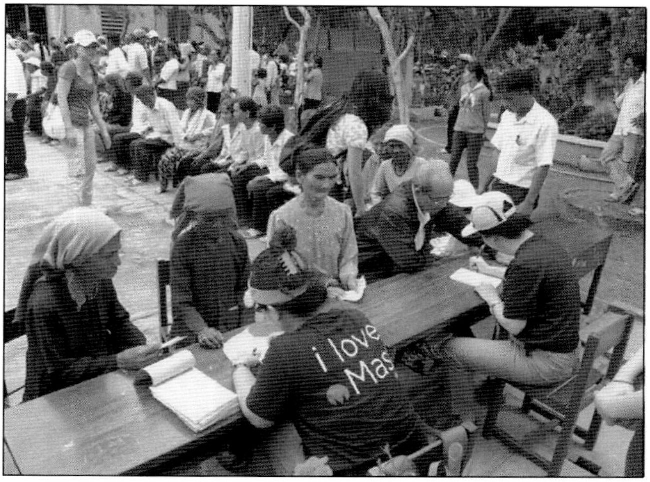

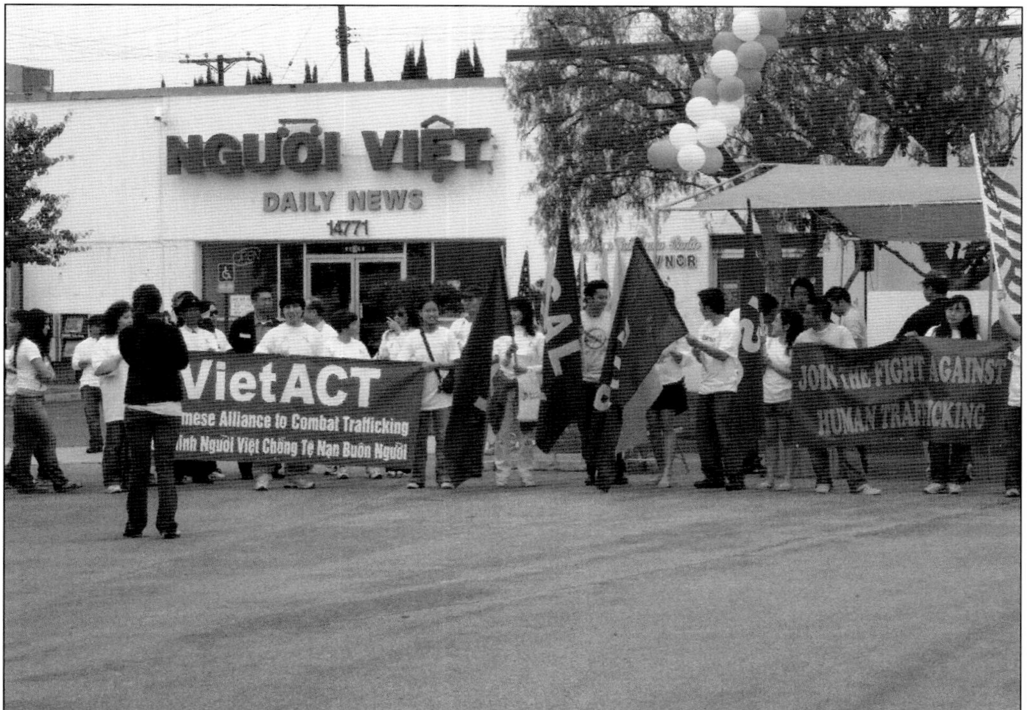

Vietnamese Alliance to Combat Trafficking (VietACT), a nonprofit organization, was founded in 2004 to raise awareness about Vietnamese children and women who were being sold or trafficked worldwide. They held rallies and fundraisers within the Little Saigon community. (Courtesy of Ben Hamatake.)

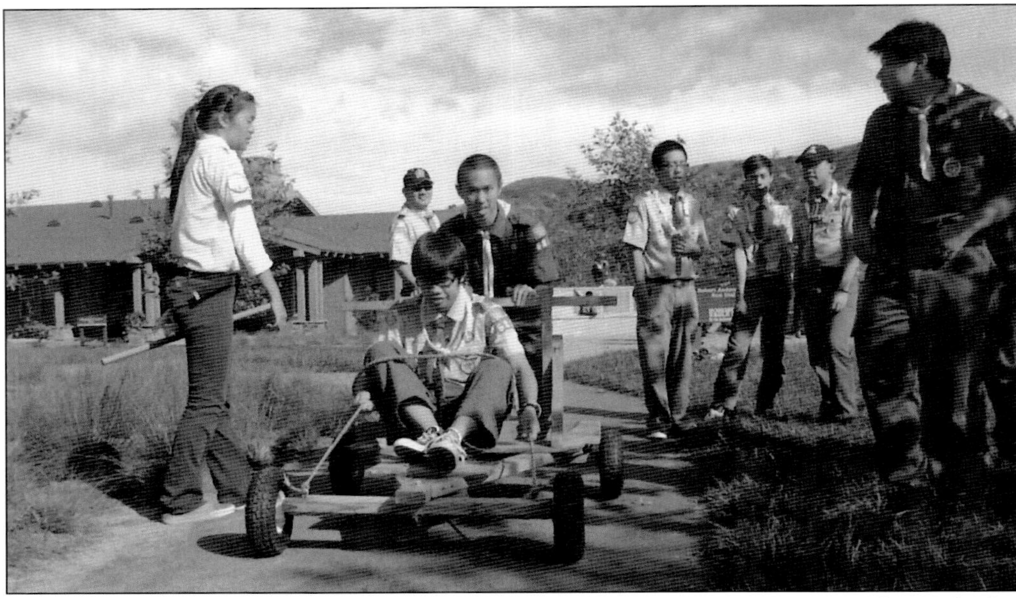

Youth scouts have existed in Vietnam since the 1930s but during various periods were banned. They have resurfaced in the overseas Vietnamese populations, including the United States, as seen in this photograph of scouts from Hoi Xuan Lien Doan Huong Dao Truong Son going through a "bridging" ritual where Webelo Scouts bridge over to become Boy Scouts. The Vietnamese Girl Scouts, although smaller, also organizes troops in the United States. (Courtesy of Diep Ngoc Vo.)

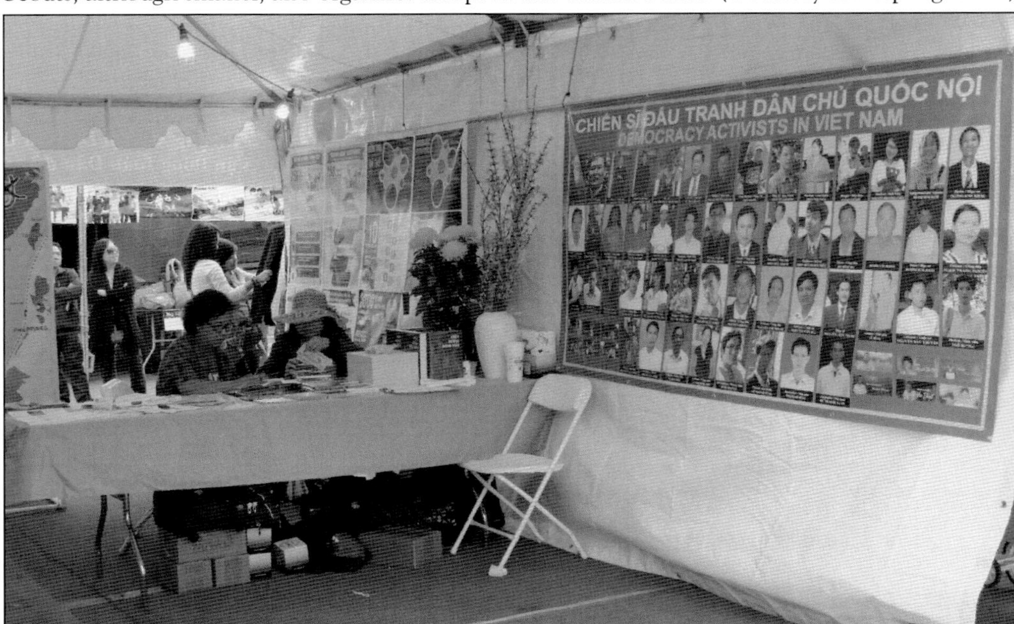

Decades after their displacement from Vietnam, refugees and immigrants still feel an attachment to their homeland. There are a number of organizations that advocate for religious and political freedom in Vietnam, such as this one that had a booth at the Tet Festival in Garden Grove. (Courtesy of Linda Trinh Vo.)

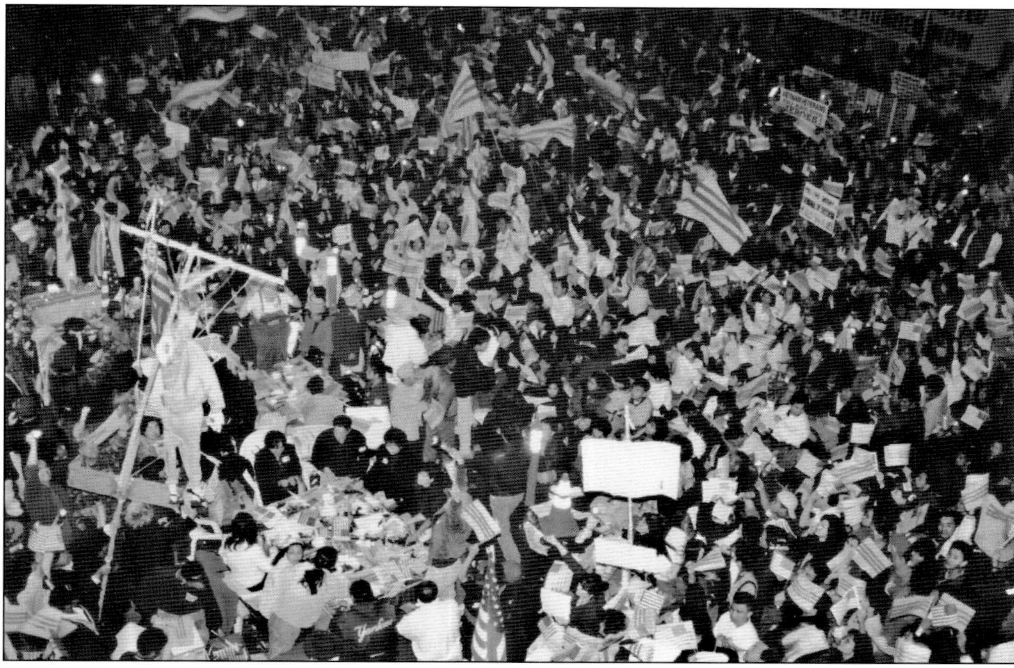

This aerial image shows the Hi-Tek video store protest in 1999 with a crowd waving the Vietnamese "Heritage and Freedom" flag along with other political imagery. The anti-communist protest was triggered by the shop owner displaying two images commonly associated with the Communist regime: a photo of Ho Chi Minh and the flag of the Socialist Republic of Vietnam. This struck a chord with many refugees who lost their livelihood, homes, and family members to the communist government in Vietnam. (Courtesy of Ly Kien Truc.)

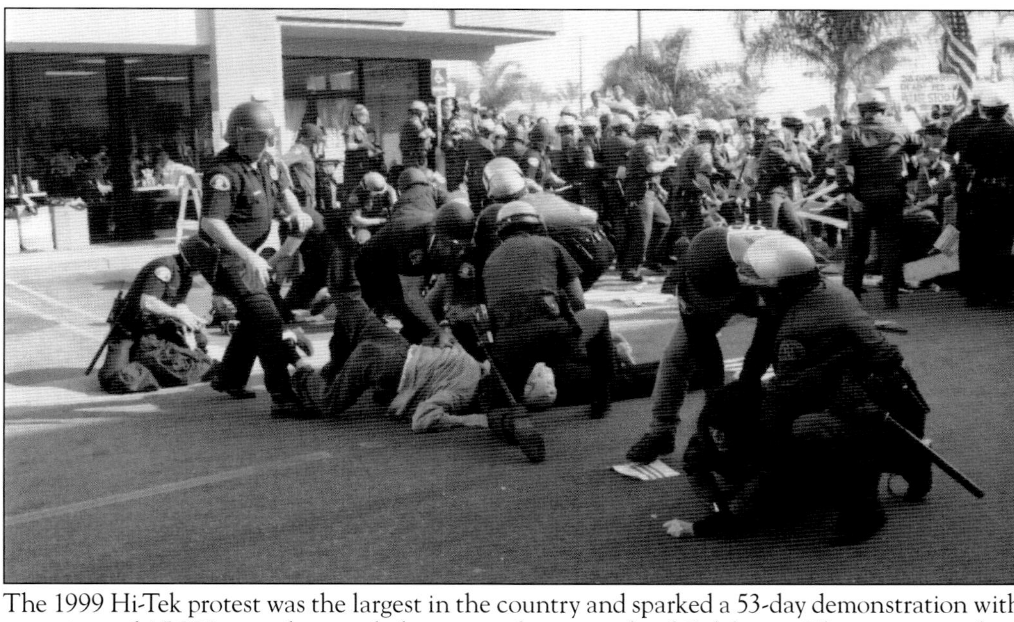

The 1999 Hi-Tek protest was the largest in the country and sparked a 53-day demonstration with an estimated 15,000 attendees, including many from outside of California. The events involved heated protests as well as peaceful vigils. (Courtesy of Ly Kien Truc.)

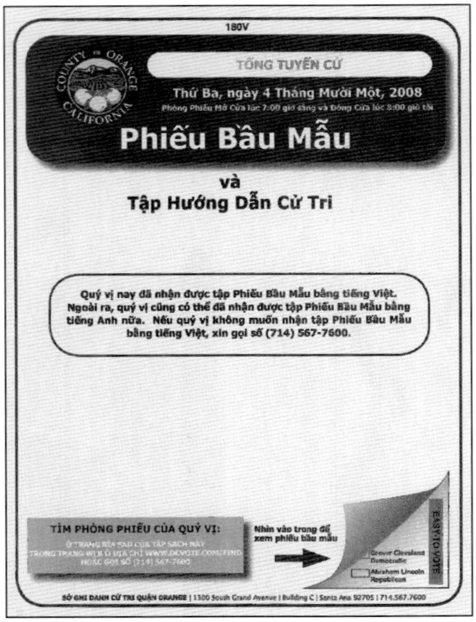

To accommodate the Vietnamese American population who have limited English proficiency (LEP), Orange County provides Vietnamese-language voting materials and ballots, as well as bilingual workers at the polls. These changes are a result of political pressure and lobbying by communities of color to enforce compliance of federal regulations. Despite their limited time in the United States, Vietnamese have high rates of voter participation and voting by absentee ballots. (Courtesy of the UCI Libraries Southeast Asian Archive, MS-SEA022, B9:8.)

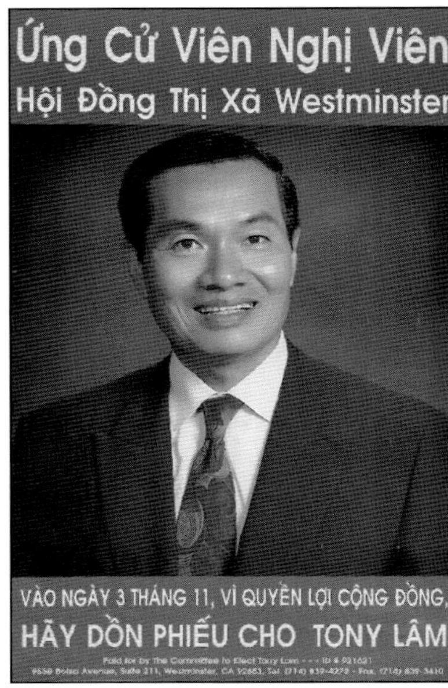

In 1992, entrepreneur Tony Lam was the first Vietnamese American elected to political office as a member of the Westminster City Council. His 1992 campaign poster in Vietnamese states his candidacy, date of election, and a bid to "cast your vote for Tony Lam." Since then, Vietnamese Americans have been seeking political office and winning elections at the city, county, and state level. (Courtesy of the UCI Libraries Southeast Asian Archive, MS-SEA020.)

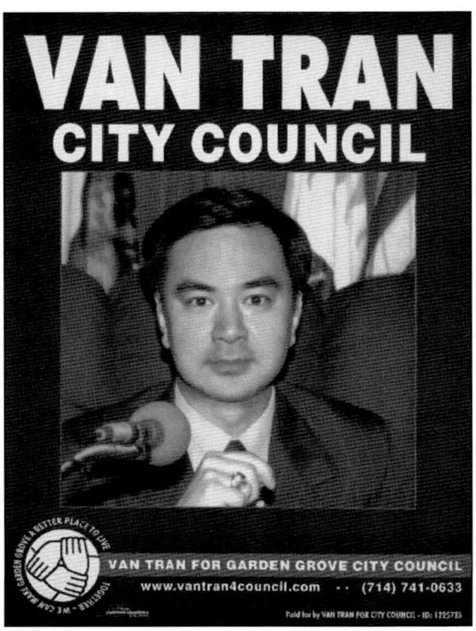

This 2000 campaign poster publicizes Van Tran for Garden Grove City Council, a seat he won with the highest number of votes in the city's history. After serving one term, he was elected to the California State Assembly in 2004, representing the 68th District, which includes part of Little Saigon. He was re-elected in 2006 and 2008 and during these terms helped other Vietnamese Republicans get elected to local office. He came to the United States as a refugee in 1975 when he was 10 years old. (Courtesy of the UCI Libraries Southeast Asian Archive, MS-SEA020.)

During election season, local politicians campaign heavily in Little Saigon since the Vietnamese are known for their voter participation. (Courtesy of Quan Tran.)

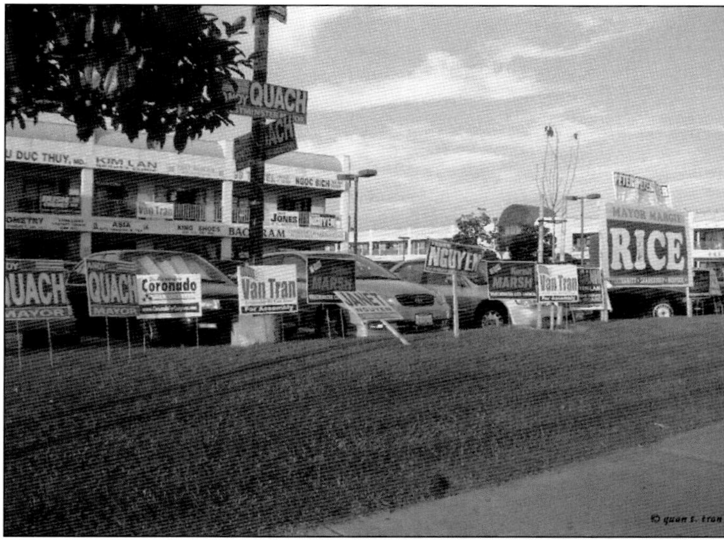

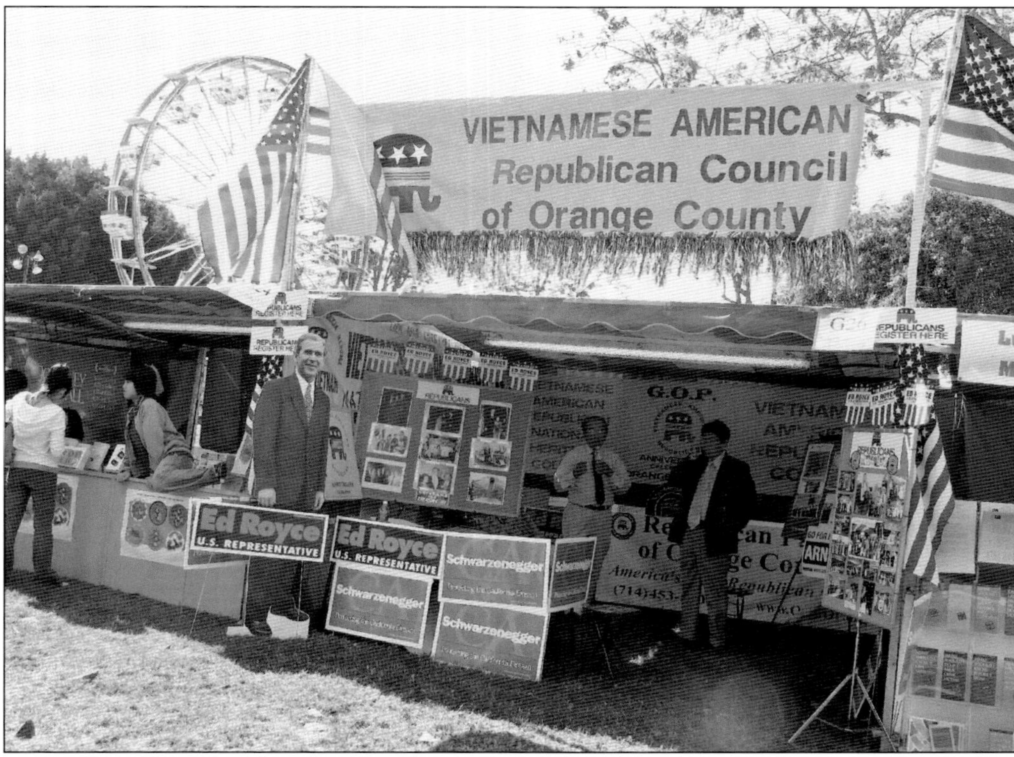

The Republican Party in Orange County usually has a booth at the UVSA Tet Festival in Garden Grove. Republican support is high among first-generation Vietnamese, many of whom support the fiscally and politically conservative stance of the party. Local and national surveys indicate generational differences among Vietnamese, with the younger generation being more supportive of Democratic Party candidates. (Courtesy of Linda Trinh Vo.)

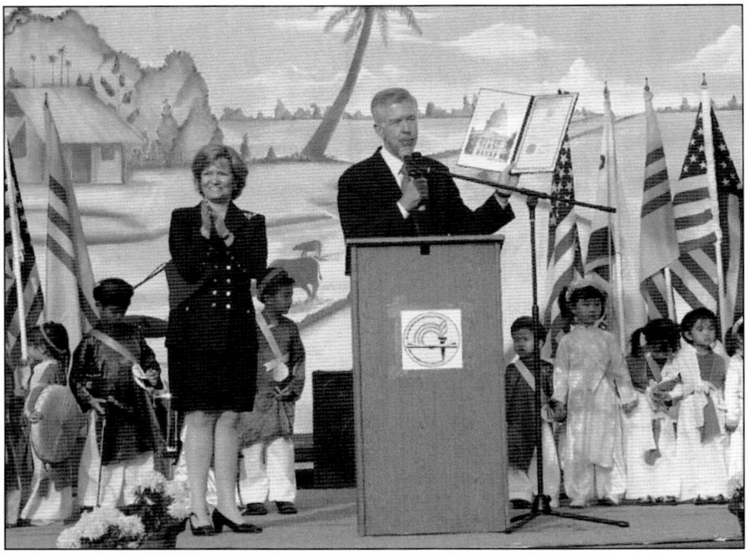

Former California governor Gray Davis and his wife, Sharon, attended the 2003 annual Tet Festival in Garden Grove Park organized by the Union of Vietnamese Student Association. (Courtesy of Linda Trinh Vo.)

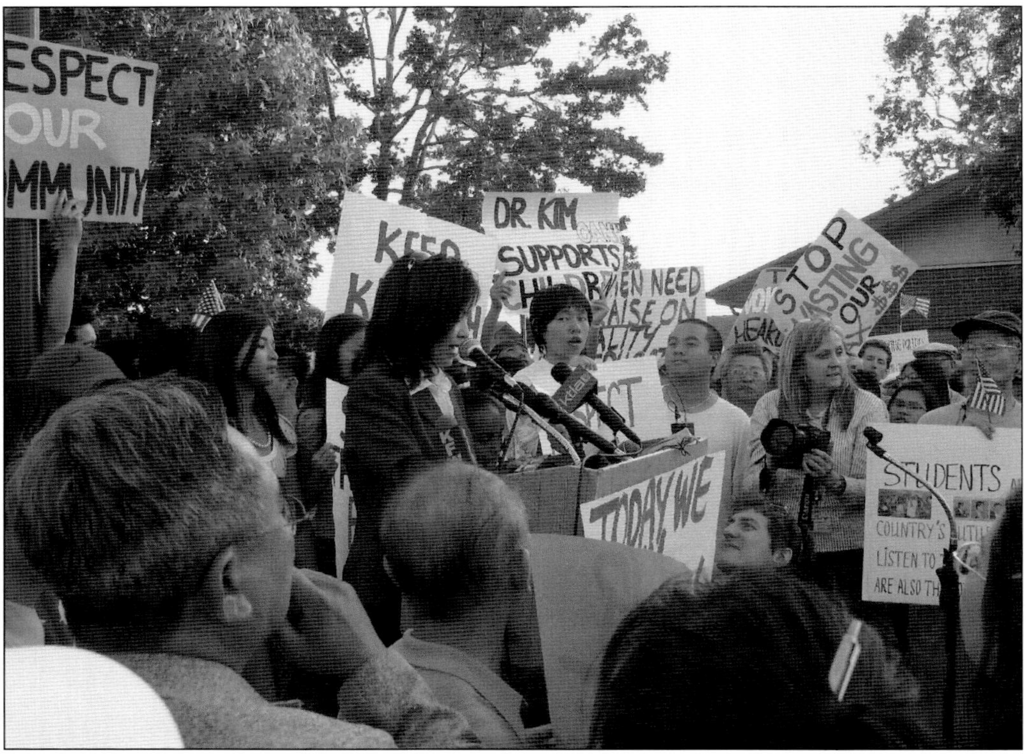

Pictured here is a 2006 rally with a diverse coalition of supporters for Dr. Kim Oanh Nguyen-Lam, who is fluent in English, French, Spanish, and Vietnamese. She was hired as superintendent of the Westminster School District, which is predominately Latino and Asian, but a week later the trustees rescinded her appointment without explanation. One of the first Vietnamese Democratic elected officials, she was elected in November 2004 and re-elected in 2008. She would later accept a post with the US Department of Education in Washington, DC in 2011. (Courtesy of Linda Trinh Vo.)

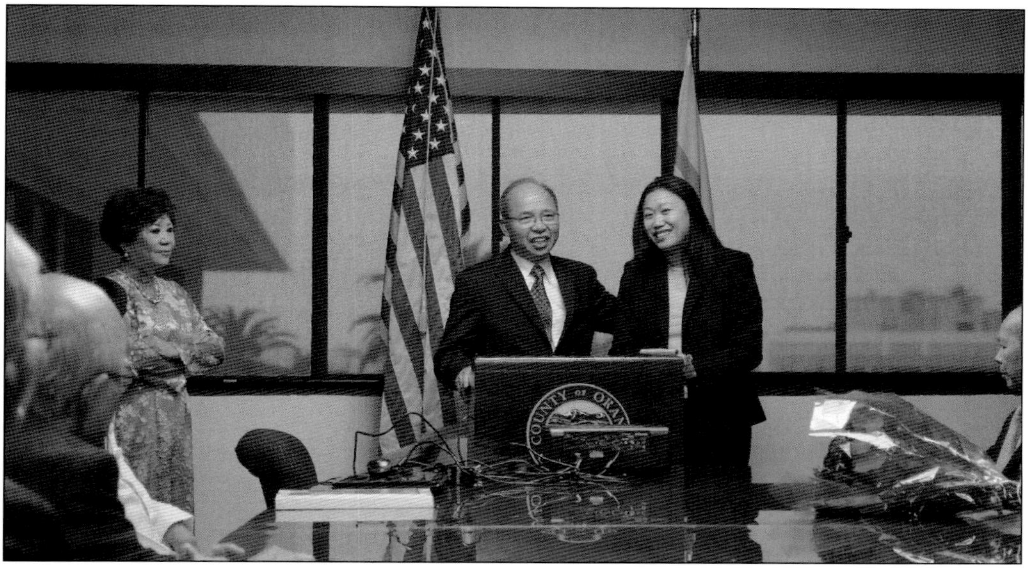

Judge Nho Trong Nguyen, the first Vietnamese American judge of Orange County, is being honored by Orange County supervisor Janet Nguyen, the first Vietnamese to be elected to this position and who was later elected as a California state senator, at his retirement ceremony in 2013. He served in the Army of the Republic of Vietnam as an infantry officer and was an elected politician in Vietnam before arriving as a refugee in 1975. To the left is his wife, Bang Van Pham, the first Vietnamese American woman to represent the 1st District on the Orange County Human Relations Commission. (Courtesy of Tram Le.)

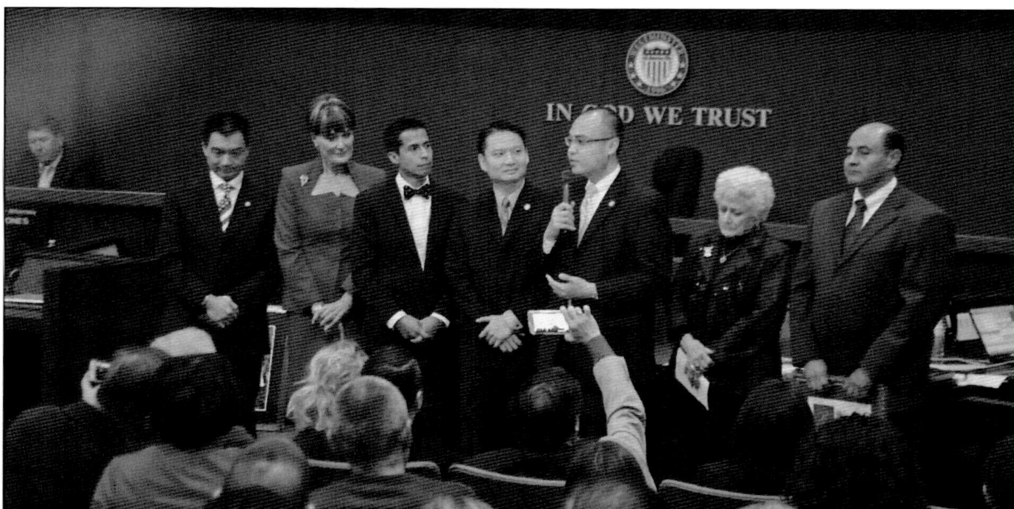

In 2013, Mayor Tri Ta (fourth from left) is being installed as the first elected Vietnamese American mayor in the country. Next to him are, from left to right, city council members Andy Quach, Diana Carey, Sergio Contreras, outgoing city council member Tyler Diep, Mayor Pro Tem Margie Rice, and state senator Lou Correa. Born in Saigon, Tri came to the United States at age 19 in 1992, works as a managing editor of *VietSALON*, a magazine for nail salon professionals, and was elected to the city council in 2006. Also, in 2014, Bao Nguyen was elected mayor of Garden Grove. (Courtesy of Kimberly Pham.)

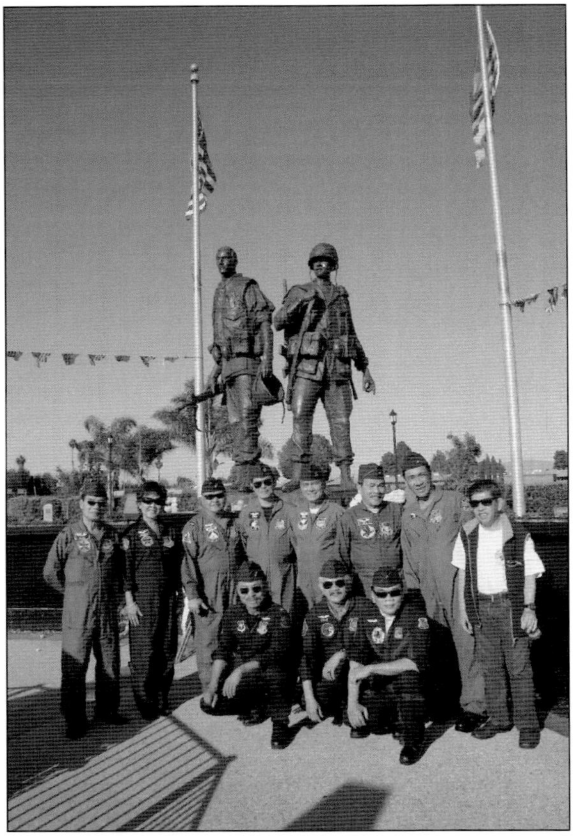

South Vietnamese military veterans, male and female, formed their own associations and participate in ceremonial and commemorative events, including the annual Black April, which marks the Fall of Saigon. Here a group of veterans with replicated uniforms and badges gathers at the Vietnam War memorial in Westminster. (Courtesy of Kimberly Pham.)

The Vietnamese American Armed Forces Association is a nonprofit association started in 2008 with a mission to provide professional development and networking for Vietnamese American service members in the US Armed Forces. Chris Phan (second in line) combines military service and a career in politics as Garden Grove city council member in 2012. (Courtesy of Kimberly Pham.)

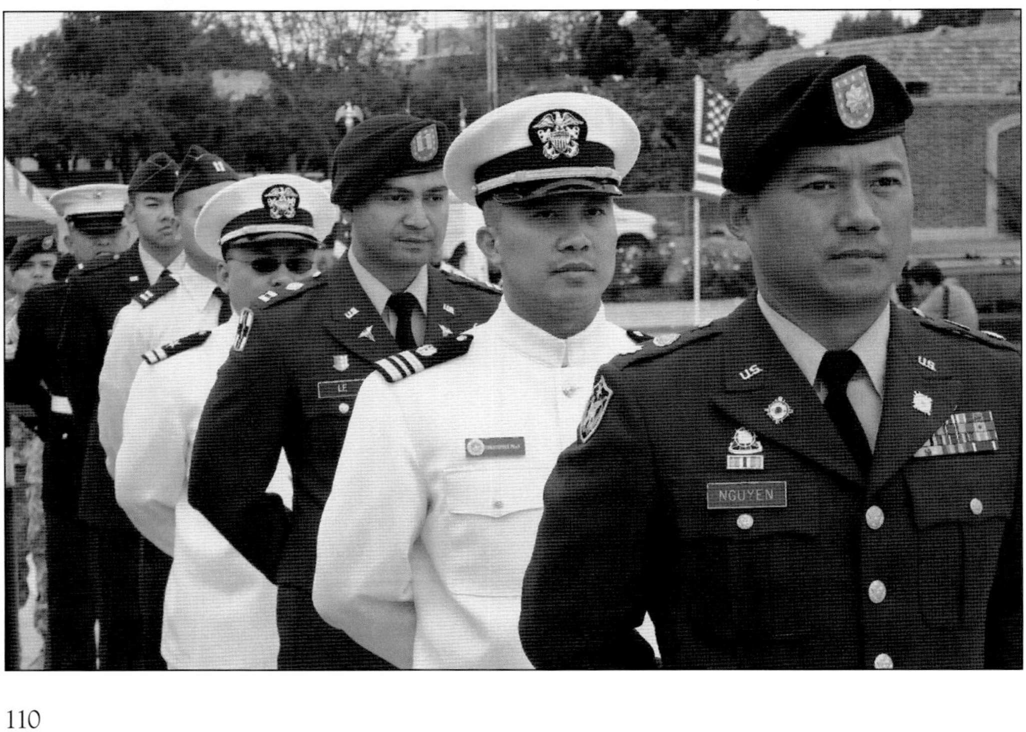

Kim Loan Ta (fourth from left) poses with her friends, many who are educated in the United States and married to professionals. Vietnamese women form their own social networks and often host or attend charity events for the Vietnamese community. (Courtesy of Kim Loan Ta.)

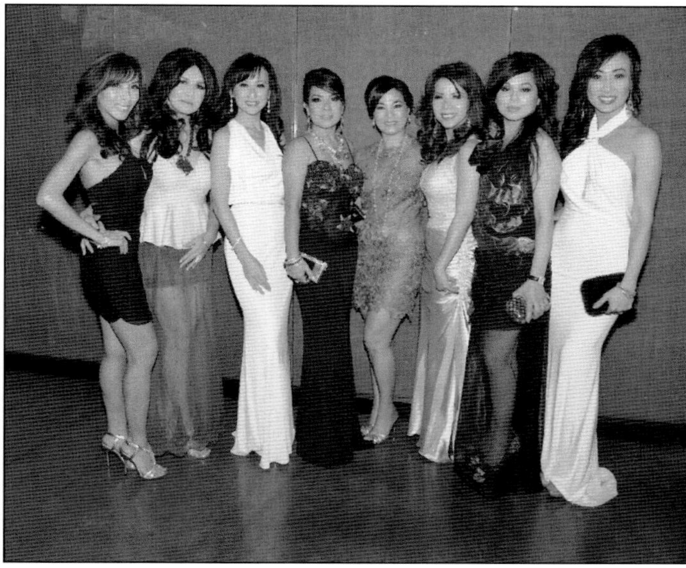

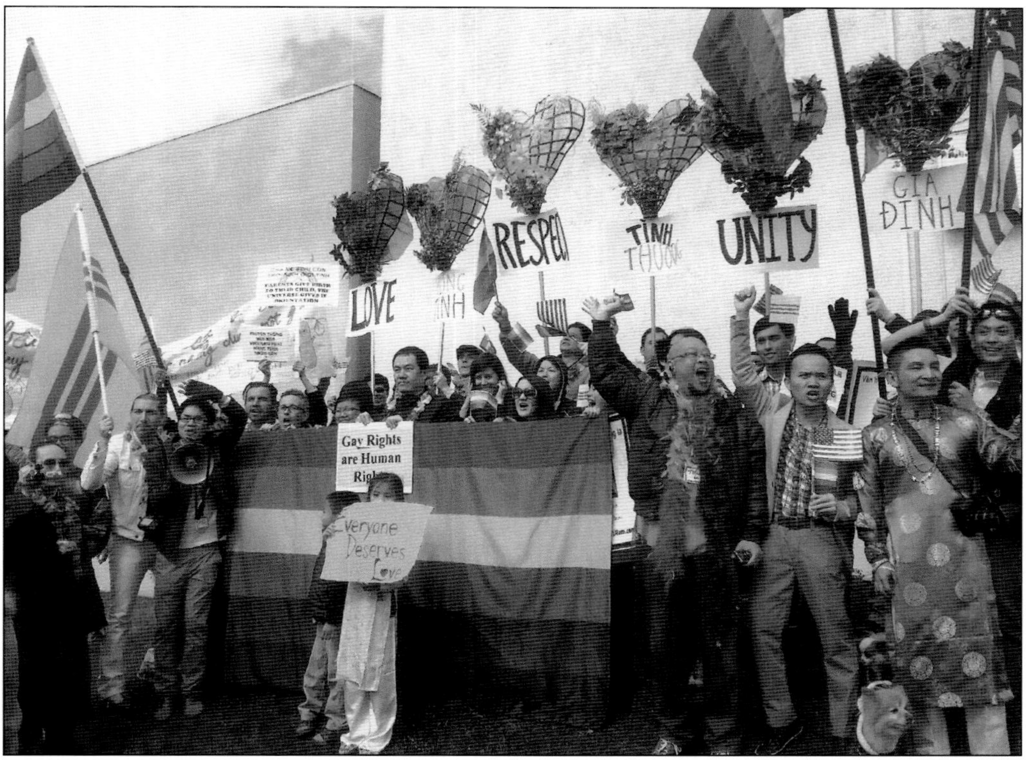

On February 10, 2013, over 250 Vietnamese lesbian, gay, bisexual, and transgender (LGBT) activists and allies attended the Tet Parade in Westminster. LGBT organizers were not allowed to participate in the parade, so they responded by creating signs and symbols of love and inclusion. Out of the Tet Parade controversy, the group Viet Rainbow of Orange County was formed to advocate for equality and representation. (Courtesy of Julie Vo.)

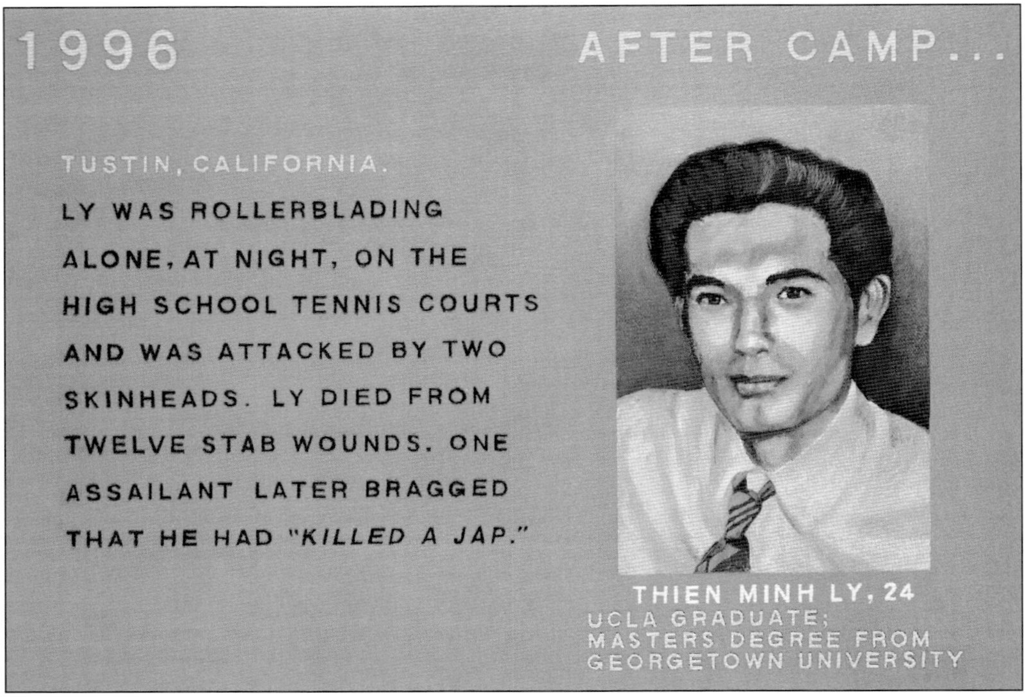

On January 29, 1996, Tustin resident Thien Minh Ly, age 24 , was found brutally murdered at a local high school where he had gone rollerblading. Thien, a refugee whose family owned a video rental shop in Santa Ana, received his bachelor's degree from UCLA, where he was president of the Vietnamese Student Union, and his master's degree from Georgetown University. Two young, male, white supremacists bragged about killing "a Jap" and were found guilty of committing a hate crime. This painting is in remembrance of Thien and connects his life to other individual and institutional acts of racial discrimination against Asian Americans. It is part of a series of 80 paintings (1999–2001) by Japanese American artist Ben Sakoguchi, who was incarcerated with his family during World War II when the US government imprisoned over 120,000 innocent Japanese Americans because of racial prejudice. (Courtesy of Ben Sakoguchi.)

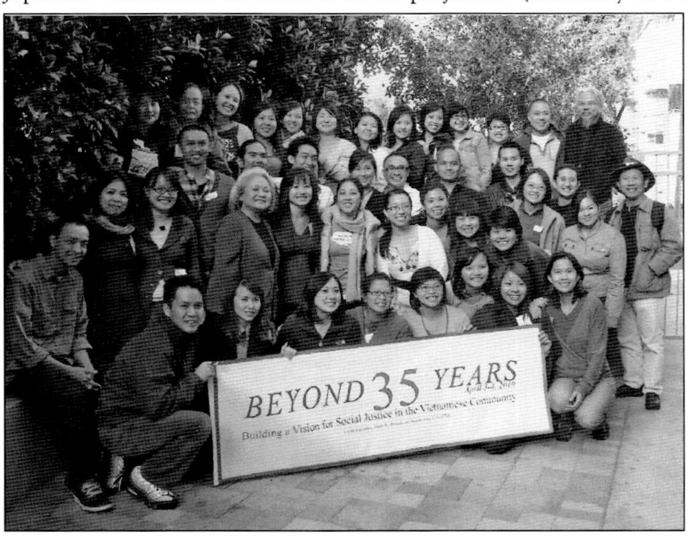

In 2010, a Southern California gathering of progressive Vietnamese Americans was held in Santa Ana and brought together established and emerging leaders from across the country for workshops and trainings. (Courtesy of Linda Trinh Vo.)

Nine

Arts and Leisure

Little Saigon in Orange County is the cultural capital of the Vietnamese overseas community and has set trends for Vietnamese arts and entertainment shared around the world. Vietnamese from across the United States and from other countries flock to Little Saigon to attend the world's largest Tet Festival, the most celebrated holiday, outside of Vietnam. The Vietnamese "Media Village" on Moran Street is where four major newspapers, a radio station, and a television station coexist on a commercial cul-de-sac. Additionally, dozens of print media outlets and 24-hour Vietnamese television and radio stations that broadcast throughout the United States are headquartered in Orange County. This region is also known as the "Vietnamese Hollywood," as it produces popular music variety shows featuring live music, dancing, and comedic sketches that are taped and circulated nationally and abroad. Little Saigon is home to the annual Vietnamese International Film Festival and a thriving community of artists that range from traditional to contemporary. For Vietnamese Americans, leisure is an important component of everyday life represented by numerous restaurants and coffee shops, sporting activities, and social gatherings.

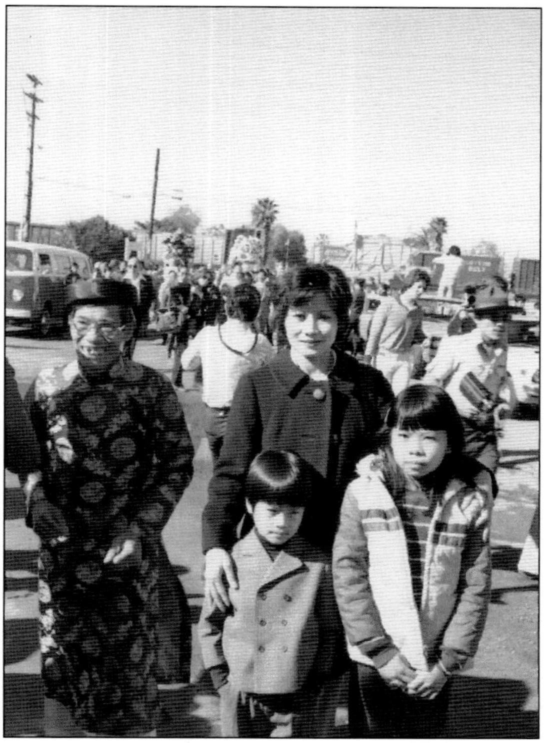

Liem Le (center) takes her children Quang (left) and Tu-Uyen (right) to one of the first Tet Festivals in Orange County, held in a Bolsa Avenue parking lot in 1981. (Courtesy of Tu-Uyen Nguyen.)

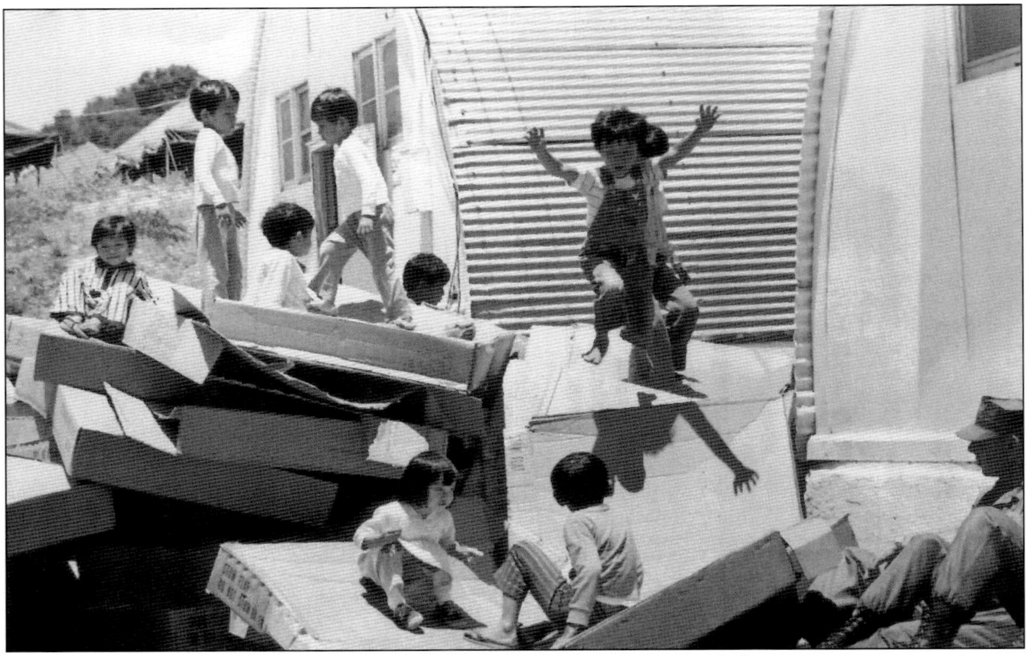

Camp Pendleton in San Diego County was open in 1975 to temporarily house Vietnamese refugees. Here children are having fun with the makeshift playground made of discarded cardboard boxes under the watchful eye of US military personnel. (Official Marine Corps photograph.)

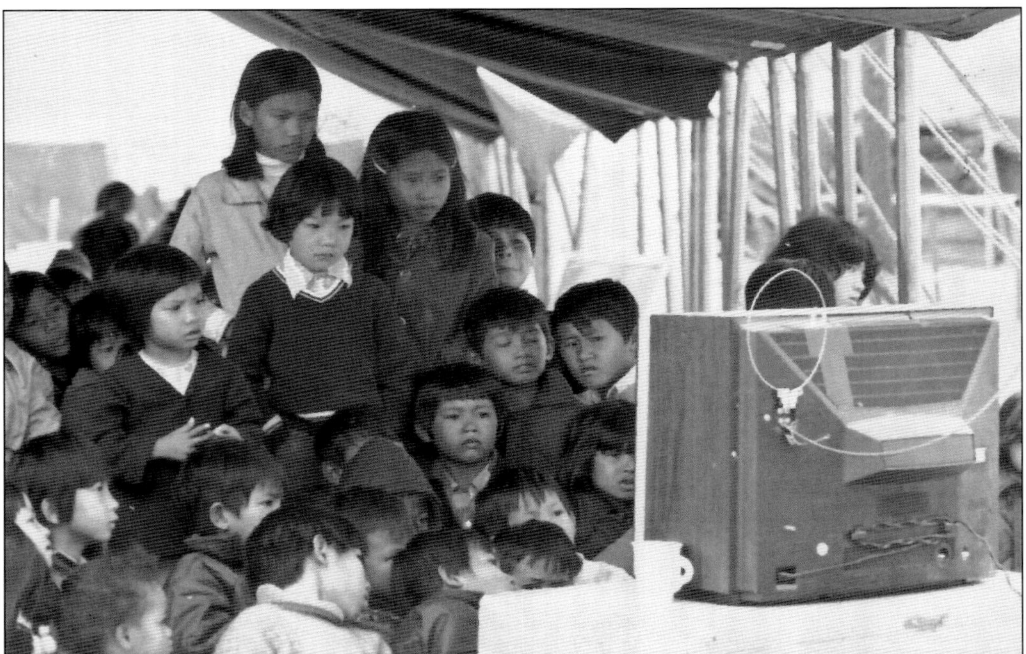

Refugee children at Camp Pendleton watch television as a form of entertainment and to learn English. (Official Marine Corps photograph.)

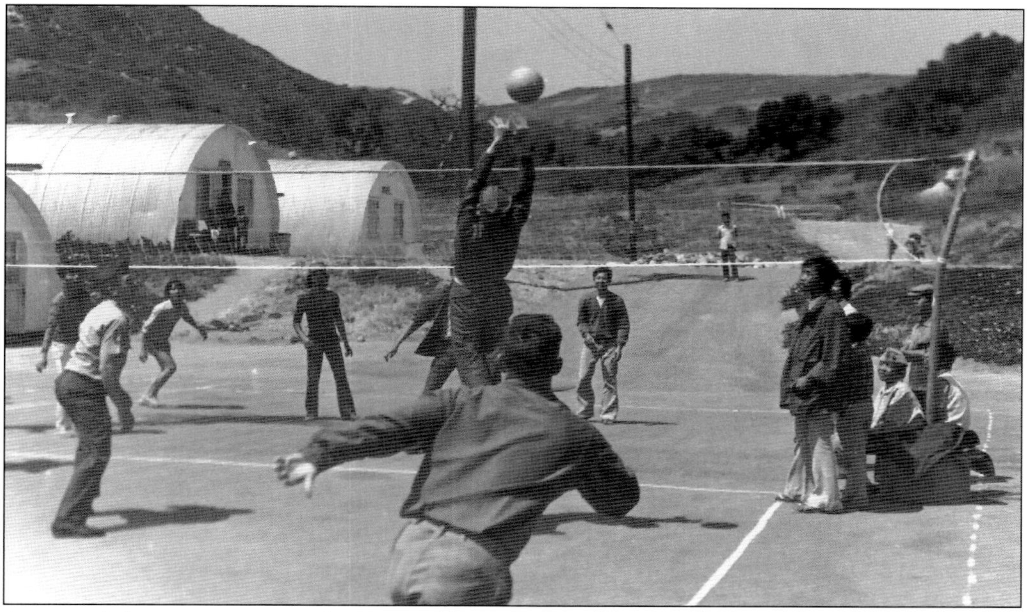

As part of their recreation in the camps, Vietnamese refugees and American military personnel engage in a game of volleyball to pass the time. The background shows converted Quonset huts provided to refugees for shelter, while other housing consisted of temporary tents set up to quickly accommodate the refugees. (Official Marine Corps photograph.)

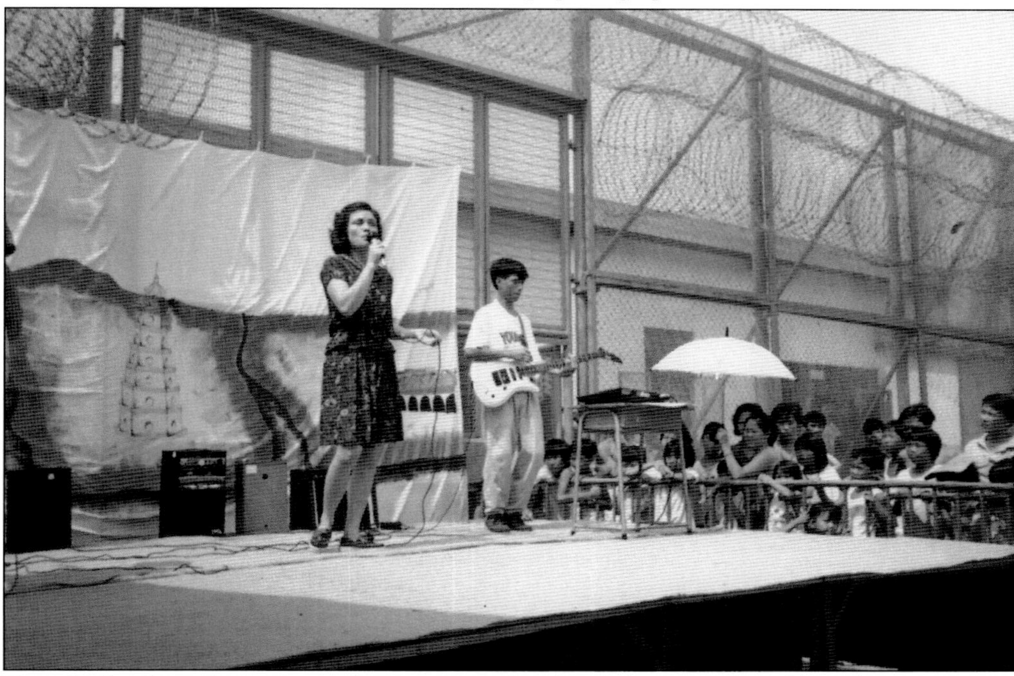

To make the days of waiting in refugee camps in Southeast Asia more bearable, refugees organized entertainment and activities. Working with camp officials, they would post signs recruiting talent and hold stage performances such as the one pictured here. (Courtesy of the UCI Libraries Southeast Asian Archive, MS-SEA016, B11:4.)

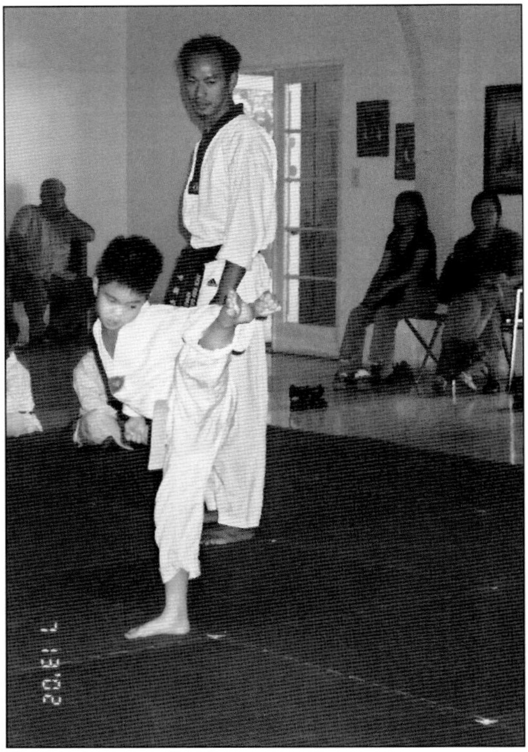

In 1999, Jack Toan started a free martial arts program, now sponsored by the Horizon Cross Cultural Center in Orange County. Every Saturday for more than a decade, Jack and a team of other instructors teach martial arts to young people, many who could not afford lessons otherwise. (Courtesy of Jack Toan.)

Vietnamese men from different parts of Orange County gather regularly for informal games of basketball at Mile Square Park in Fountain Valley. The development of the park parallels the development of the Vietnamese community. Families and organizations often host picnics and special events here, and on occasion Vietnamese wedding parties can be seen taking photographs. (Courtesy of Julie Huynh and Zed Santiago.)

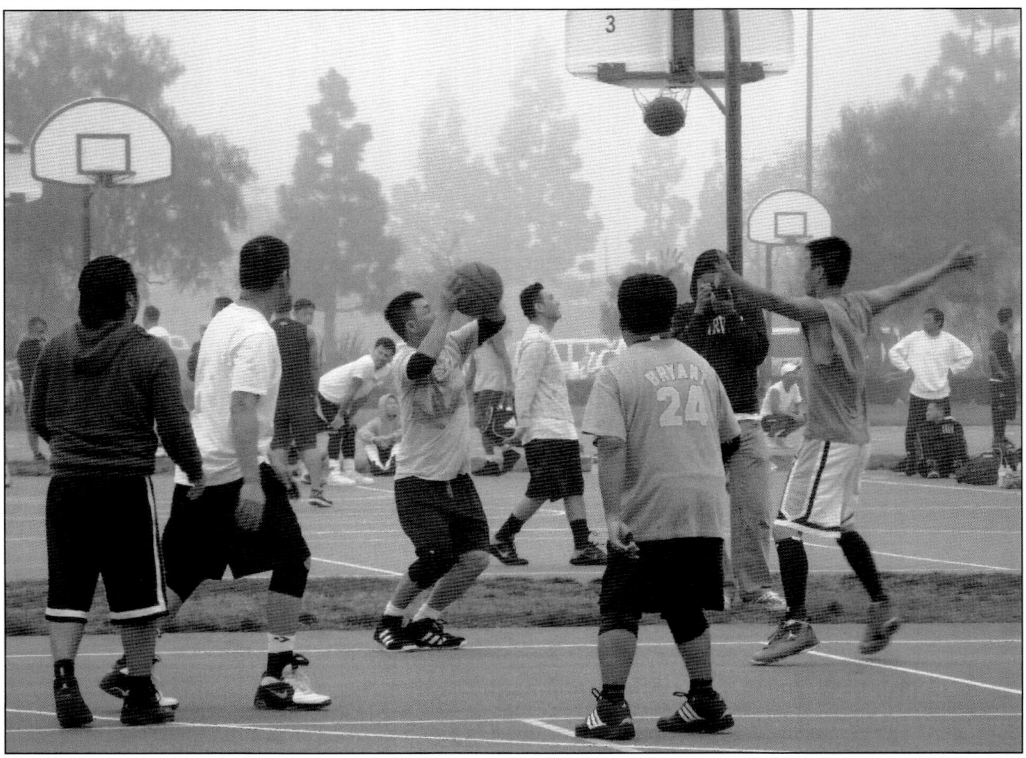

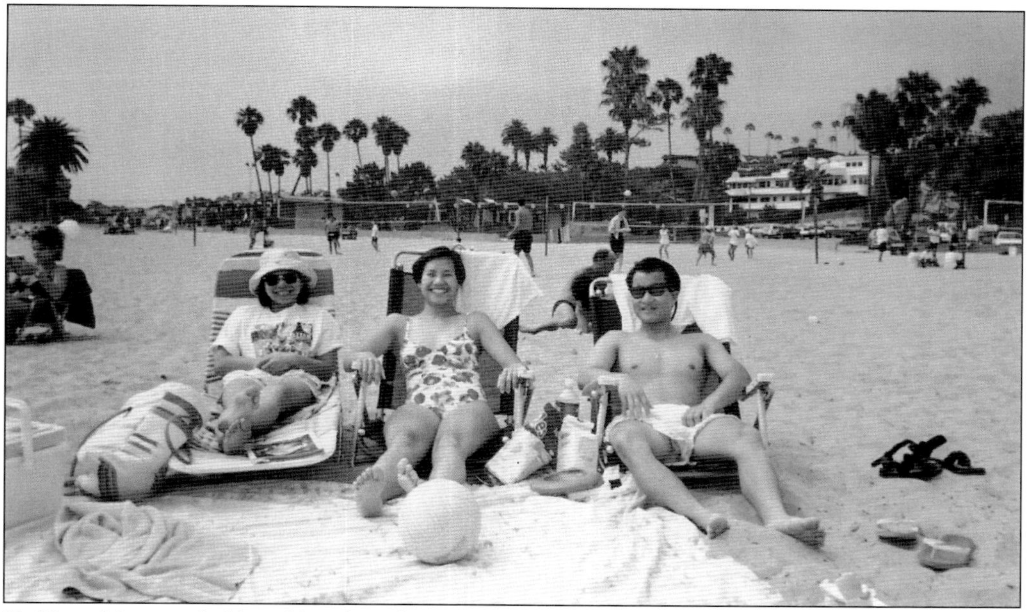

Tu-Uyen Nguyen (left) and her friends enjoy a day at Corona Del Mar beach in July 1993. The three friends were students who met through their involvement in student activism in college. (Courtesy of Tu-Uyen Nguyen.)

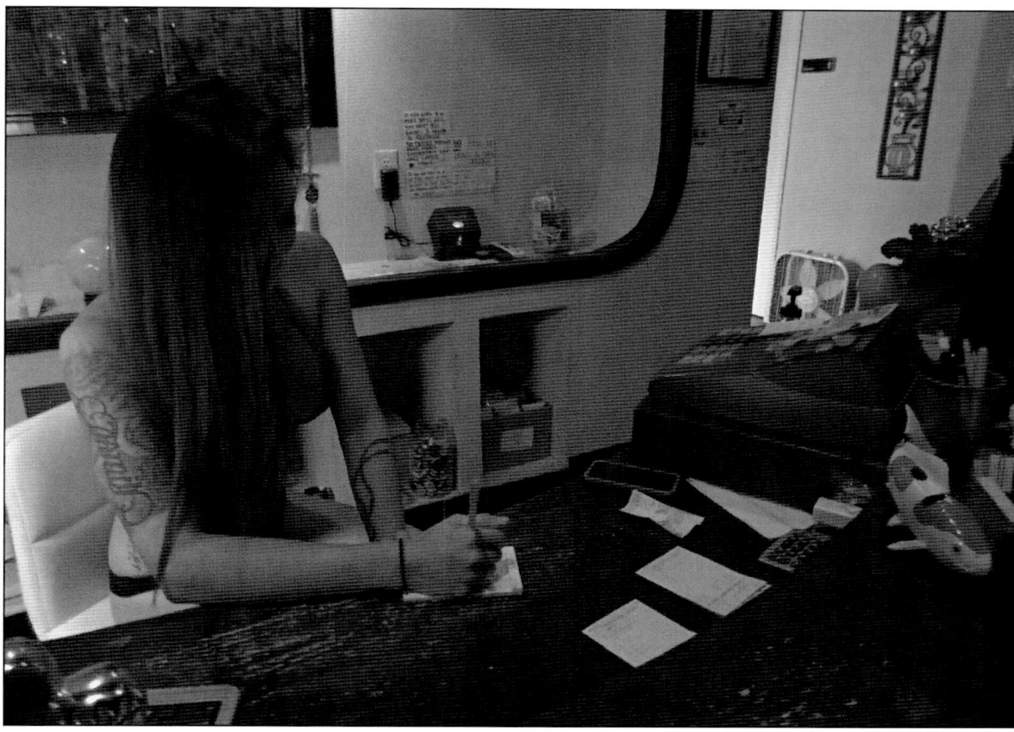

Vietnamese women, some who are recent immigrants, find employment in entertainment and specialized café businesses in Little Saigon and surrounding communities that cater to Vietnamese male patrons. (Courtesy of Taylor Weik and Eric Chau.)

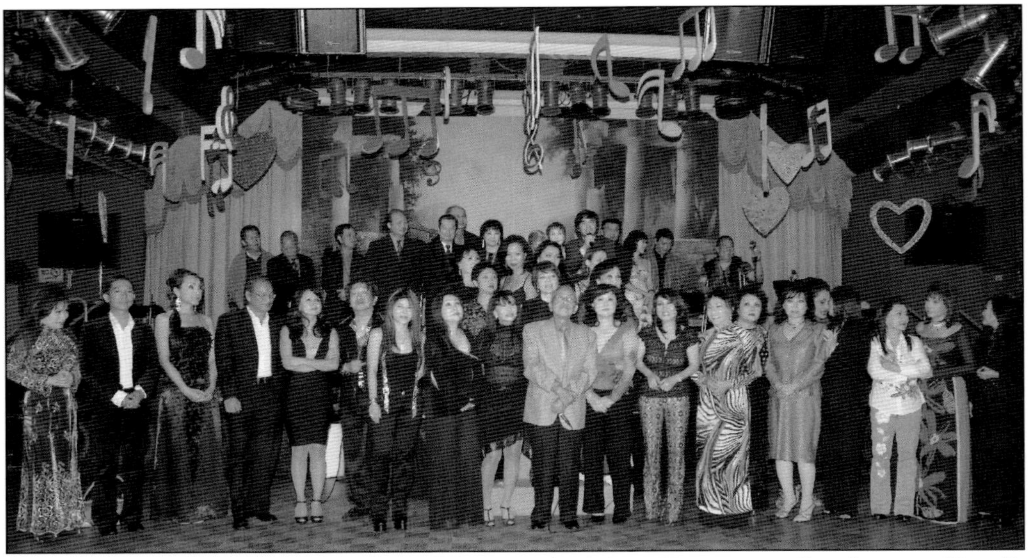

On September 14, 2008, at Majestic Dancing nightclub in Huntington Beach, over 40 well-known musicians, singers, and entertainers gathered for an evening to honor the beloved musician and composer Le Van Thien. Notable guests included Anh Bang, Huynh Anh, Vu Thanh An, Ngoc Chanh, Truc Ho, Thanh Thuy, Le Thu, Nam Loc, Truc Mai, Phuong Dung, Huong Lan, Viet Dzung, Phuong Hong Que, Tran Quoc Bao, Phong Linh, Thanh Lan, Ngoc Minh, Trang Thanh Lan, Thanh Mai, Linh Phuong, Tam Dan, Ky Phat, and Kim Tuyen. (Courtesy of Tran Quoc Bao.)

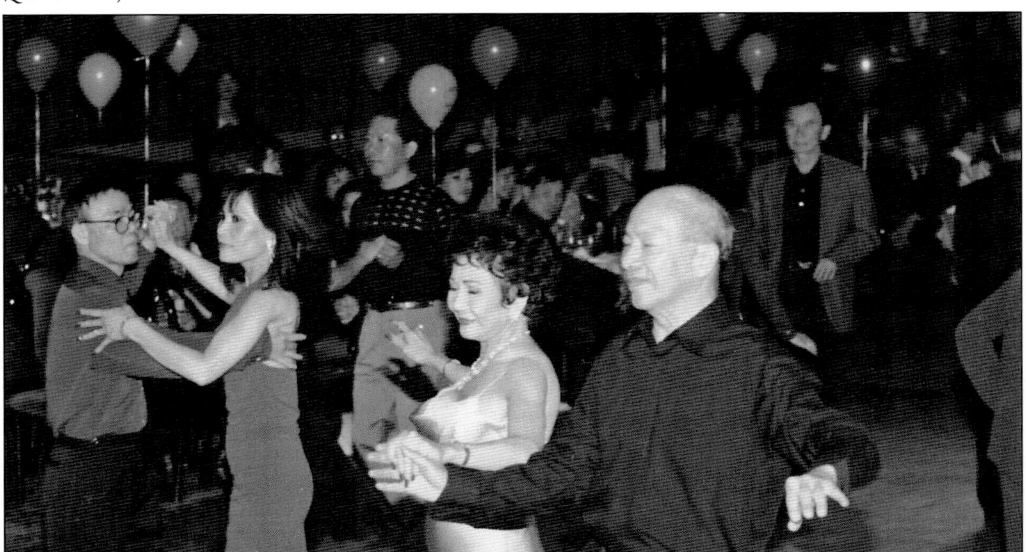

Ballroom dancing is a favorite pastime for many Vietnamese, particularly for those who enjoy listening to music composed before 1975, when French colonization brought this art form to Vietnam. At the height of its popularity in the early-to-mid-1990s, couples and groups of college students would go on a weekly basis to Vietnamese-owned night clubs, such as Majestic, Queen Bee, and Ritz, where the older generation could dance ballroom-style to a live band, and the younger generation could dance to hip-hop during the band's breaks. (Courtesy of Tran Kim Lan.)

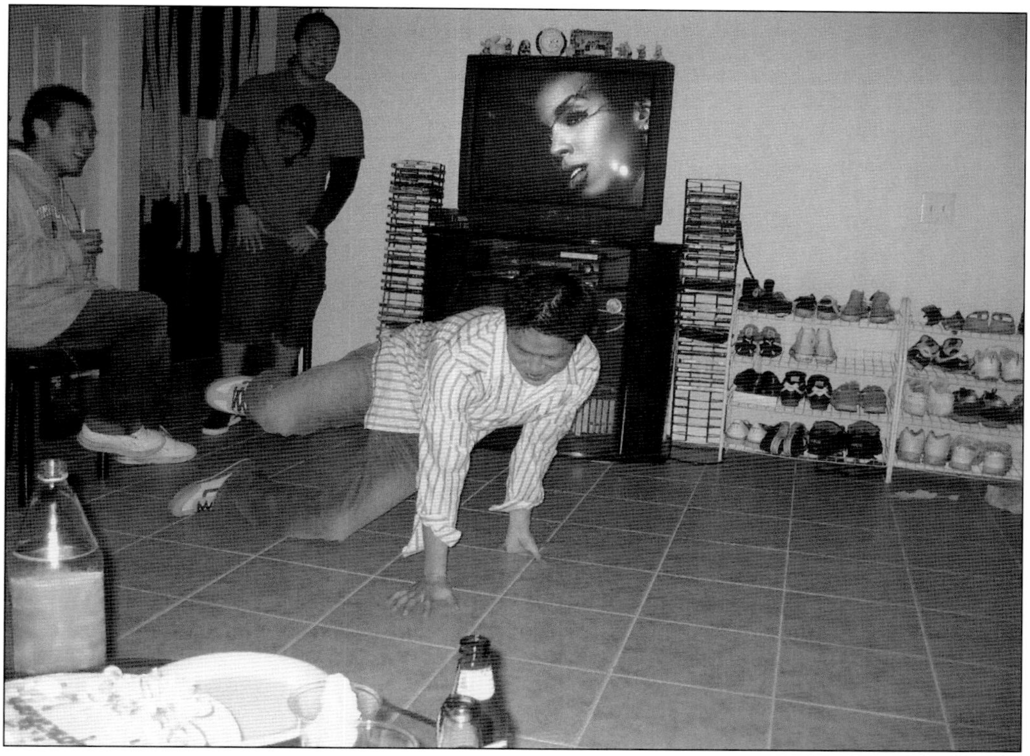

House parties are very popular among Vietnamese American youths as it is an affordable way to have fun with friends and celebrate special occasions. During the 1980s, house parties often played European New Wave music that was not played in mainstream clubs. Pictured here is Mick break dancing at a friend's house in Garden Grove. (Courtesy of Diana Nguyen.)

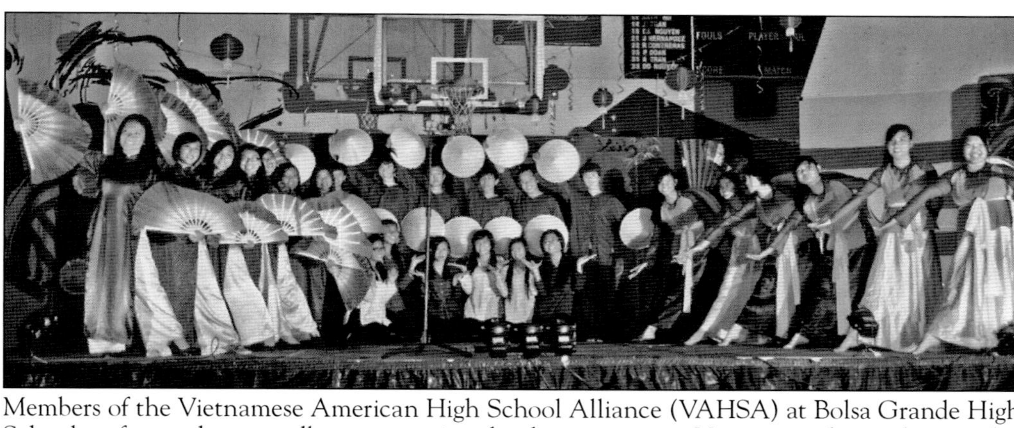

Members of the Vietnamese American High School Alliance (VAHSA) at Bolsa Grande High School perform a dance medley representing the three regions in Vietnam at their culture night, "Toi La Nguoi Viet Nam (I Am Vietnamese)," on March 1, 2013. (Courtesy of Nguyen Van Liem/ *Viet Tide*.)

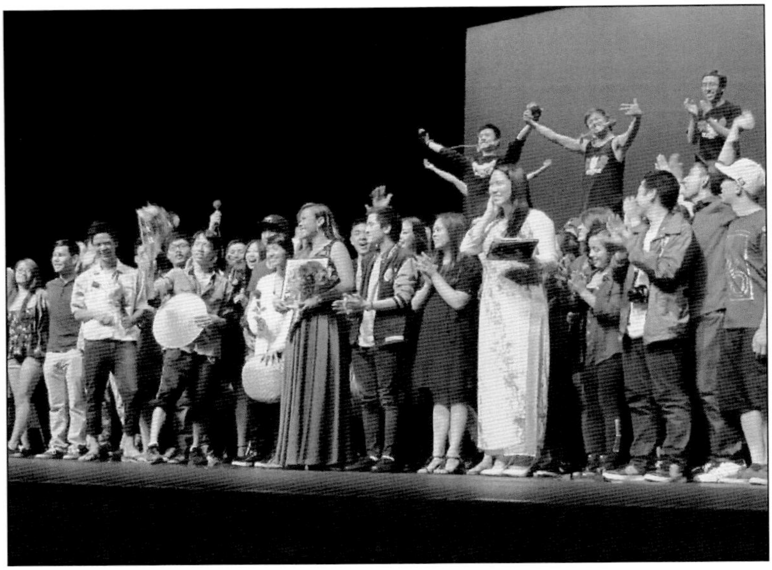

Vietnamese culture nights are organized by Vietnamese student associations at high schools and colleges across Orange County. They feature dramatic plays and comedic sketches written and performed by the students, along with traditional dances and contemporary hip-hop routines. (Courtesy of Abir Siddiqui and Julie Huynh.)

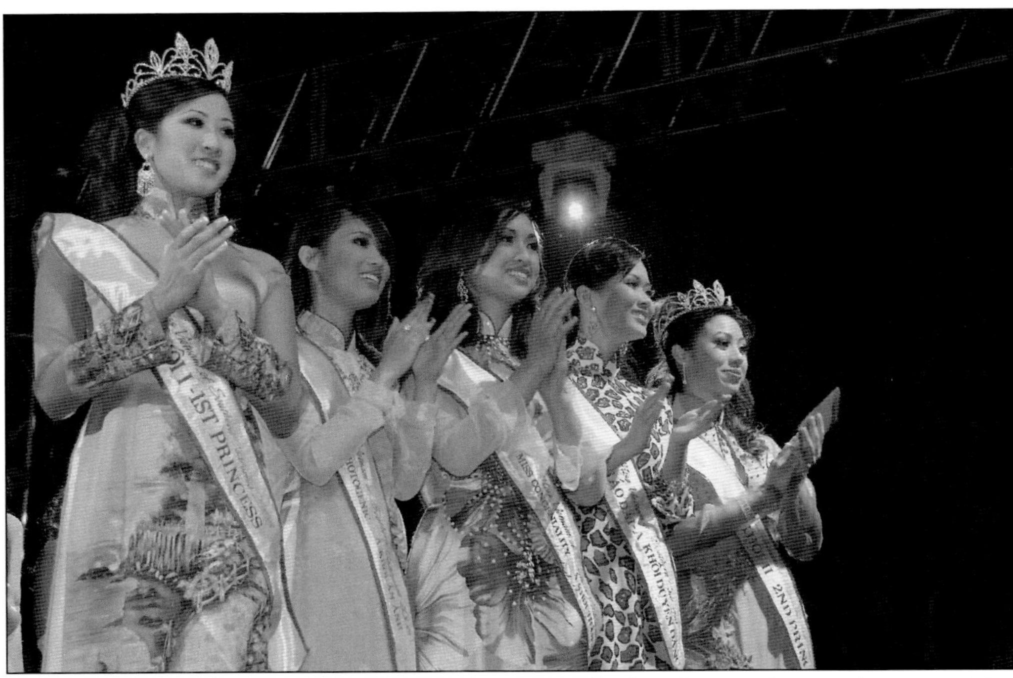

Beauty pageants in the Vietnamese community are not only about beauty; they are also competitions of linguistic and cultural knowledge featuring contestants wearing ao dai that display traditional gender roles. This pageant is Miss Vietnam Southern California, held at the annual Union of Vietnamese Student Association Tet Festival, in 2008. (Courtesy of Brian Dang.)

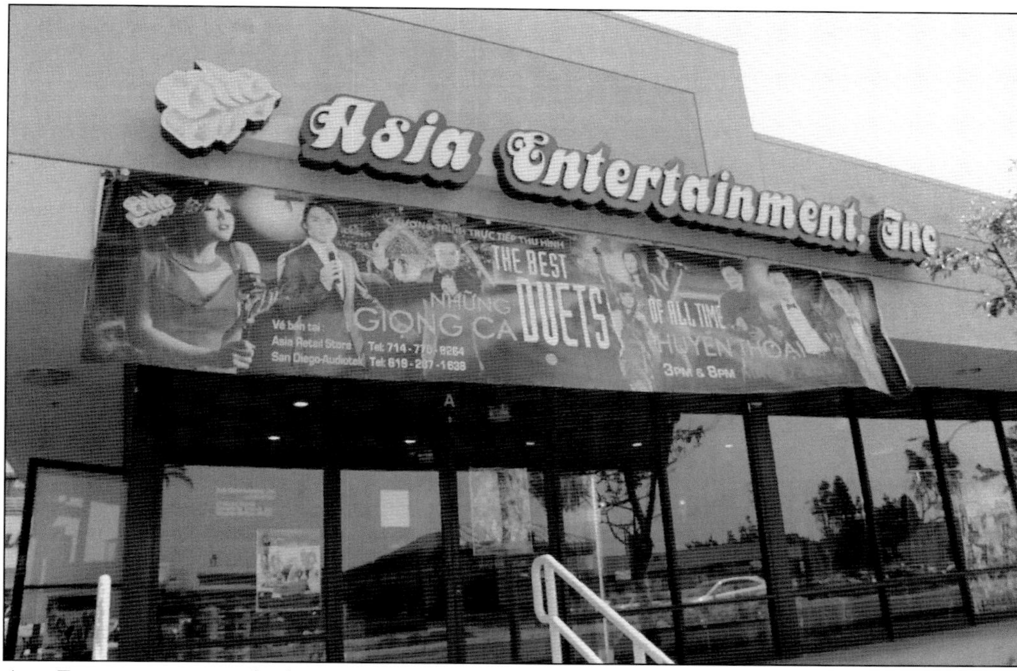

Asia Entertainment is the longest running overseas Vietnamese musical production company. It was founded over 25 years ago in Vietnam by musician Anh Bang and brought to the United States by his daughter Thy Van. Located in Westminster, the company promotes and markets live entertainment for Vietnamese audiences worldwide. They gained greater popularity when they collaborated with musician Truc Ho and leveraged their celebrity status to launch programs around the issue of human trafficking. (Courtesy of Abir Siddiqui and Julie Huynh.)

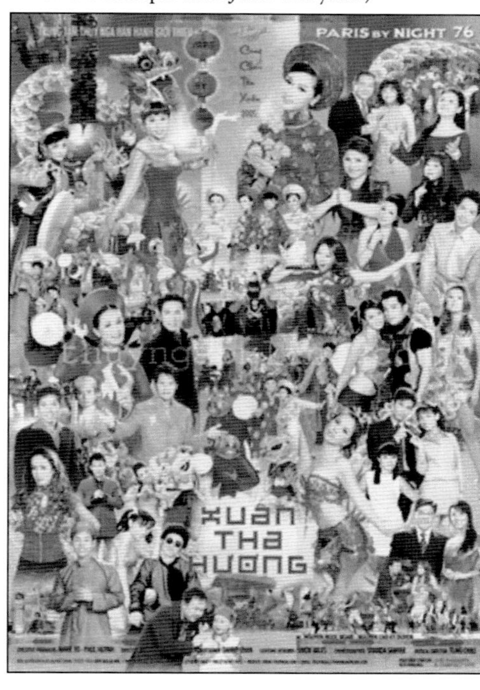

Paris by Night is a popular music variety show founded in Paris by To Van Lai, where it began as an assortment of music videos. In the late 1980s, the company shifted their headquarters to Orange County and produced live shows intertwining western and Vietnamese culture. The most recognizable emcees in these Vietnamese cultural productions are Nguyen Ngoc Ngan and Nguyen Cao Ky Duyen, the daughter of former Vietnam prime minister Nguyen Cao Ky, who settled in Westminster. (Courtesy of Thuy Nga Productions.)

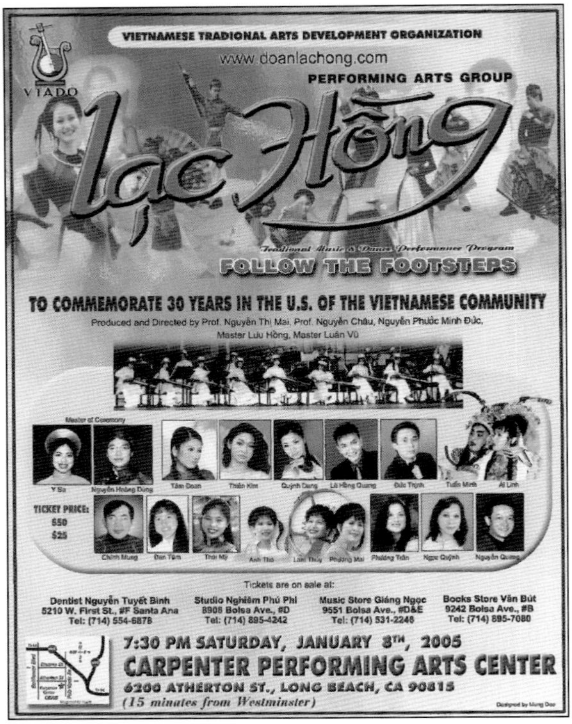

Lac Hong, also known as the Vietnamese Traditional Arts Development Organization, is located in Westminster and organizes music and dance performances. The group was formed in 1988 by former music instructors from the Vietnamese National Conservatory of Music in Saigon and other Vietnamese musicians living in Orange County. Its mission is to preserve, develop, and promote traditional music and dance throughout the United States. (Courtesy of the UCI Libraries Southeast Asian Archive, MS-SEA020.)

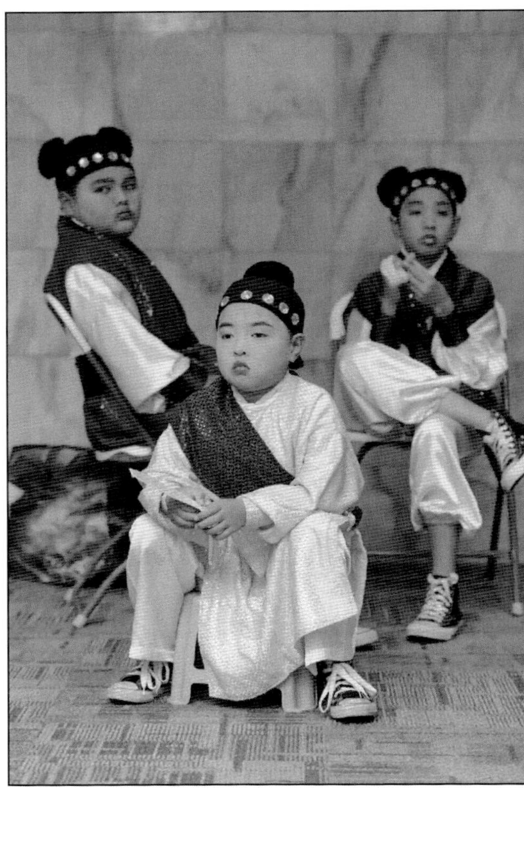

Since the beginning of the 20th century, the opera-like art form *hat boi* has been slowly fading due to competition from *cai luong*, traditional Southern Vietnamese drama and music theatre. Although imported from China in the 13th century, Vietnamese hat boi has developed its own distinct music, dance, and makeup. Master artist Ngoc Bay, the only professional hat boi performer in the United States, teaches hat boi classes to diverse age groups. Pictured here are three of her students waiting backstage to perform at Westminster Mall. (Courtesy of the Vietnamese American Arts and Letters Association.)

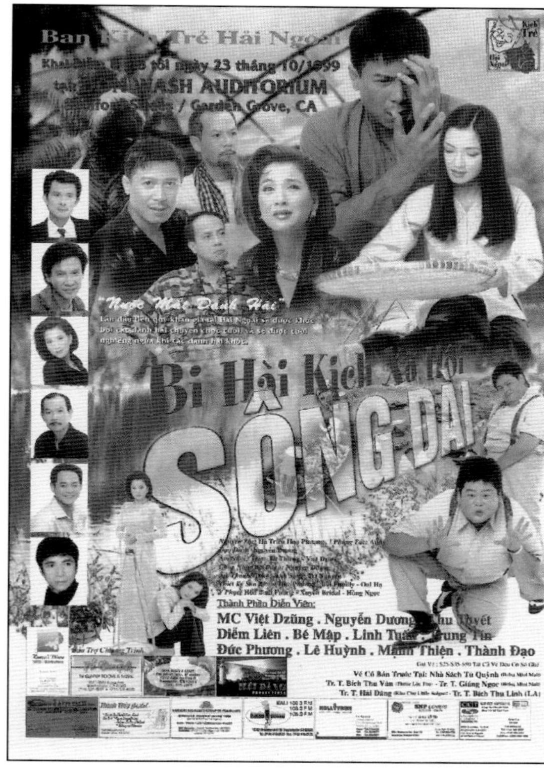

This is a flyer for the performance of *Song Dai*, a comedic drama produced by Kich Tre Hai Ngoai theatre group on October 23, 1999, at Don Wash Auditorium in Garden Grove. Theater groups made up of mainly first-generation refugees such as these were difficult to sustain financially and performed on a project-by-project basis with almost no core members. (Courtesy of the UCI Libraries Southeast Asian Archive, MS-SEA020.)

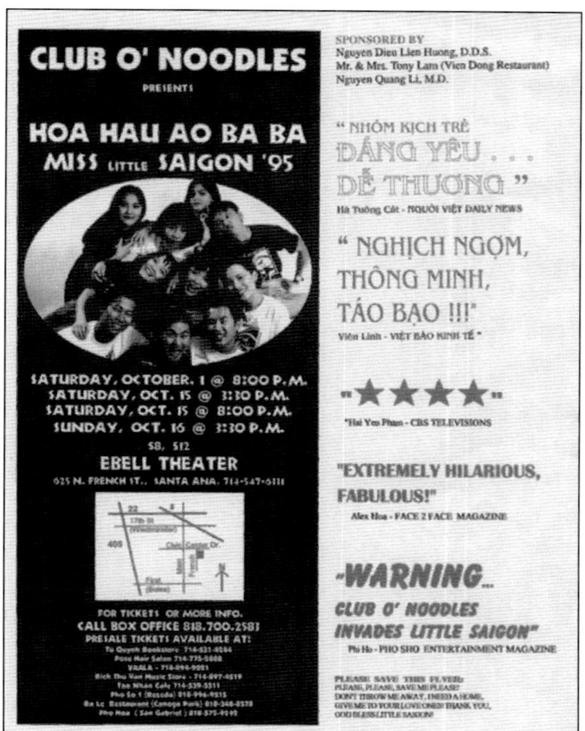

Founded in 1993, Club O' Noodles is a theatre troupe made up of 1.5 (those born abroad who came to the US as children) and second-generation Vietnamese Americans. Although started at California State University, Northridge, co-founders Hung Nguyen, Tram Le, and Thanh Nguyen recruited students from different colleges, including UC Irvine and Golden West College. *Hoa Hau Ao Ba Ba (Miss Little Saigon)*, a satirical play, was performed at the Ebell Theater in Santa Ana. (Courtesy of the UCI Libraries Southeast Asian Archive, MS-SEA020.)

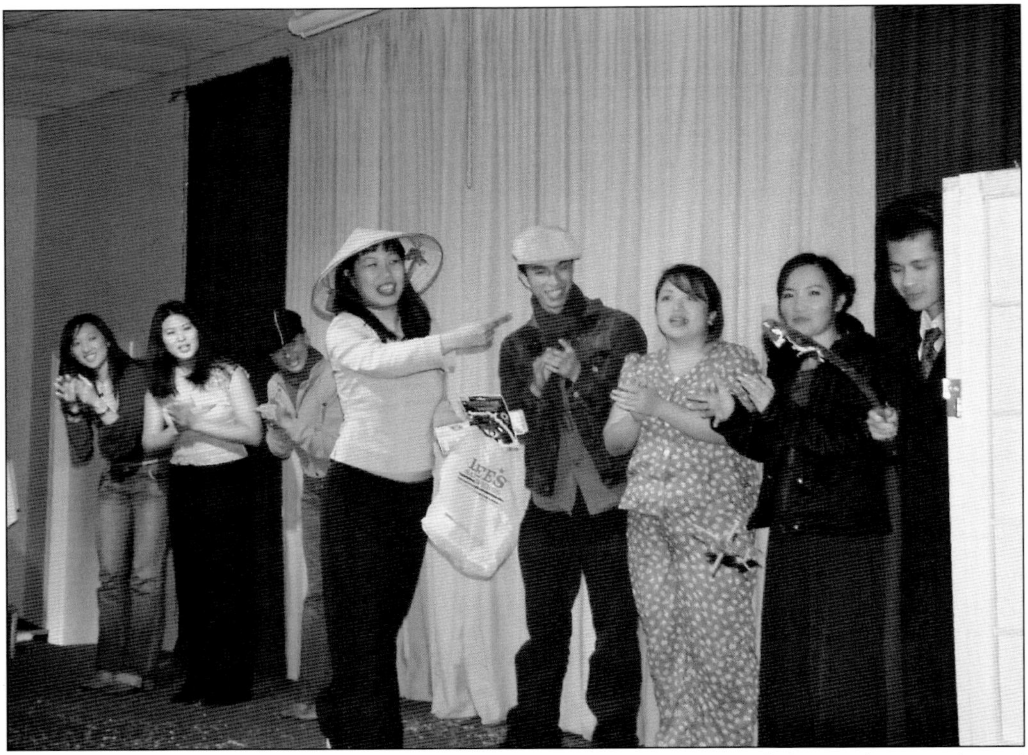

Curated by Nguyen Cao Hiep and Viet Le in January 2005, *Miss Saigon with the Wind* was performed and exhibited at Highways Performance Space in Santa Monica and Vien Dong Community Center in Westminster. According to the curators' statement, "These female performance all-stars from across the US explode stereotypes and expectations through their individual takes on love, war, sexuality, ethnicity, and fish sauce. Not identity politics as usual." Pictured here from left to right are Taylur Ngo (from Mai Piece), Lan Tran, le thi diem thuy, Kristina Wong, Shaun Nguyen, Tram Le, Uyen Huynh, and Viet Le after their performance at Vien Dong Community Center. (Courtesy of Linda Trinh Vo.)

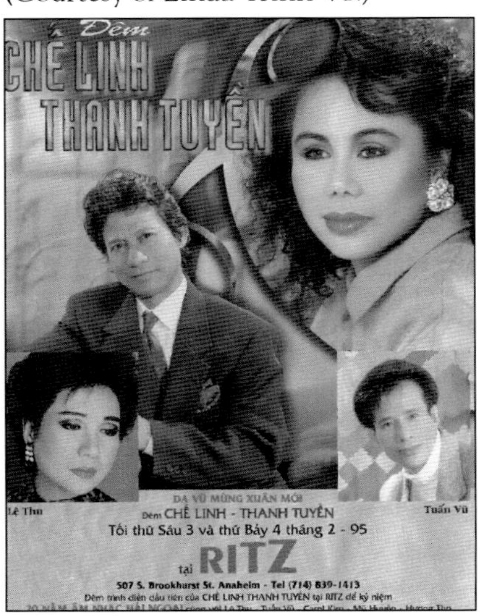

Le Thu, Che Linh, and Thanh Tuyen are beloved folk singers from the 1960s and 1970s who resettled in Orange County. They perform for the overseas Vietnamese community, and their music appeals to the nostalgia many refugees have for their homeland. (Courtesy of the UCI Libraries Southeast Asian Archive, MS-SEA020.)

Established in 1989, Ngan Khoi Chorus is a Southern California nonprofit organization promoting choral singing among Vietnamese Americans. It is the largest and most popular chorus group in the Vietnamese community and is known for blending Vietnamese folk music with Western music traditions. (Courtesy of the UCI Libraries Southeast Asian Archive, MS-SEA020.)

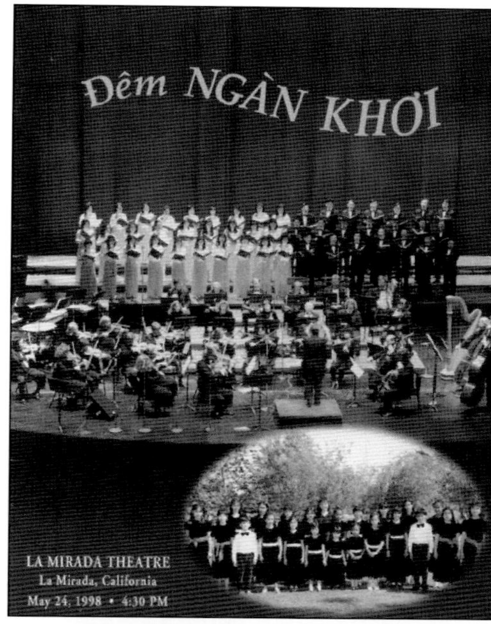

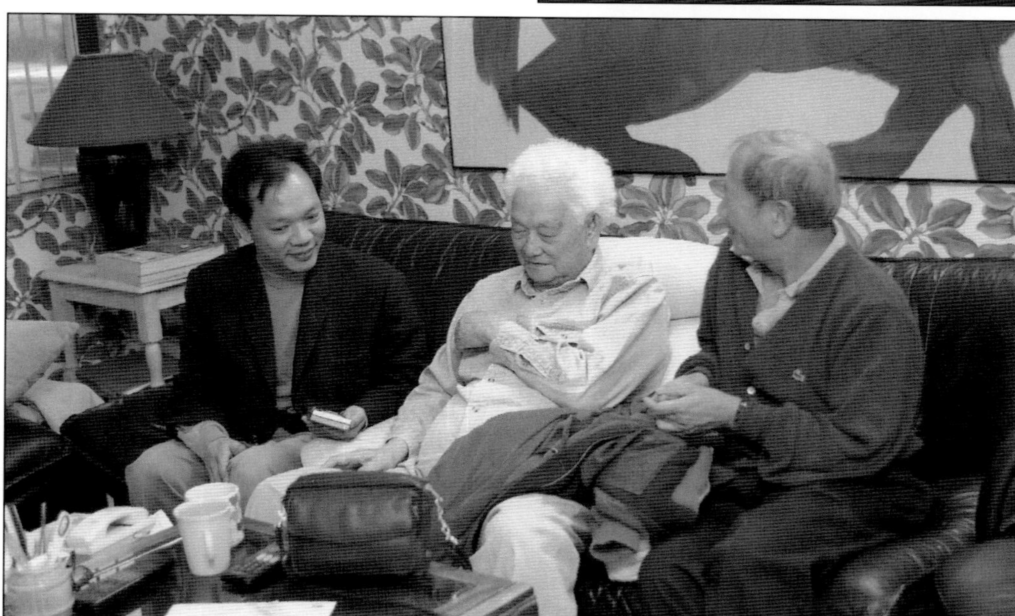

Legendary Pham Duy is Vietnam's most prolific music composer and songwriter, with a career spanning more than seven decades. His music was banned in Vietnam from 1975 to 2005, yet it continues to be performed throughout the world. He is known for incorporating themes of war, refugees, and homeland while blending traditional Vietnamese music with modern methods and melodies. Pham Duy (center) is being interviewed by Pham Phu Thien Giao, editor-in-chief of *Nguoi Viet Daily News* (left), and Do Viet Anh, former CEO of *Nguoi Viet Daily News* (right), at his residence in Midway City in Orange County. The interview was held on May 15, 2004, the day before he returned to Vietnam, where he passed away at age 91. (Courtesy of Benjamin Vu.)

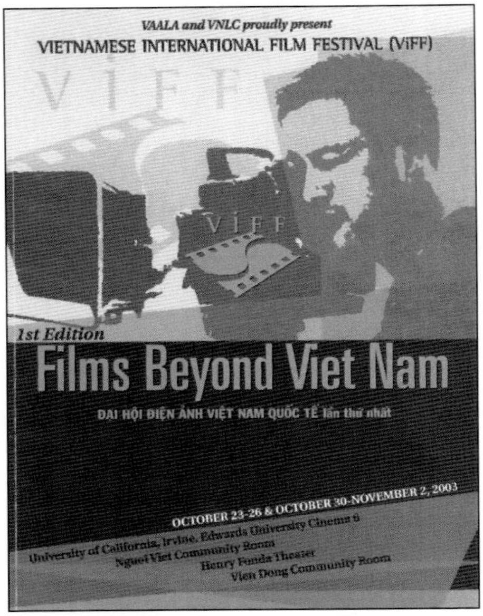

The Vietnamese International Film Festival (now renamed Viet Film Fest) was first held at UC Irvine, UCLA, Nguoi Viet Community Room, and Vien Dong Community Room in 2003. It was designed to bring together Vietnamese filmmakers and their communities by providing a support system and an alternative outlet to the mainstream film industry. The founding festival co-directors were Ysa Le, Tram Le, and Huong Ninh. (Courtesy of the UCI Libraries Southeast Asian Archive, MS-SEA020.)

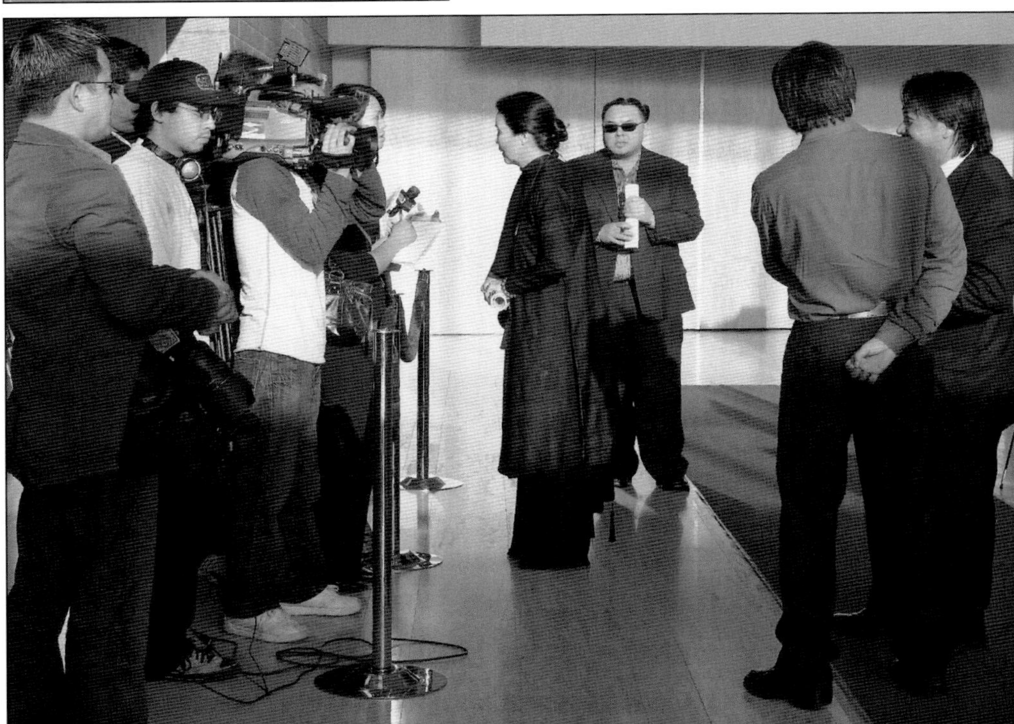

The feature-length film *Journey from the Fall*, a saga about the Vietnamese re-education camp and boat people experience, debuted in 2007 to a sold-out screening at the Rose Center in Westminster. It is written and directed by Ham Tran, a graduate from the UCLA Film School. This film was funded mostly by the Vietnamese American community. Pictured here is acclaimed actress Kieu Chinh, who has a major role in the film, giving an interview to the Vietnamese press with Ham Tran on the far right. (Courtesy of Linda Trinh Vo.)

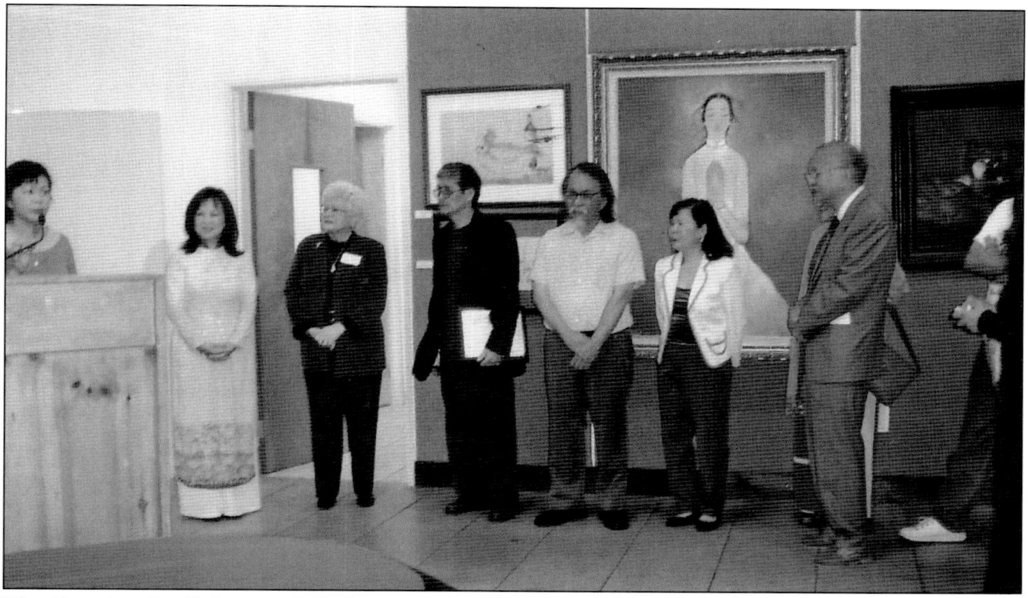

The *Reunion Art Exhibit* included paintings and sculptures by former teachers and students of the Saigon National School of Fine Arts and the Hue School of Fine Arts. This exhibition took place at Danchi Art Gallery in Westminster in April 2005. Pictured are, from left to right, Ann Phong, Kim Oanh Nguyen-Lam, Margie Rice, Nguyen Khai, Nguyen Dong, Nguyen Thi Hop, Nguyen Thi Nga (obstructed from view), and Ngo Bao. (Courtesy of Ann Phong.)

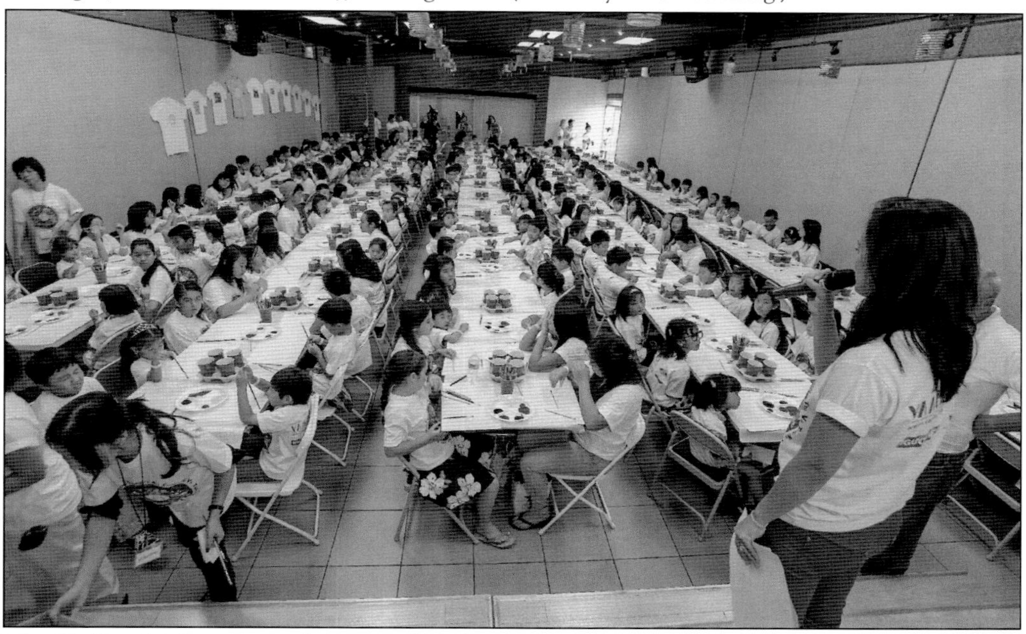

The Children's Moon Festival, organized by the Vietnamese American Arts and Letters Association (VAALA) and hosted by *Nguoi Viet Daily News*, has been an annual tradition since 2002. It celebrates the mid-autumn Moon Festival by fostering youthful creativity and bringing the festive Vietnamese holiday to the communities of Orange County. (Courtesy of the Vietnamese American Arts and Letters Association.)